Design Education ·
Sustainable Future

Sustainability is a powerful force that is fundamentally reshaping humanity's relationship to the natural world and is ushering in the Age of Integration. The move from well-intentioned greening to the higher bar of integral sustainability and regenerative design demands a new type of design professional, one that is deeply collaborative, ethically grounded, empathically connected and technologically empowered.

As a response, this book argues for a great leap forward in design education: from an individualistic and competitive model to a new approach defined by an integral consciousness, shaped by the values of inclusivity and cooperation, and implemented by a series of integrative behaviors including: an ethically infused design brief, a co-creative design process, on-going value engineering, pre-emptive engineering, design validation through simulation, on-line enabled integrated learning, and the use of well-vetted rating systems.

This book contains the integral frameworks, whole system change methodologies, intrinsic values and integrative behaviors that will assist professors and their students in an authentic and effective pursuit of design education for a sustainable future.

Rob Fleming is a LEED® Accredited Professional and a registered architect with over 15 years' experience of teaching, research and practice in sustainable design. He is the co-creator and Director of the award-winning Master of Science in Sustainable Design Program at Philadelphia University. Rob is a Sustainability Fellow at Re:Vision Architecture in Philadelphia where he consults and facilitates integrated design charrettes.

About the Cover:

Rob Fleming, The Cosmic Clock, 1995, Mixed media

The cover for the paperback edition of this title shows The Cosmic Clock, a diagram made in 1996 as part of a studio project at Virginia Tech's Washington Alexandria Architecture Consortium. The four 'rifts' depict the giant leaps of human consciousness. The cardinal points served as organizing elements for the studio project.

Design Education for a Sustainable Future

Rob Fleming

Routledge
Taylor & Francis Group

LONDON AND NEW YORK

earthscan
from Routledge

First published 2013
by Routledge
2 Park Square, Milton Park, Abingdon, Oxon, OX14 4RN

Simultaneously published in the USA and Canada
by Routledge
711 Third Avenue, New York, NY 10017

Routledge is an imprint of the Taylor & Francis Group, an informa business

British Library Cataloguing in Publication Data
A catalogue record for this book is available from the British Library

Library of Congress Cataloging-in-Publication Data
Fleming, Rob (Robert Michael)
Design education for a sustainable future / Rob Fleming.
pages cm
Includes bibliographical references and index.
1. Sustainable design--Study and teaching (Higher) I. Title.
NK1520.F59 2013
720'.47071--dc23
2012034650

ISBN13: 978-0-415-53765-0 (hbk)
ISBN13: 978-0-415-53766-7 (pbk)
ISBN13: 978-0-203-58407-1 (ebk)

Typeset in Futura by Saxon Graphics Ltd, Derby

MIX
Paper from responsible sources
FSC
www.fsc.org   FSC® C018575

Printed and bound in Great Britain by MPG Printgroup

This book is dedicated to my mom and dad

"A pioneering and visionary work which takes a hard look at design education and design today, something the profession and the schools would rather ignore. Fleming presents a clear and brilliant picture of both human culture's history and that of architecture. He presents clear models of where we must go and how to get there now!" – *Sim Van der Ryn*

"Rob Fleming has developed a strong program in sustainability education that is well supported by this work that brings together theory and pragmatic applications of sustainability principles and practices. While there are many evolving texts on how sustainability improves our built environment, Rob's work uniquely addresses how emerging designers can think about applying sustainability principles to their work far into the future. The tools of sustainability will inevitably evolve and reflect back on historical precedents; learning to think reflectively about what works best in different environments is the essence of keeping sustainability practices relevant to individual client circumstances. This is a text that should receive wide readership from educators, practitioners, and design students preparing for work in varying global situations where sustainability practices may matter most." – *Ted Landsmark, President, Boston Architectural College*

"This book has more new and powerful educational ideas than a ten year stack of architectural education journals! It positions Rob Fleming as the leading visionary voice in design education today. His work calls designers and educators to take the momentous leap to an inclusive and discriminating integral perspective that transcends the totally ineffective relativistic pluralism dominating every design school today. Instead, he offers us a way to connect and honor the often disparate design realms of human experience, cultural meaning, physical performance and systemic processes. The transformations he proposes will challenge us all, surely; yet such compelling practices are critical to solving our collective and already-dramatic environmental and social problems. If widely adopted, our world will improve exponentially. This is both the design education community's challenge and its auspicious opportunity. May we all be daring enough to embrace it!" – *Mark DeKay, author,* Integral Sustainable Design: transformative perspectives *(Earthscan from Routledge, 2011).*

CONTENTS

FIGURES

TABLES

FIGURE SOURCES

Figure 1.1
Sim Van der Ryn's "Three Ring Diagram"
Source: Re-drawn and adapted by author from Van der Ryn, S. (2005) *Design for Life*, Gibbs-Smith, Layton, UT, p122

Figure 1.2
Age of the Hunter Gatherer
Source: Re-drawn and adapted by author from Van der Ryn, S. (2005) *Design for Life*, Gibbs-Smith, Layton, UT, p136

Figure 1.3
Age of Agriculture
Source: Re-drawn and adapted by author from Van der Ryn, S. (2005) *Design for Life*, Gibbs-Smith, Layton, UT, p139

Figure 1.4
Holocene period and the Age of Agriculture
Sources: Re-drawn with additions by author from Schönwiese, C.-D.
(1997) "Anthropogene und natürliche Signale im Klimageschehen"
Naturwissenschaften, 84: 65–73; Dansgaard, W. et al. (1993)
"Evidence for general instability of past climate from a 250-kyr ice-core
record," *Nature*, 364: 218–220

Figure 1.5
Early Age of Industry
Source: Re-drawn and adapted by author from Van der Ryn, S., "Three
Ring Diagram," in *Design for Life* (2005) Gibbs-Smith, Layton, UT, p140

Figure 1.6
Late Age of Industry
Source: Re-drawn and adapted by author from Van der Ryn, S., "Three
Ring Diagram," in *Design for Life* (2005) Gibbs-Smith, Layton, UT, p140

Figure 1.7
Age of Information
Source: Re-drawn and adapted by author from Van der Ryn, S., "Three
Ring Diagram," in *Design for Life* (2005) Gibbs-Smith, Layton, UT, p140

Figure 1.8
Age of Integration
Source: Re-drawn and adapted by author from Van der Ryn, S., "Three
Ring Diagram," in *Design for Life* (2005) Gibbs-Smith, Layton, UT

Figure 1.9
Dawn of the Anthropocene
Sources: Re-drawn with additions by author from Schönwiese, C.-D.
(1997) "Anthropogene und natürliche Signale im Klimageschehen"
Naturwissenschaften, 84: 65–73; Dansgaard, W. et al. (1993)
"Evidence for general instability of past climate from a 250-kyr ice-core
record," *Nature*, 364: 218–220

Figure 1.10
Sim Van der Ryn's spiral of consciousness/culture depicting the Age of Eco-Logic
Source: Re-drawn by author from Van der Ryn, S., *Design for Life* (2005) Gibbs-Smith, Layton, UT, p126

Figure 2.1
The great "Tent" of sustainability (plan view)
Source: Created and drawn by author

Figure 2.2
The Natural Step funnel
Source: Re-drawn and adapted by author from the The Natural Step Program http://www.thenaturalstep.org/en/natural-step-funnel, Accessed: 8/9/2012 10:13PM

Figure 2.3
Trajectory of integrative thinking
Source: Re-drawn and adapted by author from 7group and Bill Reed (2009) *The Integrative Design Guide to Green Building: Redefining the Practice of Sustainability*, John Wiley & Sons Inc., Hoboken, NJ, p45

Figure 2.4
Triple Bottom Line diagrams
Sources: Image on the left: Re-drawn and adapted by author from a standard diagram that is frequently used
Image on the right: Re-drawn and adapted by author from Elkington, J. (1997) *Cannibals with Forks: The Triple Bottom Line of 21st Century Business*, Capstone, Oxford, p73

Figure 2.5
Triple Bottom Line diagram with shear zone
Source: Re-drawn and adapted by author from Elkington, J. (1997) *Cannibals with Forks: The Triple Bottom Line of 21st Century Business*, Capstone, Oxford, UK

Figure 2.6

Maslow's Hierarchy of Needs repurposed for sustainable design

Sources: Image on the left: Re-drawn and adapted by author from Maslow, A. (1964) *Toward a Psychology of Being*, John Wiley and Sons, New York

Image on the right: Re-drawn by author from Fleming, R. and Pastore, C., "The Aesthetics of Green," Proceedings, Association of Collegiate Schools of Architecture, National Conference, New Orleans, LA, 2003

Figure 2.7

Transcendent sustainability

Source: Re-drawn and by author from Fleming, R. and Pastore, C., "The Aesthetics of Green," Proceedings, Association of Collegiate Schools of Architecture, National Conference, New Orleans, LA, 2003

Figure 2.8

Quadruple Bottom Line diagrams

Source: Re-drawn and adapted by author from diagrams developed by Rob Fleming and Anne Sherman

Figure 3.1

Ken Wilber's Integral Theory

Source: Re-drawn by author from Wilber, K. (2000) *A Brief History of Everything*, Shambhala, Boston, MA, "The Four Quadrants," para. 2

Figure 3.2

Integral Ecology

Source: Re-drawn by author from Esbjörn-Hargens, S., "Integral Ecology: An ecology of perspectives," *AQAL Journal of Integral theory and Practice*, winter 2005, 1 (1): 24

Figure 3.3

The Four Perspectives of Integral Sustainable Design

Source: Re-drawn by author from DeKay, Mark (2011) *Integral Sustainable Design: Transformative Perspectives*, Earthscan, London, pxxiii

Figure 3.4
Barrett's Seven Levels of School Consciousness
Source: Re-drawn and adapted by author from Barrett, R. "The Seven Levels of School Consciousness," Barrett Values Centre, http://www.valuescentre.com/uploads/2010-07-06/The%207%20Levels%20of%20Schools.pdf, Accessed: 8/9/2012 11:42PM

Figure 3.5
Barrett's Four Quadrants of Human Systems
Source: Re-drawn by author from Barrett, R. "Fundamentals of Cultural Transformation: Implementing whole system change," Barrett Values Centre, http://www.valuescentre.com/uploads/2010-04-19/FCT.pdf, Accessed on 6/3/2012

Figure 3.6
Barrett's Four Conditions for Whole System Change
Source: Re-drawn by author from Barrett, R. "Fundamentals of Cultural Transformation: Implementing whole system change," Barrett Values Centre, http://www.valuescentre.com/uploads/2010-04-19/FCT.pdf, Accessed on 6/3/2012

Figure 3.7
Philadelphia University's MS in Sustainable Design Program: Barrett's Four Conditions for Whole System Change inscribed within Wilber's Integral Theory Framework
Source: Created and drawn by author

Figure 3.8
Integral Sustainable Design Studio Curriculum Model at Philadelphia University
Source: Created and drawn by author

Figure 4.1
Approach to diversity and inclusivity
Source: Created and drawn by author

Figure 5.7
Typical seating arrangement for design charrette vetting session
Source: Created and drawn by author

Figure 5.8
Typical schedule of a design charrette in an academic setting
Source: Created and drawn by author

Figure 6.1
Integrative studio model: the design brief
Source: Created and drawn by author

Figure 6.2
Comparison between typical design studio and proposed integrative model
Source: Created and drawn by author

Figure 6.3
The designer as the agent
Source: Created and drawn by author

Figure 7.1
Integrative studio model: integrative behaviors
Source: Created and drawn by author

Figure 7.2
The blended or flipped classroom model for support courses
Source: Created and drawn by author

Figure 8.1
Integrative studio model: the collection of certifications, standards and metrics that serve to assist designers in understanding their impact on the natural world
Source: Created and drawn by author

Figure 8.2
The forces that shape the development of design curricula
Source: Created and drawn by author

Figure 8.3
The LEED® Rating System categories organized within Mark DeKay's Integral Sustainable Design Framework
Source: Created and drawn by author

Figure 8.4
The Living Building Challenge's requirements organized within Mark DeKay's Integral Sustainable Design Framework
Source: Created and drawn by author

Figure 8.5
Organization of NAAB criteria within the Integral Theory model
Source: NAAB 2011 Criterion B.6. Comprehensive Design Ability (created and drawn by author)

Figure 9.1
Rogers' adoption of innovation curve: adapted for Integral Sustainable Design
Source: Re-drawn and adapted by author from Moore, G. (2002) *Crossing the Chasm: Marketing and Selling Disruptive Products to Mainstream Customers*, HarperBusiness, New York, p12

Figure 9.2
Culture change for design education: an integral perspective
Source: Created and drawn by author

ACKNOWLEDGMENTS

Many years ago, my wife Nica and I visited the Metropolitan Museum in New York City. After visiting a modern art exhibit which included Cubist works by Braque and Picasso, we wandered into an adjoining exhibit on African Art. The work was remarkable and the link between the so called primitive work of Africa and the European Cubist masters was undeniable. When I looked to see who the artist was for one particularly remarkable mask that caught my eye, I was surprised to see the name of an entire village in Kenya. That brought home the idea that great art is as much about the work of an inspired individual as it is about the collective achievement of a village or a community. Nothing could be truer in my case and in the case of this book. The work is as much a result of an individual effort as it is the cumulative expression of the "village" that raised me, influenced me and ultimately helped to shape the point of view and knowledge base that led to the creation and development of the book.

It was made possible because of my loving wife who withstood the scores of significant and insignificant questions from me, held down the home front and gave me the space literally and figuratively to finish this project. I am not sure why I chose the kitchen counter as my office for the last six months but somehow it was the only way to stay connected – especially to my two kids who provided the best distractions and kept me grounded. Finally the stack of books will be put away, the notes placed in a folder and the lap top closed. In the end, I am not sure how I might have completed this project without the family support. My larger family, especially my parents Aisha Bey and Bob Fleming, my stepmom, Dottie Fleming, my mother-in-law Bertha Waters, my siblings especially Kathy Fleming, uncles, aunts, cousins, nephews, nieces, and so on … all contributed to the village that made me who I am.

My current approach to sustainable design was largely formed through the work at Philadelphia University with specific influences by Chris Pastore, the Skeptic and Rob Fryer, the Stoic who co-created the Sustainable Design Program, and insisted on keeping me honest and rigorous (as much as possible for me) about the topics covered in this book – especially climate change. The MS in Sustainable Design students, alumni, staff (Maryann Spencer) and faculty were always ready to participate in any number of pedagogic experiments. Student Anne Sherman was an excellent collaborator (and clued me into Barrett). Sonam Shah and Julia Bushueva provided great research support.

From 1997 to 2009, I coordinated the sustainability studio in the undergraduate Architecture Program at Philadelphia University. My colleagues were extremely patient with me, especially during the SURVIVE! Project. I can imagine more than a few occasions when I must have annoyed everyone but as is the way at our school, we all still found a way to make it work and this book is in some part a testament to the supportive and collaborative culture in the College of Architecture and the Built Environment at Philadelphia University. My colleagues in the Landscape Architecture program have tried their best to get me to understand and appreciate what they do, and it is just now beginning to hit home. My two former deans, Gary Crowell and Vini Nathan, gave me the freedom and support to pursue new models of education which helped to open the door to many of the ideas contained within this book.

At Virginia Tech's Washington Alexandria Architecture Consortium Susan Piedmont-Palladino introduced me to the concept of sustainability way back in 1994 and helped to get me through thesis and to start my teaching career. Her early reviews of this book were critical in setting a proper direction and tone. Christine Mondor has always been willing to state her feelings about the work and her point of view has been invaluable. Howard Ways has always offered a unique point of view. Mark DeKay's book, *Integral Sustainable Design* came at just the right time and his visit to Philadelphia University along with his wife Suzanne was reassuring and energizing.

Scott Kelly who coaxed me to get started on the book, and Jenn Rezeli provided the professional environment at Re:Vision Architecture to learn and develop many of the approaches explored in the book. Many professionals and authors provided input into this book including but not limited to: Emilie Hagen, Cory Brugger, Brian Phillips, Marguerite Anglin, Tiffany Milner, Michael Spain, Scott Kelly, Sandy Wiggins, Shannon Kaplan, Rob Diemer, Kathryn Anthony, Ann Thorpe, Lance Hosey, Greg Hunt, Chris Hellstern, Stacy H. Smedley, Tom Gavin, Chris Zelov, Marvin Roseman and Steven Moore.

Finally, I'd like to thank Nicki Dennis from Earthscan, who has been very supportive and encouraging throughout this process.

PREFACE

This book is disruptive. The bedrock that supported the design and construction industry for centuries has now shifted in so many directions and has been shaken so vigorously that the basic premise of design practice and by default design education are in need of serious reconsideration. The landscape of professional practice, as driven in part by the need for financial survival and by the rise of sustainability, is changing much faster and more dramatically than anyone could have predicted. Behind it, albeit more slowly and more covertly, the foundations of design education are beginning to shake free from the shackles of decades, if not centuries, of inertia. With that comes the clarion call to leave the comfortable zone of *benign neglect*, a strategy we academics employ to deal with the most controversial and uncomfortable issues (see diversity) to a new, self-aware and more evolved consciousness. The disruptive nature of this book is not in its capacity to break things apart, but rather in its ability to convey a new mental map of design education, one that is ethically grounded, increasingly inclusive, deeply cooperative, better aligned and integrated to the core.

In that sense, this book is a polemic – an argument for the reconsideration of design education as an essential tool in the larger societal movement towards a sustainable future. The reader is driven towards a possible if not probable conclusion that sustainability is the *next great paradigm*, the foundation of a new integral world view that is and/ or will, fundamentally alter design education processes and by default the future generations of young people who will shape our built environments. But the polemic also serves as a diversion, a sleight of hand, to coax each reader to confront his or her own design consciousness – to begin the process of becoming aware of his or her own pedagogical strengths and weaknesses. Such experiences can be either deeply troubling and lead to therapy (or at least to drink); or pedagogic nirvana, the state of bliss so powerful that teaching for free would seem perfectly fine. Of course the end result will land somewhere within that very wide spectrum.

This book is horizontal in its organization – a study of the interrelationships between the values and behaviors that comprise the meta-framework for design education. The reasons for this are straightforward. Sustainability is still not widely understood or valued, and therefore continued work is required to this end. As a response, I try and contribute to the coalescing definition of sustainable design by offering a set of frameworks borrowed from Integral Theory and Integral Sustainable Design. But I also offer some concrete examples either from my own 15 years of sustainable design education experience or from others: practitioners or educators who have grappled with sustainability at varying levels and from differing directions.

The temptation by the reader will be to interpret this book as an indictment of standard design education practices. While some parts will attack some fiercely defended educational methodologies such as the design jury, the overall premise is to present the next move forward as an evolutionary jump rather than a bloody revolution. The foundations of studio based education remain sound and will continue to gain favor as more and more disciplines seek to incorporate project based learning into their core methodologies. The temptation to tear apart has been resisted through the premise of "transcend and include" – a process by which new models of organization emerge and layer on top of older models creating a wonderful palimpsest of approaches and methodologies that serve simultaneously as a critique of the old methods and as a reaffirmation of their continued efficacy.

There are no images of buildings, landscapes or interiors in this book. The purpose is simple. Designers have been trained to reach high levels of visual literacy, as in the ability to view any design expression and immediately identify its precedents, influences, visual meaning and ultimately to determine the project's value. But that perception of value is based almost solely on its visual, spatial or tectonic content and is devoid of a deeper understanding of the economic, environmental and social forces that eventually shape projects. As designers we can slice and dice any project design, breaking down even the best intentioned work, and we also elevate less worthy projects that offer little sustenance for a society starving for meaning and content in projects. Such visually astute but hypercritical processes can be traced back to their roots in the design academies where students gain an amazing depth of visual literacy and a sharp tongue often at the expense of other important aspects of design practice and of life itself.

I find myself in the position of the timid third year design student who sheepishly pins sketches to the wall and awkwardly attempts to verbally communicate intent. If *completion trumps perfection* and if a new emphasis on *intention and method* in design education is coming, then the work contained within this book will have to suffice. Like the mid review, the student hopes that the critics "get it." Agreement is optional, but hopefully the message itself was delivered well enough to drive meaningful conversation and to stir debate. In the end, if that is achieved, then this project could be considered a success. I long ago realized that people change when they are ready. My goal is to provide the nudge, the slight push to the left or right towards the very large mirror that we all must encounter at some point in our lives, the mirror that drives our consciousness to new levels, reshapes our values, changes our behaviors and in turn will hopefully make us better educators.

Please visit formfollowsworldview.com, where you will find my blog along with other information related to sustainable design education that will be useful to educators.

Disclaimers

This book is extremely U.S. centric in its views of the world and its peoples. The reasons for this are inexcusable but they are there none the less. I have yet to gain enough perspective or knowledge to properly place this book in a global context. I have unwittingly fallen victim to the misguided view of America as the center of the universe, when I know intuitively that such is not the case. Given the tight deadline for this book and the amount of research needed just to cover the main points I am left with the realization that many readers outside the U.S. may find the work provincial. I believe that the book still holds great value for the global reader and I therefore beg forgiveness in advance for the limited scope of references and examples provided.

Secondly, despite the years of effort to be more inclusive of the disciplines that comprise sustainable design education – interior design, landscape architecture, architectural engineering, civil engineering and construction to name a few – my overall approach is still defined by years of architecture practice, teaching and education. While I make attempts to offer examples from other disciplines, the inevitable focus on architecture is relentless. Given that, I ask for patience from my colleagues and from the readers.

Lastly, despite my attempt to be comprehensive, a number of important critical aspects of design education have been left out. The impact of research and the differences between undergraduate and graduate education have been excluded not because they aren't important but because something had to be excluded for the simple sake of completion.

INTRODUCTION
form follows world view

The premise of this book is remarkably simple. It is based on a series of straightforward questions that seek to uncover the context, values and behaviors necessary for effective twenty-first century design education. Is society moving towards a new sustainable or integral world view, a new set of cultural values that are reshaping the very fabric of human existence? If so, how are such profound shifts in consciousness impacting the design and construction industries? And how can design educators better reflect the zeitgeist of the new century by moving from well-intentioned but lightweight "greening" to the deeper and more impactful ideals of sustainability and resilience?

The process of answering these questions begins with the requisite historical narrative which explores cultural evolution not as a slow and gradual rise to new levels of complexity but rather through a series of hyper-accelerated jumps in human consciousness. The jump from dispersed hunter gatherer cultures to centralized agrarian societies and then to industrialized nations correlates well to the convergence of new energy sources and the invention of new communication technologies.

Jeremy Rifkin argues in his book *The Empathic Civilization: The Race to Global Consciousness in a World in Crisis* that "The convergence of energy and communications revolutions not only reconfigures society and social roles and relationships but also human consciousness itself."[1] The early twenty-first century, as characterized by unprecedented sharing of information via wireless networks and by the emergence of renewable energy technologies, demarcates a threshold from one world view to another, a jump from an industrialized conception of nature as immutable and infinite to a Gaia inspired view of nature as alive, intelligent and, most of all, fragile in the hands of man.

The principles of sustainability, which emphasize ecological regeneration and co-creative processes, comprise a new and powerful ideal that is reshaping technologically driven initiatives, especially those associated with the design and construction of the built environment. Societal conceptions of money and profit, consumerism, design and technology are radically shifting to address the superficial but useful demands of "greening," and are leading to finding deeper and more meaningful processes to meet the much higher bar of sustainability.

The unpacking of such lofty but important aspirations must include the painful but necessary establishment of the territory and domain of sustainability and sustainable design as a means of laying the groundwork for a more in-depth look at design education. For many designers, the word "sustainability" is taboo. Some refrain from using it at all due to a high level of confusion (thanks, in part, to "green washing") surrounding both the word itself and its connotations. Others use the word naïvely, as a catch-all for all things good and progressive. In addition, the meaning of the word shifts when understood in the context of different parts the world, different economies and differing cultural expectations of quality of life. Despite such complexities, the actual meaning of sustainability and its connotations comprise the epicenter of a vast paradigmatic jump from an industrialized design approach dominated by materialism, technological expression and what Thomas Friedman called *situational values* to a design approach supported by virtual simplicity, environmental regeneration and an adoption of *sustainable values*.[2] In short, the developed world is moving from a focus on raising the *standard of living via technological progress*, as defined by comfort and convenience, to a focus on a *higher quality of life* as defined by meaningful embodied experiences through relationships with each other and with nature.

The amorphous nature of sustainability is both its great strength and its weakness. As such, it allows for multiple entry points: from biophilic and emergent design expressions to tectonically inspired energy efficient designs to socially responsible activism. While John Elkington's *Triple Bottom Line of People, Profit and Planet* is now well established in the world of commerce and government, the simple yet compelling collection of words has yet to become part of the designer's mental matrix. Opportunities such as economic viability and environmental regeneration are slowly and awkwardly finding their way into the mainstream of design education thinking, while the inclusion of socially responsible design varies from school to school and from studio to studio. Susan Szenasy, editor in chief of *Metropolis* magazine, argues in the *Journal of Interior Design* that "after all, social equity is one leg of a three-legged sustainability stool; the other two legs are ecology and economy."[3] While the three-legged stool of sustainability is on one level a powerful icon of the new sense of integration, on another level it is deeply troubling for the designer. The absence of the *experience* of sustainability is problematic not just for designers but for society as a whole. Are we to be left with blocks and blocks of highly performing built projects that leave little, if any, nourishment for the soul? Lance Hosey argues in his new book, *The Shape of Green: Aesthetics, Ecology and Design*, "If it's not beautiful, it's not sustainable. Aesthetic attraction is not a superficial concern – it's an environmental imperative."[4] Indeed, the idea that buildings, landscapes and interiors must be both highly performing and also beautiful helps to form the nucleus of the proposed "Quadruple Bottom Line," a term developed in collaboration with Sustainable Design student Anne Sherman to add the experiential or aesthetic component to the existing Triple Bottom Line tenets of environment, economics and equity. The addition of experience into the now well-established collection of equity, enterprise and ecology prompts the discarding of the utilitarian three-legged *stool* of the Triple Bottom Line in favor of the more comfortable and inviting four-legged *chair* of sustainability. In this way, the entry point for designers is wide open, offering an avenue of exploration that is more familiar and therefore more accessible to the typical designer and, by default, the typical design educator.

But the need for the aesthetic pathway speaks volumes to the inability of design professionals and educators to embrace sustainability in all of its phases and meanings. The fixation on aesthetics, formalism, tectonics

3

and space making at the expense of directly addressing larger societal issues partially explains the slow movement towards more integrated and sustainable practices in both practice and the academies.

Ultimately, LEED® rated green buildings need not be ugly, while highly evocative and beguiling design expressions need not be devoid of an ethical foundation. Evolving the design professions to higher states of consciousness does not demand a paradigm shift so much as it does the *transcendence* to a new more integrated world view, and the *inclusion* of all preceding world views. The approach of "both and" or "transcend and include" recognizes the continuing value of all previous world views and plays an essential role in the establishment of new design consciousness not as a choice between the past and present, but rather as an additional motivation to pursue sustainability. The emerging integral world view is best described in Ken Wilber's *Integral Theory*, while Mark DeKay's *Integral Sustainable Design* serves as a powerful framework to organize, unite and catalyze the various forces that shape the sustainable built environment.

The implications of the new world view for design educators are staggering. Current educational models can be characterized as exclusive, competitive, formalistic and isolated and do not reflect the emerging sensibilities of the spirit of the age. As far back as 1968, Whitney M. Young, Jr., head of the Urban League, challenged the AIA on issues relating to social responsibility and diversity within the profession.[5] In 1991, Kathryn Anthony, in her book *Design Juries on Trial,* offered the first whispers of a need for changing the way projects are reviewed.[6] In 1996, Boyer and Mitgang in their publication *Building Community* recommended that architects and architectural educators assume a leadership role in preserving the environment and the planet's resources.[7] In 2001, the AIAS Studio Culture document cited "hazing" as one of the attributes of design education.[8] An exhaustive 2006 AIA sponsored report, *Ecological Literacy in Architecture Education* by Lance Hosey and Kira Gould, suggests that design educators are only just beginning to nudge at the opportunities presented by sustainability.[9] But the emergence of a new design consciousness asks: if form follows world view, and if integration is the new consciousness, then how will that impact design education?

The process begins with understanding some core values – *inclusion* and *cooperation* – and by pursuing a set of integral core behaviors:

beginning with inclusion, the question of "who designs" has new meaning in the age of collaboration, cooperation and integration. Those students marginalized due to the color of their skin, their gender or any other difference comprise generations of lost design talent for the industry and perpetuates the perception and reality of design as an exclusive club. Those without design training – clients, neighbors, engineering consultants and builders – have limited entry points in the typical design process and even less so in academic projects, despite the fact that their contributions clearly shape the overall design product. The drive towards inclusion raises many questions, including: How will the largely Caucasian dominated design academies overcome years of privilege to build more diverse and inclusive learning communities? How will the design professions let go of their tight control over discipline territory to open opportunities for meaningful collaboration?

If inclusivity sets the cast of characters for effective collaborations, the rules of engagement that govern design education must evolve to feature the intention to create highly cooperative learning environments. The shift from teaching design as a solitary creative pursuit bereft of contingencies to teaching designers to become facilitators of diverse groups, integrators of ethical content, and generators of highly evocative and beautiful places is reflected by Jeremy Till in his 2009 book *Architecture Depends*:

> This in turn suggests a move from architect as expert problem solver to that of architect as citizen sense maker; a move from a reliance on the impulsive imagination of the lone genius to that of the collaborative ethical imagination; from clinging to notions of total control to a relaxed acceptance of letting go.[10]

The integrated design process as applied to design education can allow for the horizontal and equitable participation of all students regardless of discipline, skill level or personality. Such leveling of the playing field is supported by Rifkin, who writes:

> The traditional assumption that "knowledge is power" and is used for personal gain is being subsumed by the notion that knowledge is an expression of the shared responsibilities for the collective well-being of humanity and the planet as a whole.[11]

Ultimately, the question must be asked: how will studio professors overcome the years of heredity that drive the physically punishing and emotionally draining competitive design studio for one that is uplifting, optimistic and life enriching?

Inclusivity and cooperation demand new behaviors from academics such as the realignment of studio curricula to account for the rise of flatter, more contingent, more interdisciplinary work. *Pre-emptive engineering*, for example, as enabled by early collaborative design charrettes, allows technically proficient domain experts to participate early in the process of design, leading to higher and more legitimate forms of integration. *Value engineering* through the entire process connects students to the cost contingencies of design and forces a dose of reality that is so rare in most design studios. Lastly, clients and community members can provide meaningful service to the studio project, but better at the beginning when key decisions are made and design directions are established. Jeremy Till argues in *Architecture Depends*, "The most important, and most creative, part of the process [design] is the formulation of the brief. The creative brief is about negotiating a new set of social relations."[12] Indeed, the design brief expresses the consciousness of the project, develops the necessary diverse stakeholders, determines the rules for the co-creative design process, sets the schedule of interactions and clearly illuminates the integrative goals of the project.

Finally, the conscious pursuit of higher levels of integration forms the behavior that propels the emergence of new design education practices. The gap between the intention of integration, however, and its actual operation in educational settings is as wide as it is deep and fraught with numerous structural and psychological challenges. The academically reinforced disciplinary silos serve to prevent collaboration. The makeup of disciplines necessary to pursue higher levels of collaboration not only exist in separate schools and colleges within universities, but also possess deeply territorial impulses that work against such efforts. The psychological chasms and structural barriers in place are so deep that the possibility of a more integrated and sustainable curriculum crumbles at the feet of hundreds of years of academic tradition. But the meme of sustainability persists, first gnawing at the heels of an otherwise inattentive academic community, then beginning to force the construction of bridges between the silos, and finally to the pitching of large pedagogic tents.

The use of the word *tent* in favor of *silo* is not an arbitrary metaphor because it underscores the porosity and horizontality of sustainability.

Nevertheless, the move towards the operational, while daunting, must begin. On one level, design education, especially the studio, is one of the most powerfully effective vehicles for learning across the entire spectrum of higher education. On another level, such otherwise excellent approaches often lack the inclusiveness, cooperation and alignment necessary to drive the ethical content of projects and to reach higher levels of integration. Design students already possess an extremely high visual literacy; ecological literacy, however, is essential if an overall movement towards integration is to occur. The use of on-line teaching and "flipped classrooms" presents a method to free up lecture courses to become additional centers of innovation. They can serve as portals for technology courses to enable mini integrative design studios or offer avenues of participation from students who are marginalized due to distance or financial or family constraints. The use of integrated sustainable design charrettes early and often in studio, especially in the collaborative development of the design brief, and especially prior to the generation of formal responses, can be an excellent tool in the expression of ethical and functional foundations of sustainable projects. The addition of *vetting* (collaborative feedback loops as part of the charrettes) can provide structured and useful direction for design students from a variety of stakeholder views. The immense potential of design/build projects possesses by default, the inclusivity, cooperation and alignment necessary for design integration. Lastly, design educators, with the benefit of specialized training, can evolve from *designers who teach*, to *educators who teach design*.

The rise of integrated project delivery, integrated design processes, inclusive design teams and participatory design processes all reflect the changing tides in the processes and products that comprise the formation of the built environment, and by default, demand an answer to a simple question: can design educators heed the call for change and begin the process of jumping into the compelling but difficult age of integration? The simple answer is yes, but. Yes, design educators are already excellent synthesizers and integrators and some have already begun to innovate through such programs as Illinois Institute of Technology's MS in Integrated Project Delivery, The Columbia (University) Building Intelligence Project and Philadelphia University's

MS in Sustainable Design. *But,* such early efforts must be matched by a clear intention to pursue higher levels of integration, and the persistence must be present to place such intentions into operation.

Design faculty need not carry such a burden alone. Program administrators must also advocate for change, accreditors must continue to evolve their requirements, licensing agencies must continue to clarify their definitions of practice, the professional associations need to push towards higher levels of sustainability, senior practitioners can shake away the pressures of financial survival to adopt new design processes and young practitioners can participate in thousands of tiny revolutions through the writing of green specs and the completion of drawings that express higher levels of integration.

Ultimately, the jump to a new world view is beginning to impact our collective consciousness, spurring a societal transition to more sophisticated economic models, to deeper levels of social responsibility, to higher levels of ecological regeneration and to a clear positioning of aesthetics as an integral part of sustainability. Design educators stand poised to meaningfully participate in the transition from the intuitive impulses of green design to the more holistic Integral Sustainable Design.

Design educators hold the promise of a sustainable future in the hearts and minds of the students they teach.

Notes

[1] Rifkin, Jeremy (2009) *The Empathic Civilization: The Race to Global Consciousness in a World in Crisis,* Penguin, New York, p34

[2] Green, B., "Tom Friedman and Steve Jobs: Situational Versus Sustainable Values," *Huffington Post,* August 9, 2012, http://www.huffingtonpost.com/brent-green/tom-friedman-and-steve-jo_b_1010112.html, Accessed 8/9/2012 5:56PM

[3] Szenasy S. (2012) "Reflections on Sustainable Design," *Journal of Interior Design,* 37 (1): px

[4] Hosey, L. (2012) *The Shape of Green: Aesthetics, Ecology and Design,* Island Press, Washington, p7

[5] American Institute of Architects, AIA Diversity / Then+Now+NEXT, https://sites.google.com/site/aiadiversityhistory/, Accessed 8/6/2012 9:15AM

[6] Anthony, K. (1991) *Design Juries on Trial: The Renaissance of the Design Studio,* Van Nostrand Reinhold, New York

[7] Boyer, E. L., Mitgang L. D. (1996) *Building Community: A New Future for Architecture Education and Practice,* Carnegie Foundation for the Advancement of Teaching, Princeton, NJ, p43

[8] Koch, A., Schwennsen, K., Dutton, T., Smith, D. (2002) *The Redesign of Studio Culture: A Report of the AIAS Studio Culture Task Force*, American Institute of Architects Students, Washington, D.C., p21

[9] Hosey, L., Gould K., *Ecological Literacy in Architecture Education Report and Proposal*, American Institute of Architects and the Tides Foundation, 2006, p44

[10] Till, J. (2009) *Architecture Depends*, MIT Press, Cambridge, MA, p151

[11] Rifkin, Jeremy (1) p15

[12] Till, J. (10) p169

1
A NEW CONTEXT FOR DESIGN EDUCATION

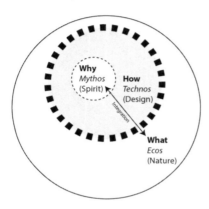

The Framework
The "Why" of design implies an ethical core that is ideally connected to the "What" (needs of Nature) through the "How" of design. The dashed circles represent barriers that will prohibit connection between the layers. The vector that connects the three rings reflects the desire for integration.

Figure 1.1
Sim Van der Ryn's "Three Ring Diagram"
Diagram depicting the relationship between societal values and beliefs, human behaviors and the natural world
Source: *Van der Ryn, S. (2005)*

It seems odd to begin a discussion about twenty-first century design education at a point in time when language was first developing and when controlled fire and simple tools were the expressions of technological process. The use of today's technologies of building information modeling, digitally enabled on-line teaching and the development of high performance facades would seem alien to the pre-analog societies of early human existence. And yet, the level of integration that was reached so organically back then is something that the current generation seeks to rediscover, to reinterpret and ultimately to place into action as part of a movement towards a sustainable future. But the path between then and now is neither gradual nor linear. The simple mantra of form follows world view requires a brief, but hopefully insightful, tour through some of the major transitions in history which will help to place the unique context of our time into clearer view. By looking at history as a series of evolutionary leaps, we can begin to understand how changes in climate, the adoption of new communication methods and the discovery of new energy sources serve to propel humanity to higher levels of consciousness and to changing societal views of the natural world. Such world views drive change in the design and construction industry and by association changes in design education.

This overview is not meant to be exhaustive and is used solely as a process to communicate and explore patterns in human development as a means to illuminate the impact of world view shifts upon design and design education. Design historians will, by default, shudder at some of the simplified characterizations of different periods of design history and therefore the passages below should be considered more as "broad brush strokes through history" than an in-depth portrayal of events, people and objects.

The lenses that will be used are built largely upon Sim Van der Ryn's "Rings" from his book *Design for Life* in which he writes, "Years ago I developed a simple three-ring diagram to help students understand that their role as designers is as mediators between what the culture and clients tell them they want and what nature tells us it needs."[1] Van der Ryn's three rings, altered and illustrated in Figure 1.1 provide, in his words, "a simple analytic and descriptive tool to relate the design of a civilization to its environment and underlying beliefs."[2] At the core, beliefs are expressed in Van der Ryn's words as *Mythos* or Spirit, or the "Why" of design. Jeremy Rifkin offers a helpful description of the core:

> What made the Romantic era unique within the context of the evolutionary history of empathic consciousness is the great stress placed on what Rousseau, and later Wordsworth and Whitman, called the "Sentiment of Being." Romantics argued that at the core of being there is an authentic self that is pure in nature, although corruptible by society.[3]

Rifkin's use of the word "nature" underscores an important aspect of the diagram – the vector that connects from the core out to nature and to the cosmos beyond – which expresses a line of potential integration, a unified design approach that links the design process to a set of core beliefs and to the natural world. *Technos* and Design, then, serve to express human activities in pursuit of survival, comfort and convenience, in short, the act of reshaping nature to suit human purposes, the "How" in Figure 1.1. Lastly, *Ecos* or Nature expresses the "What" of design. Nature provides the raw materials for construction and the ecosystem services to operate buildings and also provides the forces (wind, water, sun, contour, flora and fauna) that are shaped to create environments suitable for human habitation. Indeed, the idea of using design as a connector between humankind and the natural world as shaped by a set of core beliefs or world views is a foundational principle for sustainable design.

In Mark DeKay's 2011 book, *Integral Sustainable Design*, he shares his "Levels of Complexity," which he argues "arise from the unfolding sequence of development in human individuals, cultures and physical systems, which manifest as developmental sequences such as those for values, cognition, biological evolution, economic systems and world views."[4] His approach will help to identify and better understand different world views and their impacts on the design of the built environment, especially moving into the future. Ken Wilber's principle, "transcend and include,"[5] is a critical aspect of his Integral Theory which states that:

> in many of the developmental or evolutionary approaches, each worldview gives way to its successor because inherent limitations in the earlier worldview become apparent. This generates a great deal of disruption and chaos, so to speak, and the system, if it doesn't simply collapse escapes its own chaos by evolving to a more highly organized pattern.[6]

Jeremy Rifkin's catalytic forces of "communication and energy discoveries" as drivers of world view shifts will help to focus attention on the "dramatic impacts of social media and renewable energy systems upon our time."[7] Ian McHarg's treatise "On Values," from *Design with Nature* (first published 1969), will also help to place the discussion into clearer focus as it brings a much needed, if not essential, landscape architecture perspective. Lastly, historical analysis describes a deep rift that developed between humankind and nature – a rift so deep that only a calculated and concerted effort will begin the process of healing a planet in distress. Understanding the relationship, then, between world view, design and nature will help to illuminate the unique challenge and opportunity ahead for the current generation of built environment professionals.

Finally, a section called "Snap shots and sound bites" will be introduced to cover some of the expressions of the different world views from a design and construction perspective. In other words, how did the values and beliefs of a specific time in history change the behaviors and actions of those designing and constructing the built environment? And the question follows logically, what were the corresponding design education processes that either supported the existing behaviors or sought to change them? In short, how was design taught?

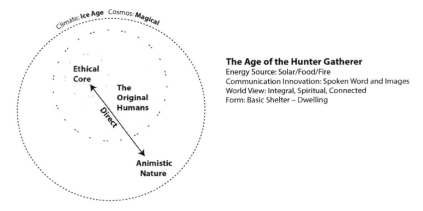

The Age of the Hunter Gatherer
Energy Source: Solar/Food/Fire
Communication Innovation: Spoken Word and Images
World View: Integral, Spiritual, Connected
Form: Basic Shelter – Dwelling

Figure 1.2
Age of the Hunter Gatherer
Diagram depicting the relationship between societal values and beliefs, human behaviors and the natural world

Source: *Van der Ryn, S. (2005)*

Early humans

The so called "primitive hut" which was appropriated by Marc-Antoine Laugier as "the origin of all possible forms of architecture"[8] is one way to think about the contribution of early humans to the development of the built environment. Laugier went on to recount a revisionist approach to design history by arguing that the "the column entablature and pediment are seen as all originating in the primitive hut."[9] In a similarly revisionist manner, the primitive hut could also be viewed as the *original sustainable structure*. The varying spatial configurations[10] and forms of early domestic architecture suggest a deep understanding of local site conditions and prevailing climatic patterns. The careful selection and processing of local materials, joined by complex tension connections, finished with layers of natural materials to shed water and shelter

13

against prevailing winds comprise a sophisticated and biophilic tectonic expression. The difference between a highly detailed and perfected eight hundred square foot Solar Decathlon house[11] and a highly detailed and perfected "hut" is negligible if one is willing to look at such structures without prejudice and without the pressures of conforming to contemporary design expectations.

While the current generation can draw inspiration and insight from the architecture of early humans, the broader lesson lies in understanding the consciousness that created such structures. The conception of humans as part of everything, as part of a food web, as part of the cosmos, without hierarchy, is perhaps the most profound lesson of all because such a world view denotes humility, innate connections to the natural world, and a deep understanding of interdependence – all of which describe modern day conceptions of sustainability. At a deeper level, the world view of early humans featured an equally deep connection to the inner self, the world of dreams, of spirit and of the imagination. In *The Things We Do: Using the Lessons of Bernard & Darwin to Understand the What, How and Why of Our Behavior*, Gary Cziko writes:

> At some point in the evolution of our species, our ancestors developed awareness of their own existence and desires as well as the strange and powerful force of life present in all living animals and humans, but obviously absent in the bodies of dead animals and humans. Therefore they developed belief in a soul or spirit that gave life to bodies and also accounted for human consciousness, thoughts, desires, and behavior.[12]

Human consciousness as defined by a strong connection to the ethical core as shown in Figure 1.2 and by an inextricable link to the world of nature comprises the nucleus of a highly integrated world view that thrived for thousands of years and continues to tenuously exist today in isolated, 'undeveloped' parts of the world. Early humans were the original sustainable architects and builders, not as a result of an abstract concept of "saving the planet" or to appear chic and stylish, but rather as a result of the simple need to survive and to provide comfort. Such direct forms of architecture appeal to our intuition as something so pure, and so unfettered by the contradictions and complexities that characterize today's built environment. The temptation to romanticize early human existence as "pristine" is tempered by research that shows that early humans used controlled burning to reduce heavy underbrush and thus prevent forest fires, and also removed trees to create favorable edge conditions known as ecotones for the purposes of security and increased biodiversity.[13] The interaction between humankind and the natural world was probably less pure than many would like to believe. The development of spoken language and visual symbols offered the first steps towards a more abstract, and by default a more objective view of the world. The assignment of words and symbols to elements found in nature signaled the beginning of a more formal ordering of the natural world and perhaps the end of a completely connected relationship between humankind and the natural world – the dawn of a human consciousness. Nevertheless, these early forms of existence continue to serve as icons of an indigenous world view that is rooted in place, culturally integrated with nature and deeply spiritual in the purest sense.

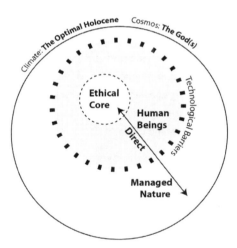

The Age of Agriculture
Energy Source: Solar/Surplus Food
Information Source: Written Language
World View: Traditional
Form: Simple

Design Education
Form: Mentorship
Teacher Student Ratio: 1:1
Values: Supportive
Behaviors: Desk Crit & Design Build

Figure 1.3
Age of Agriculture
Diagram depicting the relationship between societal values and beliefs, human behaviors and the natural world
Source: *Van der Ryn S. (2005)*

Agricultural society

While the development of language and symbols marked the first abstract building blocks of a barrier that would begin to form between humans and nature, the development of a new and more consistent

15

energy source via agriculture and animal husbandry (surplus food energy) would fuel the transition from animistic hunter gatherer societies to the next age of agrarian consciousness. Jeremy Rifkin argues:

> The cultivation of cereals some ten thousand years ago in North Africa, the Middle East, India, and China, marked a turning point for human society. The cereals have been called "the great moving power of civilization." The food surpluses provided an energy endowment to sustain growing populations and the establishment of kingdoms, and later of empires.[14]

The development of writing and arithmetic to manage the new energy regimes of surplus food forms the second component of Rifkin's recipe for a cultural leap in human evolution. He writes:

> Managing an increasingly complex energy regime necessitated a concomitant communications revolution. The Sumerians' invention of cuneiform – the first written script – was equally important to the invention of hydraulic technology in the production, storage, and distribution of grain. Cuneiform made it possible to oversee and supervise the vast complex operations required to maintain the whole hydraulic enterprise. Record keeping allowed the Sumerians to track all the operations, including monitoring the day-to-day storing and distributing of the grain.[15]

While writing and math provided great value in the overall evolution of human culture, it also reflected the ability to think abstractly to begin to pull further away from the direct connection to the natural world. The ability to assign a written word and an economic value to each natural object accelerated the adoption of the perception of elements of nature as a set of accumulated resources that would lead to comfort, wealth and greater security.

Lastly, the onset of the Holocene (Figure 1.4) provided a warmer and more hospitable climate for human development. The end of long and harsh ice ages thanks to early global warming aligns well with early agricultural practices and the rise of a higher level intellectual capability of humankind. While the ebbs and flows of nature via the passage of the sun and moon, yearly flooding patterns, and the coming and going of the seasons served as consistent connections to

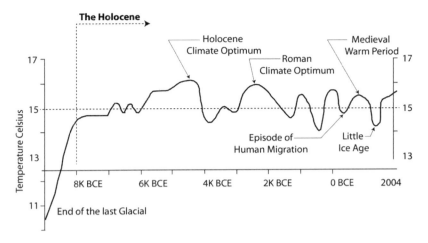

Figure 1.4
Holocene period and the Age of Agriculture
Average near-surface temperatures of the northern hemisphere during the past 11,000 years compiled. This is a chart often used by climate change deniers

Source: *Schönwiese, C.-D. (1997)*

nature, the invention of an accurate calendar by the Egyptians stands as one of many examples of the mapping of the natural world in defined abstract terms. The ability to store food (solar energy), and the communication regime to manage the energy (writing and arithmetic) converged to ignite the flame of technological process. Sadly, early solar energy, in the form of food, could only be converted to use in large quantities via animal and human labor (slavery). The added invention of money, or of abstract value to natural objects such as wheat or cattle, and even people, constituted a further and deeper objectification of the natural world and an increasing distance from the ethical core as shown in Figure 1.3. Plants and animals, once considered sacred within an animistic world view, could now be viewed as resources, as commodities to be bartered and leveraged to gain access to other commodities. With the advent of map making, the Earth itself (the landscape) could now be understood through abstract two-dimensional images that were used to define land ownership, serving to more deeply sever the ties between humans and the natural world because now the land itself could be understood as having monetary value. The emergence of abstract polytheistic gods and then to various monotheistic gods, offered an explanation for the organization of the cosmos and functioning of nature which further eroded the animistic understanding of nature as

17

intrinsically spiritual. Finally and perhaps most importantly, humankind, now freed from inconsistent and dispersed food sources and better shielded from the forces of nature, could now begin the long pursuit of increased comfort and convenience via scientific discovery and technological progress. The benefits of such progress are unquestioned. However, the objective view of the reality that would further separate humankind from the natural world and from the ethical core led, in part, to collateral damage to the natural world and increased subjugation of humans as slaves.

Snap shots and sound bites

During the Age of Agriculture in Europe, architecture and design existed within the tight hierarchical organization of the guilds. Design and construction was completed by stonemasons or carpenters who sometimes became the master builder, and the distinction between architect and engineer was commonly blurred.[16] This "blurring" speaks to the obvious benefits of disciplinary alignment but also to a deeper unity between qualitative thought processes (design) and quantitative thought processes (engineering and construction). The union between the two as an underlying capability of the iconic master builder is referred to quite often in sustainability courses partly because the entirety of a built project, from conception to completion, could be comprehended by a single mind, thereby allowing for the continued integration of design, engineering and construction. The approach of the designer builder is captured by the following quote from the 2008 Oxford Conference: A Re-Evaluation of Education in Architecture:

> One has observed that whether the lives of the people are directly bonded with the source of materials like forests (timber), village ponds (mud), or mountains (stone), there is a respect for nature and an understanding which proclaims that use only what you need. There are generations after you that are going to need the same things and therefore the responsibility lies with you.[17]

Domestic architecture, often classified as *traditional* or *vernacular*, expressed a close relationship to nature through careful selection and organization of sites, logical building orientation, manipulation of natural forces, the use of local materials and associated construction technologies and practices, all of which continue to comprise a significant set of contemporary sustainable design practices. Not surprisingly, some liken current day sustainability efforts to this approach with oft heard quotes such as, "Sustainability is not new and it's been around for a long time." The poetry of vernacular architecture continues to captivate even the most contemporary human, supporting the assertion that understanding the evolution of design is not about one set of expressions replacing another as some of the Modernists have argued, but rather a rich palimpsest of styles, approaches and technologies which continues to bring value to the present day.

The civic forms of the Age were designed and built as an abstract expression of an organized cosmology, a clear departure from the previous biophilic expressions of the hunter gatherer. Sim Van der Ryn calls such expressions, "metamorphic," and he writes:

> The form derives not from nature as before, but from a transcendent mythology or cosmology. The process and its rules are executed by craftsmen and master builders, probably without any written rulebook, but rather carried in their memory and experience, the great cathedrals of the Middle Ages are good examples.[18]

Design education in the Age of Agriculture

In Europe, the education of the designer and architect occurred through the apprentice model. An apprentice would serve a master for years, learning the totality of the trade through spoken word and direct experience. In that sense the ability of the designer to approach a project from all of its dimensions is passed down – a holistic model. Central to that process was a one to one relationship between teacher and student: "It is commonly understood that prior to the mid-19th century, architectural education existed as an apprentice system where aspiring architects would serve under the guidance of an experienced architect."[19] One can imagine the desk crit of today originating from such a deep and personal form of instruction. Because the architect was also the master builder, the instruction also formed a one to one relationship between the conception of an idea and its execution in built form – thereby reaffirming the tight linkage between an abstract idea drawn, perhaps in plaster, and the actual built work – a connected educational approach that balanced the subjective and objective aspects of human functioning.

Eventually the pupillage model came into existence where the relationship changed from a trade between the services of the master and apprentice to something resembling the current day model of paying for design education. Gary Stevens writes in *The Favored Circle: The Social Foundations of Architectural Distinction*, "We must start with the 'natural mode' of education for the Anglo-American system of professions, which is the self-controlling mechanism of apprenticeship or, strictly, pupillage."[20] Some states in the U.S. still allow for this model of education as means to gain licensure. The requirement of a professional degree as the sole pathway to registration is still novel when considering the way it has been done for centuries. Stevens continues his discussion on the Anglo origins of design education:

> Probably something like one-half of all entrants to the occupation were trained through pupillage by 1800, rising very quickly in the opening decades of the nineteenth century to displace other entry points into the occupation, such as through the building trades. Pupillage usually lasted five or six years, and often included attendance at a local arts academy, and perhaps foreign travel.[21]

Now, the education of designers was beginning to be released from the guilds and move into a fee-for-service model.[22] It should be noted that the pupillage model ensured a close relationship between the profession of architecture[23] and the associated educational process, an organic relationship, which again reinforces the theme of this section on holistic systems: between the profession and the educators, between the educator and the students and between the student and the actual built work.

While the descriptions of early forms of design education are beguiling and romantic, the pathway to becoming a master builder and an architect was typically reserved for the wealthy who could afford to pay for pupillage, travel and university courses. It was virtually impossible for a person from a lower economic class to become an architect; also troubling is the idea that social connections were as valuable as actual talent in terms of gaining employment with top architects.[24]

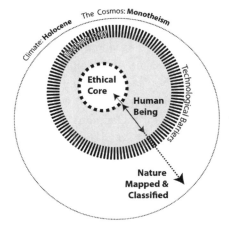

Early Industrial Age
Energy Source: Wind and Water
Communications Innovation: Printing Press
World View: Early Rationalism
Form: Symmetrical, Hierarchical

Design Education
Form: Atelier + The Academy
Teacher Student Ratio: 1:1 + 1:12
Values: Competitive
Behaviors: The Closed Design Jury

Figure 1.5
Early Age of Industry
Diagram depicting the relationship between societal values and beliefs, human behaviors and the natural world

Source: *Van der Ryn, S. (2005)*

The Early Age of Industry

It is hard to pinpoint the exact moment when one grand age transitions to another. Some argue that the transition to the Age of Industry from the Age of Agriculture began during the Renaissance, when humanity began to elevate itself above nature through technological innovation as fueled by scientific advancement and innovations in philosophy. The knowledge of the Greeks as stored and translated by the Persians, along with a series of important mathematical innovations such as algebra, were disseminated back into Europe via the invading and conquering Moors in Southern Spain. The now emerging abstract mental processes necessary to conceive of machines to harness the latent energy potential of wind and water through the use of windmills, sailing ships and water wheels, comprised a giant leap in the ability to put the forces of nature to work for the benefit of humankind. At roughly the same time, the invention of the printing press relieved the arduous process of hand copying books and exponentially increased the rate at which information could be shared. Lastly, despite a few mini ice ages and warming periods, the highly beneficial climatic stability of the Holocene served to provide the last ingredient of a recipe to transform human consciousness and by default create the conditions for the establishment of a new world view. The advent of the Scientific Method, the move towards reason over superstition and the later thrust of Positivism contained a new conception of the cosmos that shifted from a theological understanding of nature to one that was increasingly more reductionist, mechanistic, materialistic and secular. An example of this profound shift includes Descartes' opinion that "inanimate objects as well as plants and all animals were purely physical machines with no consciousness, desires, or purposes of any kind."[25] Descartes' dualistic philosophy would serve as one of the building blocks of a very long and very deep process of the disengagement of large segments of humanity from the natural world. Sim Van der Ryn writes "It [nature] is seen as a collection of separate and unrelated resources to be used to improve the human and economic condition."[26] However, such a separation has proven a valuable philosophic underpinning in the pursuit of scientific advancement which has led to dramatic increases in wealth (for some); improvements in human health (for many but not all); and ultimately higher levels of comfort and convenience for the developed world – in short, a culture of progress. Rifkin argues that:

> Progress was a revolutionary new idea for which there was little precedent. Time, in the new scheme of things, was no longer to be used in preparation for the Second Coming of Christ but rather as a means to advance the new temporal idea of progress. To believe in progress is to believe in a future that is always improving, enlarging and, above all, enduring. There is no end to progress. It is unstoppable, relentless.[27]

Leonardo Da Vinci's invention of perspective contributed to the rising tide of individualism over collectivism as a dominant theme that still persists to our time. The following quote from Jean Gebsner, author of *Ever-Present Origin*, serves to underscore this point:

> Leonardo's development of perspective with its emphatic spatialization of man's image of the world marks the beginning of the deficient phase of the mental structure ... the late European world and particularly its derivative cultures, the American and the Russian, are worlds of immoderation.[28]

The association of technological advancement with increasing levels of human comfort, "immoderation" and happiness (for some) would not just constitute the basis of the despoiling of the now "inanimate" natural world but would also set the stage for widespread social injustices across the globe through the auspices of colonialism, "settlement" and widespread enslavement. The individualistic entrepreneur, armed with a new, more rational world view, shielded by fledgling corporate law and driven by an intense desire for wealth, comfort and notoriety, could overlook the inhumane and barbaric treatment of human beings in order to build the lucrative slave trade. In this way, the despoiling of the natural environment in combination with the subjugation and oppression of indigenous peoples, serve as a reminder to understand that the human tendency to destroy nature and oppress humans comes from the same mind-set. McHarg writes, "The aboriginals whom they [the colonialists] confronted bore no such resentment [towards nature]. They had other views of human destiny and fulfilment."[29] The juxtaposition of the individualistic "explorers" versus the "collectivist" indigenous populations serves as an example of the quantum jumps of each successive world view transition.

While materialism, individualism and reductionism would eventually define the dominant world views (in the developed parts of the world at least), a persistent thread of counter views provided an antidote, offering the seeds of a sustainable future. Johann Wolfgang von Goethe, a prolific writer, scientist and philosopher, questioned the value of a purely rational approach to the world.[30] Goethe sought to account for subjective and objective perspectives in his work[31] and he outlined his method in the essay "The Experiment as Mediator between Subject and Object" (1772).[32] Later the Romantic Movement came into full force. Rifkin argues:

> Shortcomings aside, the Romantic Movement offered a sophisticated counter cosmology to the mathematical and mechanical universe of Rene Descartes and Isaac Newton. While Descartes found cosmic unity in mathematical laws and Newton in the laws governing gravitation, the Romantics saw it in the divine interconnectedness of all living beings. Their views anticipated the scientific vision of twentieth-century ecology.[33]

Snap shots and sound bites

Exponential population growth and increases in wealth via shipping, trading and enslavement formed the nucleus of an increasingly complex

European society. The individual architect, artist and designer began to leave the tightly controlled guilds, signaling a transition from designer as skilled craftsman to designer as individual professional. In a 2002 paper on the topic, K. L. Burns writes:

> During the nineteenth century, construction projects began to grow in complexity and scale. Growth led to new technology and techniques. New technology and techniques then led to specialization. As a result, the apprentice-trained master builder began to lose his expertise in all the building disciplines. This was when the master builder separated into two distinct professionals; the designer and the builder.[34]

Buildings, landscapes and interiors were of course larger and more complex, but also offered the opportunity to express the rationality and order of the new age. Perhaps the gardens of the Renaissance best reflected the changing design expressions of the time. Ian McHarg writes:

> In [Villa Aldobrandini and Mondragone] the authority of man was made visible by the imposition of a simple Euclidean geometry upon the landscape, and this is seen to increase within the period, man imposes his simple, entertaining illusion of order accomplished with great art, upon the unknowing and uncaring nature. The garden is offered as proof of man's superiority.[35]

The regimented, symmetrical and highly stylized gardens symbolized man's increasing mental and physical separation from the natural world. Buildings during this period, although geometric and perfected, still included a sense of nature through divine proportions – a remaining connection to the natural world. Over time the rise of mannerism and eventually the Baroque period would counter the harsh orthogonal lines of increasingly rationally derived design.

Design education in the Early Age of Industry

In 1789, when the École des Beaux-Arts was re-established and the Ecole Polytechnique[36] was formed, a fissure emerged between the architects who were associated with the fine arts and the architects associated with engineering. The split on some levels made sense as the technological revolution was producing new materials with new properties, and also large and complex infrastructure projects such as bridges. A deeper focus on the performative aspects of design was in order. However, the split also reflected a severing of the once connected qualitative and quantitative aspects of design through the master builder or more pointedly a divide between the subjective and objective approaches in design. Of course it's never that clean. Spiro Kostof, author of A History of Architecture: Settings and Rituals, softens the argument: "The split between building art and building science has probably been overdrawn. Nineteenth-century architects were not innocent of modern technology, nor were engineers devoid of a formal sense of design."[37] The passage below will delve a bit deeper into aspects of each school and some of the ramifications of the split between the two for our time.

The École des Beaux-Arts was famous for its highly competitive and rigorous processes.[38] The jury system, which is still in use today, was highly formal, often behind closed doors. Thomas Fisher, in an essay entitled "Critiquing the Design Culture," wrote:

> Studio culture pedagogy originates, in part, from 18th and 19th Century French rationalism, which held that through the analysis of precedent and the application of reason we could arrive at a consensus about the truth in a given situation. This rationalism underlays the teaching methods of the École des Beaux-Arts, brought to the first schools of architecture in the United States by architects such as William Ware and Richard Morris Hunt.[39]

Fisher's argument should not be a surprise by now as the relationship between world view and design expression naturally carries through to the educational processes that served the professions. The reliance on "rationalism" and the "application of reason" as the core tenets of design education both reflect and perpetuate the reductionist world view that was dominant in European culture at that time. Furthermore the emphasis on individuality and competition that continues to characterize contemporary design educational culture is reflected in an additional quote by Fisher:

> Many of the features of today's design studio – the unquestioned authority of the critic, the long hours, the focus on schematic solutions, the rare discussion of users or

clients – were begotten by that 150 year-old system. Specifically, the Prix de Rome personified the competitive culture as young architectural students vied for the prize, finding ways to please the closed jury.[40]

Later German influences further shaped design education. Fisher continues:

> The attention paid to star designers, the focus on current styles, the striving for freedom from constraints, the historicist nature of architectural theory, the tendency to polarize education and practice all echo the Hegelian beliefs that history moves through the world of a few great individuals, that every period has its characteristic styles, that history is moving towards a maximization of freedom of every person, and that cultures progress by a process of synthesizing polarities.[41]

The Ecole Polytechnique was overseen by Jean-Nicholas-Louis Durand. Durand's approach has been widely defined as "rational,"[42] and he himself preferred to be called an engineer rather than an architect even though he was placed second in the Prix de Rome in 1779 and 1780.[43] Gottfried Semper characterized his work as "a chess Grand Master of empty ideas,"[44] indicating that the rational approach to design was, perhaps, devoid of spiritual content. Furthermore Durand was one of the first to abandon the classical/natural proportioning systems in favor of the metric system adopted in France in 1795.[45] Durand's rejection of aesthetics[46] and his statement that "Architects should concern themselves with planning and nothing else"[47] suggest at least a partial origin for the conception of design as disconnected from nature among other things. In fairness, Durand's fixation on the plan was connected at least to the end users as he argued that, "A building will please if it serves our needs well."[48]

The split between the two sides, the rational/objective and the emotional/aesthetic (with an undercurrent of rationalism), in many ways made sense considering the increased complexities of new materials and new construction systems. The divide between the schools could also be viewed as a separation between the conception of design as satisfying the *wants* of society for imaginative expressions of privilege, good taste and beauty (École des Beaux-Arts) versus the *needs* of society for environments that support basic human functioning (the Ecole Polytechnique). The claim made here is bold and is offered as a prelude to a deeper exploration on the subject later in the book.

The ability of a single person to contain all of the necessary knowledge in one mind was becoming increasingly rare, making the appearance of the classic master builder increasingly rare. Furthermore, the tacit awareness of different personality types who possess different interests (some for art and some for science) makes a split a logical, if not inevitable conclusion. The impact, however, upon contemporary education and practice is dramatic when considering the desperate need for engineers, building scientists, architects and designers to work together to solve complex contemporary sustainability problems.

The French model was highly structured and state sanctioned, in contrast to the British pupillage model. While wealth and privilege were still the prerequisite for entry into the academies and by default the most prominent firms, the seeds of twentieth century educational models, which would hold much greater potential for individuals of all classes, was born. However it should be noted that the origins of western design education as emanating solely from the wealthy class continues to have implications for design education in the twenty-first century.

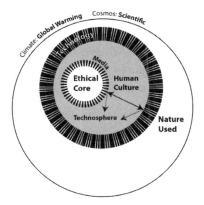

The Late Age of Industry
Energy Source: Fossil Fuels
Communication Innovation: Telephone, Radio, Film, TV
World View: Rational, Mental
Form: The Neutral Grid

Design Education
Form: The Studio
Teacher Student Ratio: 1:1 + 1:12
Values: Competitive
Behaviors: The Open Design Jury

Figure 1.6
Late Age of Industry
Diagram depicting the relationship between societal values and beliefs, human behaviors and the natural world

Source: *Van der Ryn, S. (2005)*

The Late Age of Industry

There is no certain method for identifying the transition between the early industrial revolution powered by wind and water to the next phase of development powered by fossil fuels. Perhaps The U.S. Civil War is an example of a defining moment in history when the Southern forces representing agriculture, slavery and food energy, where defeated by the Northern forces representing industrial processes, abolition and fossil fuel energy. On one level, the great injustice of slavery had finally been addressed first in Europe and later in the U.S., but on another level the use of coal and later oil and gas would once again exponentially increase the rate at which humanity could plunder the resources of the natural world. The simple equation of the Industrial Age – strip resources from the Earth, put them into production in the form of energy and products, consume those products and let the waste fall where it may – has come to represent an acceptable level of collateral damage necessary to deliver Progress. This linear conception of progress continues to be wildly profitable for companies and delivered convenience to the throngs of consumers seeking to maximize comfort. Underneath this *Cult of Progress* lies the simple philosophic view that nature is immutable, and its supply of resources infinite. Couple this underpinning with the continued rise of the corporation where individuals could separate their personal wealth and their conscience from decisions that generated unimagined profits and rampant destruction, the fuel to kindle widespread environmental destruction was complete. In the context of that time there really was no cause for concern as each destructive act, in isolation, was a mere pin prick in the Earth's natural beauty and a tiny portion of its otherwise vast store of resources. As populations grew, the number of pin pricks also grew, beginning to form a larger and more indelible mark on the planet.

In Figure 1.6, the term "media" is used as a definer of a second barrier between human culture and the ethical core. The barrier, labeled technology, forms a divide between ourselves and a natural world. Jean Gebser offers the following:

> In everyday life, few are aware that the motorization, and
> the technologization impose quantitative conditions on man
> that lead to an immeasurable loss of freedom. Machines,
> film, press, radio [today we can add to these the electronic
> time sinks of TV, video games and the Internet] lead not

> only to mediocrity and a dependency relationship, but also
> to an increasing de-individualization and atomization of
> the individual.[49]

The reference to "de-individualization" in the quote above speaks also to the following, from McDonough: "We have moved from people with lives, to consumers with lifestyles."[50]

Snap shots and sound bites

The International Style of architecture perhaps best reflected the now solidified rational world view (at least in the developed world). The expression of emerging technologies of steel and concrete structural systems, a new focus on horizontality versus verticality, a predilection for asymmetry, the pursuit of the building as a stripped down object floating on piloti perched in the neutral landscape, serve as characteristics of the then new Modern Architecture. As the pattern goes, the design expressions of the time were a reflection of the larger Modern world view of technological progress, individualism and increasing comfort. At the same time, the seeds of sustainable design were slowly finding their way into the message of the new, liberated design approach. Considerably larger window openings, increased natural light and fresh air, and larger and more expansive views to the natural landscape would constitute an increase in quality of life for many.[51] Therefore, the demonization of Modern Architecture as an enemy of nature, a common perception among sustainability professionals, is extreme. The rise of the landscape architect, specifically through the work of Olmsted, signaled the beginning of a more sophisticated relationship to the natural world and a larger cultural understanding that natural elements such as trees, water and open space are intrinsically connected to human health and well-being, hence the great expansion of urban parks around the world.

The iconic greats of the twentieth century – Wright, Le Corbusier, Aalto, Gropius et al. – come with such strong preconceptions that to discuss them in a shortened space would only serve to obfuscate the larger message. The temptation to paint Wright as a "early sustainable designer" is naïve; the desire to discuss the Bauhaus' interest in social equity as an ethical component of architecture is too risky; and the exploration of Le Corbusier's garden roofs in his Five Points may overstate the connection. In short, many seeds of sustainability can be found in the work of early Modernists but each reader comes to the greats with such preconceptions that a further discussion may derail whatever progress has been made so far.

The meteoric rise of Modern architecture and design, while liberating and seductive, also continued the expansion of the Cult of Progress across the world, and took unique form in America with the development of the suburban ideal. Armed with more powerful machines, clear dominion over nature and a desire to "sell" comfort and convenience, the suburban developers of the 1950s and 1960s waged war against the bucolic American landscape. McHarg writes: "Show me the prototypical anthropocentric, anthropomorphizing man and you will see the destroyer, atomic demolition expert, clear feller of forests, careless miner, he who fouls the air and water, destroys whole species of wildlife: gratified driver of bulldozers, the uglifier."[52] Indeed, the widespread "development" of the otherwise pristine natural landscape with a literally flattened ground plane covered in endless antiseptic lawns and dotted with nonindigenous ornamental trees reflected a final conquest of wild nature in the U.S. Ironically, the visually repetitive houses that marched relentlessly across the banal landscapes were, in many cases, traditional in form and expression, reminding the architects that the rest of the world had not yet adopted a preference for contemporary aesthetics. The post war housing developments of the U.S., first envisioned and built by the Levitts, were "fit for whites only," reaffirming the desire for homogeneity and leading to demonstrations and protest.[53] The overarching point of this diatribe on suburbia is to help reinforce the tight connection between world view and design expression. Sim Van der Ryn writes: "I describe the morphology of Mental design as mechamorphic – form follows the mechanical processes of production. The clockwork precision of the machine of parts is the ideal."[54]

Design education in the Late Age of Industry

The basic tenets of reason that underlie the Age were now joined by a fascination with new materials and new manufacturing processes. These forces, along with a continuing drive towards greater levels of freedom for wider groups of people, would also help to encourage changes in design education. While the long held tradition of the hierarchical and rational design education models of France continued to exist well into the twentieth century,[55] new organizations and models emerged as a response to the changing times. Most notably, the design jury evolved from a closed door event to an open process. Students now had the opportunity to publicly present and hear the responses from the jury, a major movement forward in terms of transparency and equity. However, the otherwise competitive aspects of design education continued to exist in full force.

The Bauhaus educational model possessed a dual nature. In one sense the school was still linked to the past through its manifesto: "the school was to teach crafts, and all the artists and architects were to work together towards the greater goal of building the future."[56] And Gropius proclaimed his goal as being "to create a new guild of craftsmen, without the class distinctions which raise an arrogant barrier between craftsman and artist."[57] In fact the Bauhaus awarded the Master-Builder's Diploma, further connecting its future oriented activities to the traditions of the past. Also embedded in the intention was the idea that the profession of architecture was, in theory, now open to those without wealth but who possessed great skill, a major move forward in breaking down the class barriers that dominated architectural education.

At the other end of the spectrum the Bauhaus was clearly the home to the new expression of the increasingly powerful industrial world view. Not surprisingly, it was the only art school to teach the development of industrial products during its time.[58] The clear focus of the school was towards the future, as indicated in its manifesto, and so the diminishment of history as a subject to be explored is not surprising (very little emphasis on history was a vast departure from the precedent model employed by the French schools) and the dedication to a rationalist approach to design was clearly on the agenda.[59] However, Gropius himself took umbrage at the accusation that his work and educational methodologies where part of a tabula rasa and blind to the traditions that came before.[60] He wrote, "Craft was taught as a preparation for mass production."[61] Contrary to the increased specialization that was beginning to take place in the design, engineering and construction industries, the leaders of the Bauhaus sought higher levels of collaboration towards a more unified and integrative design process. The school was remarkable in its ability to transcend disciplines; as Kenneth Frampton argues, "Gropius succeeded in keeping together in happy co-operation such dissimilar artists as Kandinsky, Feininger, Klee and Schlemmer."[62]

While the focus also rested upon the progressive goals of increasing the standard of living through increased use of technology, Gropius was aware of one possible negative end game and suggested that architects should "avert mankind's enslavement by machine by giving its products a content of reality and significance and so saving the home from mechanistic anarchy."[63] Clearly Gropius and others of his time understood the great paradox of what they were working on: on the one hand they embraced all the great principles of the current world view – efficiency, rational thought and purity – but on the other they also understood that the trend if not interrupted by talented designers such as themselves would doom society to a banal existence. The educational process employed by the Bauhaus, then, hinged upon a balance between the qualitative and quantitative aspects of design – a holistic approach.

Also, it should be noted that a sense of equity follows threads through the statements and work of the Bauhaus – in this case a reference to class distinctions in the quote earlier but also clear references to socialism and social responsibility[64] by the time Adolph Meyer came to control the school and pressed his socially responsible agenda through the design of inexpensive furniture.[65]

As is now well known, the great masters of Germany migrated to the U.S. and of course had immediate impact. Thomas Fisher writes:

> With the advent of Modernism, American architecture schools were greatly impacted ... Most notably, Walter Gropius went on to serve as the head of the architecture school at Harvard and Mies van der Rohe became the head of the architecture school at the Illinois Institute of Technology.[66]

The power of the industrial world view now coupled with an influx of Modern masters catapulted the U.S. design education system hurtling towards the future at great speed. It wasn't long before many U.S. schools abandoned the Beaux-Arts style in pursuit of new architectural expressions, but the driving philosophy of hard work, competition and the use of precedents remained a cornerstone of design education, for better or worse.

The Taliesin School offered a different pathway towards education of the designer. The great depression reduced commissions for Frank Lloyd Wright and forced him to open a school of architecture. In 1931 Frank and Olgivanna Lloyd Wright circulated a prospectus to an international group of distinguished scholars, artists and friends, announcing their plan to form a school in Spring Green, Wisconsin to "Learn by Doing."[67] The couple's unique educational experiences as children led in part to the project based learning curriculum. However the idea was taken much further at Taliesin, with students spending time working in the fields, preparing meals and building structures. In fact, design students were sometimes required to build or renovate their own domiciles out in the desert at Taliesin West, providing a connection between design, construction, available materials and the local climatic conditions.[68] The Wrights clearly sought an integral model of education, one that was not isolated from other more mundane aspects of life – a grounded approach. Furthermore, the Wrights' inclusion of dance and theater as required elements of the curriculum suggests a desire to create a well-rounded student, a departure perhaps, from the competetive models adopted in the U.S. from Europe.[69]

The school's methodologies continue to be considered unique, suggesting that the Wrights' educational model is almost cult like in its core beliefs and its associated behaviors.[70] Like the Bauhaus, the Taliesin school was multidisciplinary, although still architecture centric in its approach. "The fine arts, so called," they asserted, "should stand at the center as inspiration grouped about architecture [of which landscape and the decorative arts would be a division]."[71] Education at Taliesin would emphasize painting, sculpture, music, drama and dance "in their places as divisions of architecture."[72]

Wright's approach to design and design education was at odds with the mainstream. While the rest of the world moved towards an increasingly pure form – to a level of orthodoxy – Wright continued to explore aspects of site integration, "natural materials," nature inspired decorative arts and organic plan geometries, which all led to deep levels of complexity in form and expression. More importantly the approach reflected a thrust towards integration – a union between the qualitative and quantative approaches to design. Wright's work, then, existed outside of the prevailing direction of architecture of the time, which leads to the supposition that Wright's *forms* were in fact *following world view* – just one that did not yet exist. This in part might explain why the International Style, with its clear expression of the dominant world view, defeated Wright's organic approach and became the de facto style and expression for the twentieth century and beyond.

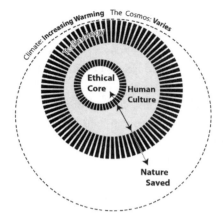

Age of Information
Energy Source: Nuclear
Communication Innovation: The Internet
World View: Pluralistic, Relativistic, Postmodern
Form: Negotiated

Design Education
Form: Design Studio
Scale: 1:1 + 1:12
Values: Diversity + Environmentalism
Behaviors: Participatory Design

Figure 1.7
Age of Information
Diagram depicting the relationship between societal values and beliefs, human behaviors and the natural world. Notice that the barriers between the rings are still increasing in width but openings are beginning to appear
Source: Van der Ryn, S. (2005)

The Age of Information

The 1960s sowed the seeds of a conflict between one world view fueled by the unparalleled benefits of technological progress versus a second emerging view focused on a paradigm based on ecological balance and social equity. Over the next 45 years the two opposing world views would begin to express themselves in different ways, each twisting around the other to generate a tumultuous time. Conflicts arose, including sprawling materialistic suburban communities versus the long and hard struggle for civil rights; the unprecedented dumping of chemicals into waterways versus the awareness of man's negative impact on the planet via Rachel Carson's *Silent Spring*; and the amazing technological achievements of the Apollo missions versus the new found understanding of the Earth as a "big blue marble."[73] It's not surprising that the Age of Information also includes the movement of society towards a more pluralistic, relativistic Postmodern world view. The sacrifice of lives and livelihoods by the civil rights leaders in the 1960s opened the door to a new found, yet awkward, connection between ethnic groups previously separated by the strict walls of racist society. It also propelled the legitimacy of the subject into the mind-set of larger numbers of people who were also willing to take action on the issue as citizens began to awaken from the hypnotic trance of the Cult of

Progress. The fact that both widespread social and environmental movements started at the same time is not coincidental, as the same mind-set that would allow corporations and governments to despoil the natural world could also allow for oppression of one set of human beings by others. The ability of the human mind to rationalize its actions via philosophy and/or religious convictions is a theme that runs through history. The 1960s represented a time when that kind of thinking was called into question. People began to ask the hard but simple questions: Why should one group of humans experience such brutal discrimination and oppression while others freely enjoy all that Progress has to offer? Why should the Earth with its rich abundance of resources and infinite beauty fall victim to destruction in the name of Progress? Why should corporations be allowed to amass huge profits without consideration for basic human rights or the health and well-being of the planet? The Age of Information reflects the great awakening of larger society from the long slumber induced by the comforts provided by the industrial idiom.

By the 1970s several civil rights Acts had been passed by the U.S. Congress, followed by the Clean Water, Clean Air, and Species Endangerment Acts. At the same time the legacy of the Age of Industry continued to impact the planet, most notably through the Union Carbide plant explosion in Bhopal in 1984, and the Exxon Valdez oil spill in 1989. These examples demonstrate that environmental destruction and human suffering are intimately connected and underscores the realization that issues of economics, environment and equity are difficult, if not impossible to separate.

At the same time the United Nations worked steadily during the 1970s and 1980s to resolve the competing motivations of technological progress in pursuit of profit and wealth versus environmental protection and equitable treatment of all people. The creation of the Brundtland Commission and its now famous report, *Our Common Future*, published in 1987 laid the groundwork for a unification of the two competing world views. The now overly familiar definition of sustainable development contained within the report reads, "Sustainable development is development that meets the needs of the present without compromising the ability of future generations to meet their own needs."[74] The idea of limitations imposed by the definition implies a protection of environmental resources far into the future. But, the definition clearly denotes "sustainable development" as a de facto reality now and into the future. The definition seeks to build a framework in which the Cult of Progress can continue but not without limitations and not without a commitment to long term thinking and intergeneration equity.

By 1993, the response to the Brundtland Report and the general call of sustainability began to take further shape in the design community. William McDonough delivered the "Centennial Sermon: Design, Ecology, Ethics and the Making of Things" at the Cathedral of St. John the Divine in New York City.[75] His speech marked the first time that the design professions were so publicly linked to the processes and products that contribute to environmental degradation. He also introduced the role of the chemist Michael Braungart in sustainability work, underscoring the importance of knowledge based design (i.e. quantitatively understanding the impact of different design decisions), and also the importance of interdisciplinary design where individuals with radically different skill sets work together to solve problems. At the same time Susan Maxman, President Elect of the American Institute Architects, chose sustainability as the theme for the "Architecture at the Crossroads" conference held by the AIA and the International Union of Architects. Not only was she the first woman president of the organization, she was willing to set the vision of sustainability for a very large national organization. The founding of the Green Building Council also occurred in 1993, paving the way for an organized and targeted approach to promoting the growth of the green building industry – a clear response to the need for higher levels of environmental responsibility among the design and construction professions. The interdisciplinary nature of the organization underscores the kinds of groups that would become so common in the twenty-first century and filled a significant societal need that the existing professional organizations were either unwilling or unable to provide. Lastly, President Clinton launched the "Greening of the Whitehouse" initiative that marked a string of government generated requirements for green and sustainable practices and techniques in the built environment. Then in 1994 Paul Hawkin's *Ecology of Commerce* offered the public an evolved sensibility to the financial aspects of sustainable design. Looking at these events in retrospect, one would assume a meteoric rise of sustainability into the mainstream. Instead a quiet but consistent growth occurred and finally accelerated with the creation and adoption of the LEED® Rating System in 1998. Soon after, the green building market began to grow at a much more reliable pace.

Snap shots and sound bites

If in fact form follows world view, then the Age of Information should witness the emergence of new design approaches and new expressions. The late 1950s and early 1960s witnessed a rise of ecologically minded designers anchored most notably by Buckminster Fuller who was able to explore the desire for technological progress (Dymaxion House) but also new biomimetic approaches to structure and form (geodesic dome). Frank Lloyd Wright began to more directly address energy efficiency in his Hemisphere House. His work and teachings would spawn a thread of ecological design which would carry well into the current day in the work of Bruce Goff and Paolo Soleri. In parallel, Ian McHarg published *Design with Nature*, a seminal text in ecological design that would influence generations of built environment professionals including John Tillman Lyle, Leslie Saur and Carol Franklin – who now serve as bridges to the twenty-first century's sustainable design movement.

While the majority of designers and planners maintained their strict allegiance to orthodox Modernism, others broke from the mold. Jane Jacobs, in *The Death and Life of Great American Cities* in 1961 offered "messy vitality" as something to be desired as opposed to the clean, sanitized and ordered vision of urban renewal. Denise Scott Brown and Robert Venturi advocated for a new, pluralistic avenue of expression through projects that not only directly related to the surrounding context (Sainsbury Wing) but also explored adorned architecture through the design of Woo Hall on the Princeton Campus. Michael Graves' Portland Building remains the iconic image associated with Postmodernist architecture. James Wines of SITE Architects, Artists and Designers, explored early green aesthetics with a pop culture flavor. Glen Murcott's work perhaps best reflected a growing interest in Critical Regionalism, while the members of the firm Jersey Devil literally lived on site during the design and construction of their projects.

Perhaps most indicative of the changing emphasis of design as influenced by the new world view was the emerging field of adaptive reuse and historic preservation. The long standing rejection of historical precedent, a cornerstone of orthodox Modernism, was turned on its head by the emergence of adaptive reuse and the rise of the Interior Designer. In terms of sustainability, the restoration of old structures is both a laudable energy efficiency approach but also provided much needed cultural nourishment – a reaction to the refined but relatively neutral boxes of Modern Architecture. One could argue that historic preservation served as an early form of sustainable design.

Architects, Designers and Planners for Social Responsibility (ADPSR) was established in 1981 to promote nuclear disarmament and correct the imbalances caused by military excesses overshadowing domestic needs. Throughout the 1980s, ADPSR initiated numerous peace projects including peace parks, conferences, exhibits and citizen diplomacy exchange programs with the former Soviet Union. Since 1990, ADPSR has focused much of its effort on ecologically and socially responsible development. Soon a range of overtly ecologically minded design projects came to fruition. Susan Maxman's Women's Humane Society Animal Shelter began to explore the ethical content in architecture and their highly sustainable project the Cusano Nature Center predated the LEED® Rating System. Finally, the construction of the Chesapeake Bay Foundation Headquarters reflected the latest thinking of its time and received the first LEED® platinum rating in the U.S.

The emergence of the participatory design process began to replace the hierarchical and destructive practices that led to urban renewal and signaled the drive towards greater equity in the design and planning processes. Christopher Alexander promoted his computer programming and user centered approach to design.[76] Alexander writes:

> At the core ... is the idea that people should design for
> themselves their own houses, streets and communities. This
> idea ... comes simply from the observation that most of the
> wonderful places of the world were not made by architects
> but by the people.[77]

These emerging design processes which would become increasingly common in the next age have their roots in a pluralistic, networked world view where increases in social equity and ecological awareness set the stage for the next Age of Integration.

Design education in the Age of Information

In the late 1970s and early 1980s scores of "energy efficiency" studios and programs cropped up as a response to the then significant issue of energy independence in light of the OPEC oil scare. The studios disappeared just as quickly as oil prices dropped. In 1993 Samuel Mockbee founded the now well-recognized relationship between design build and social responsibility through the invention of the Rural Studio.[78] The idea that students could learn design in a direct, one to one method while simultaneously helping people in need (end users) and by the creative and sustainable use of repurposed materials is now commonly understood, or at least respected by the majority of design educators. Mockbee's following quote best describes the act of design as a vehicle for connecting to the ethical core: "Love your neighbor as yourself. In so doing, an architect will act on a foundation of decency that can be built upon. Help those who aren't likely to help you in return, and do so even if nobody is watching!"[79] After the watershed year of 1993, when sustainability as an overarching ethic and framework entered into the zeitgeist of the majority of design professions (landscape architecture was already there), several initiatives were launched with the aim of catalyzing a wider adoption of sustainability, among other progressive agendas, in the curriculum in design schools. In 1995, Marvin Rosenman launched the ambitious EASE project (Educating Architects for a Sustainable Environment), pulling together many top thinkers and educators of the time to formulate a cohesive and clear plan to move sustainability forward in architecture schools. One of the great accomplishments of the EASE project was its dedication to inclusivity (multiple voices in the process), its cooperative spirit, and its innovative and open approach to sustainability. While much was accomplished, including an insightful collection of "entry points" to sustainable design education, and despite the presence of many top thinkers, the EASE project never had the impact upon the overall design education community that Rosenman had hoped to achieve. In the end, Rosenman argued that even his home institution at Ball State wavered on its commitment to sustainability after his retirement.[80] Such lurches forward followed by such profound periods of silence from design educators express a series of conflicting but disturbing realities. Perhaps sustainability was not perceived as a clarion call to action by the majority of faculty. Perhaps sustainability was just another hindrance in an otherwise dogmatic pursuit of theoretical exploration and deeper manipulation of form, space and skin. Perhaps design faculty were already burdened by the existing weight of their responsibilities and sustainability meant not only a change to the syllabus but also a change in mind-set. In that sense, the ideas and concepts explored at EASE were more characteristic of the next, more integral world view.

Age of Integration
Energy Source: Renewable Energy
Communication Innovation: Social Media + Cloud Networks
World View: Integral
Form: Emergent Design, Bio-integrated, Living Systems

Design Education
Form: The Collective
Teacher Student Ratio: 1:1 + 1:12 + 1:144
Values: Sustainability, Cooperation, Inclusiveness
Behaviors: Co-creative Integrated Project Delivery

Figure 1.8
Age of Integration
Diagram depicting the relationship between societal values and beliefs, human behaviors and the natural world. Notice that media and technological barriers have become more porous and lighter, suggesting an era of integration and wholeness
Source: *Van der Ryn, S. (2005)*

The Age of Integration

If the 1960s held the seeds of a green world view, the beginning of the twenty-first century featured the blossoming of sustainability. It can be argued that the decade starting with Y2K and ending with the BP oil spill marked a profound and final transition from the previous eras of Industry and Information to the Age of Integration, a move from an unsustainable, fossil fuel driven society to a new sustainable society, powered by renewable energy, coordinated through advanced communication systems and built upon the Age of Information's newly found ethical framework. The favorable climate of the Holocene was coming to an end, largely due to the impacts of high levels of human generated carbon and methane in the atmosphere. The new era, dubbed the Anthropocene, features rising temperatures, severe drought, frequent and intense natural disasters, sea level rise, loss of biodiversity and desertification – in short a far less favorable climate for the continued support of human activities as they are currently constituted. While the possibility exists for a downturn in the warming of the planet (see Figure 1.9), the overwhelming scientific evidence points towards a continued rise of greenhouse gasses and a continued trend of global warming and climate change.[81]

Notice that the "hockey stick" made famous by Al Gore and the Intergovernmental Panel on Climate Change (IPCC), is not present in Figure 1.9. Instead, this diagram is adapted from the models most used

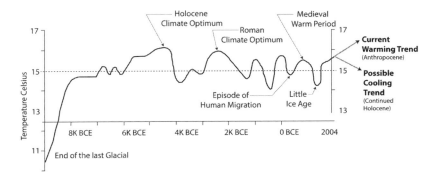

Figure 1.9
Dawn of the Anthropocene
Average near-surface temperatures of the northern hemisphere during the past 11,000 years compiled. This is a chart often used by climate change deniers
Source: *Schönwiese, C.-D. (1997)*

by climate change deniers which purport to demonstrate that even with the intense warming period over the last few decades the current period is still cooler than previous times in history. However, if the current warming trend continues as predicted by the IPCC, humanity will find itself in literally new territory as existing land masses will be redefined by changing coast lines, flooding rivers and sinking islands.

Between 2005 and 2012 a series of cataclysmic events would place into view the precarious state of the relationship between humanity and the natural world and further drive home a growing perception of the Earth as fragile, finite and precious. In 2005, Hurricane Katrina followed quickly by Rita sent shock waves through American culture because it exposed the relatively meager attempts at technological protection through levees that broke and through mechanical pumps that failed. In addition the rampant destruction by the oil industries of the barrier islands and coastal wet lands that normally serve as buffers against high winds exacerbated the damage and loss of life in New Orleans. The slow emergency response by national agencies called into question whether the U.S. had, in fact, evolved to higher levels of social consciousness. While the amazing outpouring of assistance post hurricane by thousands of religious and humanitarian groups underscored the growing levels of empathy in society. In the end, Hurricane Katrina served as an example of the growing perception of the public regarding the connection between global warming and intense weather patterns. A few months later, the devastating tsunami in

Banda Aceh, while not connected to global warming or climate change, contributed to the growing awareness of the relative helplessness of humans in the face of the destructive power of nature. Again, the empathic sensibility of the Age of Integration was expressed by unprecedented financial giving and global rescue efforts. The publication of Al Gore's book and movie, *An Inconvenient Truth*, while lambasted by climate change deniers, offered a stark vision of a high carbon environment that would become increasingly inhospitable and deadly to humankind. At the same time, a spike in gas prices in the U.S., partly due to the loss of oil and gas infrastructure in the Gulf of Mexico from the hurricanes, coupled with the war in Iraq, began to solidify a growing perception that oil and gas might be a more finite resource than previously thought. This new view of nature's bounty as scarce began to accelerate the movement of governments and companies to address a growing expectation for energy efficient systems and products.

The great recession which began in 2007 increased the gaps between rich and poor and exposed the low moral fiber of Wall Street. In addition, the increased suffering of the world's poor, the development of new, more austere lifestyles of the middle class and the decline of hedonistic consumption in developed countries have served to build a new economic reality. The emerging green economy that features the green jobs movement, huge investment in clean technologies such as wind and solar and unprecedented government incentive programs around the world provide the only bright spot in an otherwise dismal economic landscape. Barack Obama gained office by lassoing the disparate elements of the Triple Bottom Line to build a campaign based on new conceptions of environment, economy and equity. His support for the clean tech industry (solar and wind), as catalyzed by public and private investment, and populated by living wage green jobs, formed a hopeful proposition for the future not just of America but for the world as a whole (his tours where sold out in Europe). Furthermore, the fact that an African American could be elected president in a predominately Caucasian country pays homage to the efforts and sacrifices of so many civil rights leaders and participants.

The 2010 BP oil spill once again revealed the stark twenty-first century contrast between the continued quest for high profits in the corporate world and the realities of peak oil, and environmentally destructive practices. The dialectic between profit and planet still playing out, despite a changing world view, would be called into question once again via accusations of corporate negligence. But the BP oil spill also brought to light, once again, the relationship between social equity and environmental degradation. Eleven men died in the explosion and countless businesses were ruined – by an explosion and oil spill that has its roots in corporate negligence. But the twenty-first century attributes of empathy, social responsibility and environmental awareness forced BP to pursue quick and fair repayment, a contrast to the highly litigated and ineffective reparations for the victims of the Exxon Valdez oil spill in the 1980s.[82] The pattern of cataclysmic events continued beyond 2010 with the Fukushima nuclear disaster, which caused untold human suffering, and called into question the efficacy of nuclear power as a viable transitional energy source to renewables such as wind and water. The record breaking 2010 summer in Russia led to the loss of hundreds of lives. Moreover, the hottest decade on record has set in motion a long anticipated methane release from the Russian Tundra, with an anticipated impact 20 times greater than carbon emissions.[83] Lastly the record breaking 2012 droughts in the U.S. continued to bring home the dramatic changes in climate that were taking place around the world.

As a result of these and many other events, the first dozen years of the twenty-first century were nothing short of tumultuous, a wild ride through strange weather, near economic collapse, political firsts and an emotional rollercoaster brought on by terrorism and war. In addition, the emergence of Rifkin's factors for the rise of a new consciousness – new energy sources (wind and solar) and new communication technologies (social media) – combined with the emergence of the first new climatic era in twelve thousand years has brought humanity to the doorstep of the Age of Integration.

Global society is now beginning to move to a new world view, a new paradigm complete with fundamentally different means of technological progress, revolutionary new financial models (Google, Wikipedia, Facebook, eBay, et al.), evolving sensibilities of empathy and equity and lastly, and perhaps most importantly, a fundamentally new understanding of our relationship with the natural world. The statistics and facts bear this out. Paul Ehrlich's $I = PAT$ equation is more relevant today than ever. Population rise (P) and the emergence of an increasingly larger global middle class (A), along with dramatic technological advancements requiring huge amounts of energy (T), continue to increase the impacts (I) upon the Earth's ability to adequately provide eco-system services. The technology variable (T) of Ehrlich's equation has been attacked through the development and adoption of green technologies. The Population (P) variable has been attacked by social policies such as China's One Child Policy, and the variable Affluence (A) was attacked via socialism and communism. The premise of this simple equation communicates the tenuous position of humans on the planet. Clearly the levels of comfort and convenience enjoyed for centuries by some, at the expense of others, are now in jeopardy. The United Nations, large multinational corporations, government agencies at all scales, have begun to take the threats seriously. At the same time, large and well-organized grassroots movements geared towards sustainability have sprouted up all around the world. The convergence of the top down and bottom up efforts to express the new consciousness of integration have created a new context for designers, and in turn have set the stage for the development of new and more effective approaches to design education.

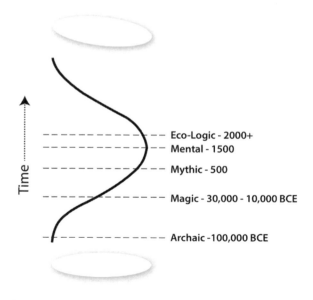

Figure 1.10
Sim Van der Ryn's spiral of consciousness/culture depicting the Age of Eco-Logic
Source: *Van der Ryn, S. (2005)*

Coming full circle

Figure 1.10, by Sim van der Ryn, explains in as clear terms as possible the dawn of the new age, which he dubs Eco-Logic. For orientation purposes, the term "Magic" in the diagram parallels the hunter gatherers referred to earlier. Van der Ryn writes:

> The diagram visualizes the perennial philosophy as a cylinder of four-dimensional space. Humankind is like a spiralling gene through time and space. Each turn represents a new epoch, a nonbiological mutation of consciousness superimposed on existing form, all previous forms are transparent and accessible. Everything is experienced as a self-similar (fractal) aspect of the whole.[84]

He continues:

> Chaos theory and fractal geometry provide additional support for the view that the world that the rational mind assumes is fixed and knowable and separate from us is not. I have faith in the possibility of human culture and consciousness transcending a long obsession with objects, quantities and control, moving towards an ecological intelligence and compassion for everything that is changing. Including each of us.[85]

Snap shots and sound bites

The clues that lead to the expression of the new world view of integration are all around us, next to us and inside us. Like the Holy Grail, integration exists as an ideal, an attracting force that drives the more meaningful efforts of process and method over the seemingly insistent demand for the perfected product. Imperfection, in the Age of Integration, is accepted and celebrated, because the application of an ethical foundation will, by default, make things very messy and uncomfortable and therefore the examples must be understood in that context.

The Living Building Challenge[86] and the Sustainable Sites Initiative[87] offer the first glimpse at the definition of holistic and integrated design. Although problematic, the requirement for *Beauty* in the Challenge and the request for *Social Equity* in the Initiative begin to build a larger and more comprehensive vision of design from the sustainability sector. Perkins+Will released its *Precautionary List*[88] that contains, among others, bio-accumulated toxins and reflects a shift from the previous era's greening efforts to a new emphasis on restorative and regenerative processes and products. In the new model, the mantra of "do no harm," is a baseline position. Harvard University, for example, built its one hundred and fiftieth LEED® rated project by 2012,[89] thereby completing its greening efforts, as a means to lay the groundwork for more ambitious regenerative initiatives in the future. Andropogon landscape architects and Kieran Timberlake Associates designed a project at Sidwell Friends School in Washington D.C. that collects, treats and reuses all water on site, an integration between land and form that generates a highly functioning ecologically minded project.[90] Re:Vision Architecture, among others, has moved from the mechanized linear design process to the deeply integrative design charrette as a core practice in pursuit of higher levels of integration.[91] The designers, engineers and builders of Masdar City in Saudi Arabia continue their long march towards a net zero energy city of 40,000.[92] The pathway towards integration is inclusive, meaning that there are multiple entry points to success: from Norman Foster's and Renzo Piano's "technophilic" approach to Emilio Ambasz's biophilic architecture, to the financially responsible, sustainable and evocative work of Morphosis, and to the ecological designs of Sim Van der Ryn and Andropogon Associates.

Design education in the Age of Integration

The central theme of this chapter has been to study the linkages between world view, design expression and design education. The changes occurring in the design academies in the early part of the twenty-first century are nothing less than profound. The Solar Decathlon began its long run of popularity with the design community and the general public, as evidenced by the 2011 session which received over 350,000 visitors.[93] The Decathlon resonates on many levels, from the simple, almost primitive program of a small living space, a twenty-first century *hut*, perhaps, to the proposition that highly performing buildings can also be beautiful, to the high levels of corporate sponsorship which reflect the move from green washing to actual financial investment in sustainability and finally, to the idea that students and faculty from design schools can effectively collaborate with engineering, marketing and construction departments. The Decathlon continues to remind us of the close connection between the ethic of sustainability and the real world application of design build education. The two are often linked, not just at the Decathlon but also in

John Quale's EcoMOD homes, in the continued success of the Rural Studio and the work of Dan Rockhill and his students in the remarkable revitalization of Greensburg Kansas.

In 2006, Kira Gould and Lance Hosey completed a deeply insightful and thorough study of the state of sustainability in design education entitled Education for a Sustainable Future. Funded by the AIA and the Tides Foundation, the report identified ecological literacy as a key component of a student's development towards becoming an effective sustainable designer.[94] While their study focused primarily on architecture schools, many of the lessons are transferrable to interior design and less so to landscape architecture. The report collected many examples of highly functioning design curricula but in the end lamented the overall lack of initiative and movement towards wider adoption of sustainability in design programs.[95]

In 2008, the Oxford Conference: A Re-evaluation of Education in Architecture provided a wide array of points of view on the subject of design education and sustainability. R. Bennetts offered the following statement:

> My hope, then, is that the 2008 Oxford Conference will recognise the significance of sustainability as a vehicle for change, not simply in the rapidly evolving design of architecture for a better environment, but in the way buildings are conceived, crafted and procured. If architects wish to be at the centre of things once again – and I would argue that they cannot afford to be anywhere else – the arrival of sustainability as the issue of our age requires an educational manifesto of equal stature.[96]

The conference was largely unprecedented in its scope and depth regarding sustainable design education and revealed on one level broad agreement that changes must occur, but at another level the wide diversity in views on what constitutes sustainability and what approaches should be used in education. They ranged from the ambitious "The Carbon Neutral Design Project" by the Society of Building Science Educators (SBSE)[97] to the pursuit of biomimicry as a model for sustainable design[98] to John Quale's "Real Buildings with Real Budgets."[99]

Today, educational institutions are beginning to express the new mantra of integration. Columbia's Building Intelligence Project (C-BIP) aligns highly capable professionals from a variety of disciplines and companies with the faculty to take on the hugely challenging problem of low performing sky scrapers in New York City. Illinois Institute of Technology is promoting its Master of Integrated Building Delivery program which unites builders, engineers and architects through the use of building information modeling software. In the UK a similar approach is used at the University of Salford Manchester's BIM and Integrated Design degree program. The founders of Philadelphia University's MS in Sustainable Design have consciously created an entirely new educational approach based on Ken Wilber's Integral Theory and Mark DeKay's Integral Sustainable Design and features the use of highly collaborative integrative design charrettes as a core behavior to pursue sustainability. William Braham at Penn Design's new Master of Environmental Building Design is actively exploring the application of Howard Odum's theories of Emergy and Maximum Power. The Boston Architectural College and Philadelphia University are evolving the use of digitally enabled on-line teaching to connect the societal imperatives of sustainability to a wider and more diverse audience. This is not an exhaustive list. It's clear that, by now, most schools have at least reached the level of "greening" with dedicated studios or "woven curricula" that begin to attack the higher bar of sustainability. The bifurcated and highly regimented departmental and compartmental approaches so common in most universities inhibit and often deny deeper attempts to attack higher levels of integration. The impetus then is pushing towards the creation of entirely new structures for delivery of education and/or dramatic transformations of existing curricula.

The mantra *form follows world view* asks each of us to examine our intentions, personal values and behaviors in pursuit of sustainability. Ken Wilber offers the following as a descriptor of the larger context of our time:

> This transformation is being driven by a new techno-economic base (informational) but it also brings with it a new world view, with a new mode of self and new intentional and behavioural patterns, set in a new cultural worldspace with new social institutions and anchors. And, as usual, specific individuals may, or may not, live up to the possibilities.[100]

Design educators, administrators and accreditors are up to this challenge and will evolve. But will the response continue to be *reactive* in its position, as in design schools playing catch up with the rest of society? Or will the response be proactive – an embracing of the vast potential of sustainability and integration not just to restore a damaged ecology or to move towards a more equitable society but also to improve design education itself? The following chapters will attempt to answer this important question by: digging deeper into the origins and meanings of sustainability; studying integral consciousness and Integral Sustainable Design as new and powerful frameworks for design education; looking deeper into *inclusivity* and *cooperation* as empathic core values in design education; looking closer at the *design brief*, as the holder of ethical content for studio projects; studying some of the emerging integrative behaviors that characterize the new terrain of design education; and lastly, realigning our perceptions and feelings about third party ratings systems and standards.

Notes

[1] Van der Ryn, S. (2005) *Design for Life*, Gibbs-Smith, Layton, UT, p132

[2] *Ibid.*

[3] Rifkin, Jeremy (2009) *The Empathic Civilization: The Race to Global Consciousness in a World in Crisis*, Penguin, New York, p361

[4] DeKay, Mark (2011) *Integral Sustainable Design: Transformative Perspectives*, Earthscan, London, pxxiii

[5] Wilber, K. (2000) *A Brief History of Everything*, Shambhala, Boston and London, section "World Transformation and the Culture Gap," para. 6

[6] Wilber, K. (5) ("World Transformation and Culture Gap," para. 2)

[7] Rifkin (3) p34

[8] Kruft, H. W. (1994) *Architectural Theory: From Vitruvius to the Present*, Princeton Architectural Press, New York, p152

[9] *Ibid.*

[10] Kostof, S. (1985) *A History of Architecture: Settings and Rituals*, Oxford University Press, New York, pp23–41

[11] The Solar Decathlon is a bi-annual event where universities compete to construct the most efficient small home. Each year, thousands come to see the homes.

[12] Cziko, G. (2000) *The Things We Do: Using the Lessons of Bernard & Darwin to Understand the What, How and Why of Our Behavior*, MIT Press, Cambridge, MA, p14

[13] Williams, G. W. (2000) "Introduction to Aboriginal Fire Use in North America," *Fire Management Today* (USDA Forest Service) 60 (3): 8–12

[14] Rifkin (3) p33

[15] Rifkin (3) p36

[16] Burckhardt, J. (1985) *The Architecture of the Italian Renaissance*, University of Chicago Press, Chicago, p11

[17] McClean, D. (2008) "Architectural Education for an 'Age of Sustainability'," *The Oxford Conference: A Re-Evaluation of Education in Architecture*, WIT Press, Boston, p100

[18] Van der Ryn (1) p138

[19] Edwards, J., McCommons, R., Eldridge, K. (1998) *Guide to Architecture Schools*, Sixth Edition, Association of Collegiate Schools of Architecture, ACSA Press, Washington, p1

[20] Stevens, G. (1998) *The Favored Circle: The Social Foundations of Architectural Distinction*, MIT Press, Cambridge, MA, p174

[21] *Ibid.*

[22] *Ibid.*

[23] *Ibid.*, p175

[24] *Ibid.*

[25] Cziko (12) p14

[26] Van der Ryn (1) p142

[27] Rifkin (3) p163

[28] Gebser, J. (1991) *The Ever-Present Origin*, Ohio University Press, Athens, p92

[29] McHarg, I. (1992) *Design with Nature*, John Wiley & Sons, New York, p76

[30] Friedenthal, R. (2010) *Goethe: His Life and Times*, Transaction Publishers, New Brunswick, NJ, p395

[31] Goethe, J., Eastlake, C. (1840) *Goethe's Theory of Colours*, translated from the German, John Murray, London, p40

[32] *Ibid.*

[33] Rifkin (3) p343

[34] Burr, K. L. (2002) "What Happened to the Master Builder? Implications for the Built Environment," Brigham Young University, Provo, UT

[35] McHarg (29) p71

[36] Kostof (10) p576

[37] *Ibid.*

[38] Edwards et al. (19) pp69–70

[39] *Ibid.*

[40] *Ibid.*

[41] *Ibid.* p70

[42] Kruft, H. W. (8) p274

[43] *Ibid.* p273

[44] *Ibid.* p274

[45] *Ibid.*

[46] Kostof (10) p577

[47] *Ibid.*

[48] *Ibid.*

[49] Gebser (28) p537

50 McDonough, W. (1993) "Centennial Sermon: Design, Ecology, Ethics and the Making of Things," given at the Cathedral of St. John the Divine, New York
51 Gropius, W. (1965) *The New Architecture and the Bauhaus*, MIT Press, Cambridge, MA, p43
52 McHarg (29) p76
53 Lacayo, R. (1998) "William Levitt," *Time Magazine*, http://www.time.com/time/magazine/article/0,9171,989781,00.html, Accessed: 8/7/2012 4:00AM
54 Van der Ryn (1) p141
55 Edwards et al. (19) p1
56 Fleming, J., Honour, H., Pevsner, N. (1999) *The Penguin Dictionary of Architecture and Landscape Architecture*, Fifth Edition, Penguin Books, London, p44
57 Frampton, K. (1980) *Modern Architecture: A Critical History*, Oxford University Press, New York, p123
58 Fleming et al. (56) p44
59 Gropius (51) p38
60 *Ibid.* p111
61 *Ibid.* p126
62 Frampton (57) p124
63 Gropius (51) p54
64 Frampton (57) pp124, 129
65 *Ibid.* p129
66 Edwards et al. (19) pp1–2
67 Taliesin Fellows: Alumni of the Frank Lloyd Wright School of Architecture, http://taliesinfellows.org/i/taliesin-fellows/, Accessed: 8/7/2012 7:10AM
68 I learned of these practices during an extended stay at Taliesin West in Scottsdale Arizona in 2002.
69 Taliesin Fellows: Alumni
70 Committee members (some of whom had no architectural background) decided who would graduate, and Mrs. Wright was known to choose dating relationships for the students. I learned this during some time spent at Taliesin North and West a few years back during sabbatical.
71 Taliesin Frank Lloyd School of Architecture: Historical Legacy, http://www.taliesin.edu/history.html, Accessed: 8/7/2012 8:25AM
72 *Ibid.*
73 United Nations: Global Issues: Environment, http://www.un.org/en/globalissues/environment/, Accessed: 8/4/2012 9:35AM
74 *Our Common Future*, Chapter 2: Towards Sustainable Development: Report of the World Commission on Environment and Development, http://www.un-documents.net/ocf-02.htm, Accessed: 8/1/2012 4:28AM
75 McDonough (50)
76 Alexander, C., Ishikawa, S., Silverstein, M. (1977) *A Pattern Language: Towns, Buildings, Construction*, Oxford University Press, New York, pxviii

[77] *Ibid.* front book flap

[78] Samuel Mockbee, Rural Studio, http://samuelmockbee.net/rural-studio/, Accessed: 3/12/2012 4:00PM

[79] Moos, D., Trechsel, G. (2003) *Samuel Mockbee and the Rural Studio: Community Architecture*, Birmingham Museum of Art, Birmingham, AL p14

[80] Phone interview with Marvin Rosenman on June 4, 2012

[81] Solomon, S., Qin, D., Manning, M., Chen, Z., Marquis, M., Averyt, K. B., Tignor, M., Miller, H. L. (eds.) (2007) *Contribution of Working Group I to the Fourth Assessment Report of the Intergovernmental Panel on Climate Change*, Cambridge University Press, Cambridge

[82] Nostrand, J. "BP vs. Exxon: The Oil Spill Cleanup: How BP's Reaction to Its Gulf Oil Spill Contrasts to Exxon's Efforts During Its Valdez Spill," Yahoo News, http://voices.yahoo.com/bp-vs-exxon-oil-spill-cleanup-6137862.html, Accessed: 8/6/2012 3:05PM

[83] Zimov, S., Schuur, E, Chapin, F. (2006) "Climate change. Permafrost and the Global Carbon Budget," *Science*, June: 312

[84] Van der Ryn (1) p127

[85] *Ibid.* pp125–126

[86] International Living Futures Institute, *The Living Building Challenge Standard*, https://ilbi.org/lbc/standard, Accessed: 8/1/2012 3:40PM

[87] *The Sustainable Sites Initiative: Guidelines and Performance Benchmarks*, American Society of Landscape Architects, Lady Bird Johnson Wildflower Center at The University of Texas at Austin, United States Botanic Garden, 2009, http://www.sustainablesites.org/products/, Accessed: 8/8/2012 3:00PM

[88] Perkins+Will, *Precautionary List*, http://transparency.perkinswill.com/Main, Accessed: 8/8/2012 3:09PM

[89] Trimble, A. (2012) "Harvard Achieves a Record 75 LEED Certifications," Sustainable Cities Collective, http://sustainablecitiescollective.com/node, posted May 7, Accessed: 8/8/2012 4:00PM

[90] *Sidwell Friends School, Middle School Addition, Master Plan & Site Design, Washington, D.C.*, Andropogon, http://www.andropogon.com/sidwell-friends-school-middle-school-addition, Accessed: 8/8/2012 3:07PM

[91] Miller, G. W. (2011) "A Natural Build," *Grid Magazine*, November, 32: 22

[92] http://www.fosterandpartners.com/Projects/1515/Default.aspx/, Accessed: 8/5/2012 6:00PM

[93] U.S. department of Energy, Solar Decathlon, http://www.solardecathlon.gov/about.html, Accessed: 8/4/2012 5:10PM

[94] Hosey, L., Gould K. (2006) *Ecological Literacy in Architecture Education Report and Proposal*, American Institute of Architects and the Tides Foundation, p1

[95] *Ibid.* p44

96 Bennetts, R. (2008) "Reasserting the Architect's Position in Pursuit of Sustainability," *The Oxford Conference: A Re-Evaluation of Education in Architecture*, WIT Press, Boston, p15

97 Boake, M., Guzokowski, M., Wasley, J. (2008) *The Oxford Conference: A Re-Evaluation of Education in Architecture*, WIT Press, Boston, pp77–82

98 Altomonte, S., *Ibid.* pp315–320

99 Quale, J., *Ibid.* pp149–153

100 Wilber (5), "World Transformation and Culture Gap," para. 2

2

UNDERSTANDING SUSTAINABILITY AND SUSTAINABLE DESIGN

TOP DOWN: (Triple Bottom Line Compliance)

Economic Viability
Energy Efficiency
Resource Allocation
Human Productivity

Ecological Regeneration
Bio-climatic
Design

Social Responsibility
Design Activism
Open Design Processes

Changing Climate
The Anthropocene

SUSTAINABILITY
(Quality of Life)
(Well-Being)
(Resilience)

Cataclysmic Events
BP oil spill
Peak oil

Technophilic
Rogers, Piano

Biophilic
Wright, Ambasz

Eco-Design
Van der Ryn
McDonough

Design Build
Jersey Devil
Yestermorrow
Solar Decathlon

BOTTOM UP: (Experiential Bottom Line, Voluntary)

Figure 2.1
The great "Tent" of sustainability (plan view)
There are many entry points to sustainability
Source: *Created and drawn by author*

At the deepest level sustainable design is not the next disciplinary *silo* disconnected from its relatives (although some have tried to make it become that). Rather, it is more like a giant *tent*, under which a wide range of world views, as expressed through different design approaches, can all co-exist simultaneously and comfortably. Figure 2.1 offers a model for sustainability that is both amorphous and comprehensive. The multilayered meanings and interpretations of sustainability make it difficult to build consensus among groups of individuals, which leads to paralysis for some. For others, the confusion regarding the term provides openings for new approaches to design or practice – an easy entry point into sustainability. For designers this freedom is expressed by the way that those with different world views can find a place within the context. For example, Modern Architecture continues to command the attention of many designers and finds its place in the dialogue via highly refined and highly efficient "technophilic" projects such as those of Foster or Piano. Green design takes the form of a more fuzzy, less streamlined approach as supported by James Wines' comical but accurate portrayal, "Buildings are landscapes in drag." The work of Emilio Ambasz is perhaps the best example of biophilic design.[1] Eco-design or Integral Sustainable Design can be seen in the work of Sim Van der Ryn or in the Sidwell Friends project by Kieran Timberlake Associates and Andropogon which unites land, form and interiors into a highly performing, didactic and transformative human experience. All of the above approaches and expressions can and should have a place in the world of sustainable design.

From a larger perspective, individuals and organizations can shape their attitudes and actions towards sustainability, which has allowed for greater overall impact and for continued growth of the movement. However, over time the term sustainability does require more definition and agreement so that higher levels of energy performance, ecological regeneration and social equity can be reached. Currently, society has relied on a set of *relative* metrics based on varying levels of good, or less bad, but, as this chapter will describe, a growing sense of agreement is emerging, an agreement that is increasingly being adopted by larger corporations, government agencies, nonprofit organizations and educational institutions.

Before moving forward it is critical to understand the premise of sustainability as fundamentally different than environmentalism. Environmentalism is commonly defined as "Advocacy of the preservation, restoration, or improvement of the natural environment; especially: the movement to control pollution."[2] Armed with this mission, environmentalists have been quite successful in helping to drive the creation of laws and ordinances that limit or negate the environmental impacts caused by industrial processes. For example, in the U.S., the passage of the Endangered Species Act, the Clean Water Act and the Clean Air Act, and the creation of the Environmental Protection Agency all served to "protect" the environment from its apparent downward spiral and set the stage for the process of environmental restoration. The U.S. EPA 2012 categorization of carbon as a "pollutant" is a continuation in the long battle between those seeking to protect the environment versus those promulgating the continued dominance of nature through industrial processes. The dualistic nature of the discourse – good versus evil, depending on which side of the table one is sitting – reflects the last fragments of a rational Modernist world view that depended upon this dialectic as the framework for engagement. As we move further into the twenty-first century, new and exciting models of environmental action are emerging. Now, companies, nonprofits, government agencies and citizens are beginning to see long lasting partnerships as a means to address long standing environmental issues. Also, the innovation of sustainability offers the premise that the benefits of economic development are weighed alongside and *equal to* environmental concerns and social responsibility. Timothy O'Riordan, in the *Scottish Geographical Magazine*, writes:

> Environmentalism was always a necessary first step. The shift towards sustainability is beginning to take place because the mood of the times is now ready to promote its early stages. However, as we contemplate more fully the fuller significance of sustainability, the very ethos of livelihood and lifestyle enters the frame of enquiry.[3]

Indeed the transition to the new model of sustainability is on one level very hopeful and intriguing, but on another level remains an enigma, a confusing and often contradictory anthem for future generations.

The Razor's Edge: green versus sustainable

As a means to sort out the consistently confusing questions surrounding sustainability and in turn sustainable design, a simple *Razor's Edge* is proposed (see Figure 2.2). On one side of the Razor stands the idea that sustainability constitutes a set of green practices that can easily be incorporated into the prevalent systems of the day and that by becoming more efficient and less destructive, the impacts of an otherwise comfortable, but consumptive lifestyle can be reduced. In that sense, greening becomes "just part of good design," another element to be taken into consideration among the many elements that the design community has proven themselves capable of assimilating. This side of

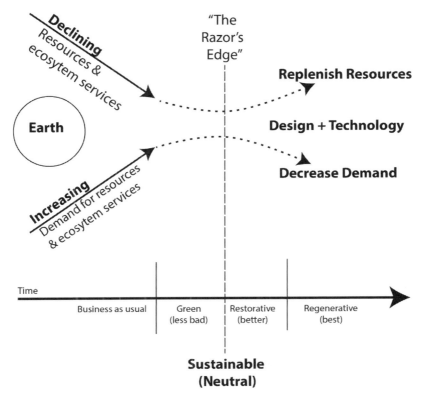

Figure 2.2
The Natural Step funnel
The Razor's Edge defines the left side of the diagram (green) versus the right side of the diagram (sustainable and restorative)

Source: *The Natural Step Program (accessed 2012)*

the Razor can be characterized as green design. Most design school curricula fall on this side of the Razor, as faculty attempt to "incorporate" green elements into an otherwise mainstream design curriculum. On the other side of the Razor's Edge, which will be discussed in more detail later, one can find sustainability, which exists more as an ideal, an ethic, a set of values that will drive humanity into the next age through increasingly higher and more effective levels of integration.

Definition of green design

Green design is the act of mitigating otherwise environmentally destructive and excessively consumptive processes and practices associated with the creation, use and disposal of products or projects. In Figure 2.2 above the converging angles of increasing demand for resources versus declining ecosystem services illustrates the problem quite clearly and positions green as "less bad," meaning that the arc of the curves will soften as societies begin to reduce impacts. But softening the curve will only prolong the eventual crossing of the two forces.

The Toyota Prius, for example, is a great example of *green* design. The car features an aerodynamic shape, lightweight construction, a hybrid engine, regenerative braking and excellent biofeedback information loops to slow drivers down. Given all of the innovation packed into the design and construction of the car, it performs, at best, double the standard, nongreen cars[4] but still uses significant amounts of gas to run the car. So the improvements, while laudable, have served only to mitigate the overall impacts upon energy supplies and air pollution. In fact the battery necessary to power the car serves as a wakeup call to green enthusiasts, as the embodied energy, environmental impact and disposal difficulties are cause for concern. Having said that, the Prius is a breakthrough car because it demonstrated that consumers were ready for a greener lifestyle and perhaps more importantly were willing to pay extra. It exemplifies the beginning of the shift from a lifestyle of *consumption* to a lifestyle of *consumption* + *mitigation*. In this way and others the act of "greening" helps move society towards sustainability, towards the other side of the Razor, like a ladder that helps someone to climb over a fence. Green buildings offer a similar proposition, an opportunity to mitigate the damage caused by the construction, operation and demolition of built projects. LEED® is a Green Building Rating system, with both the Green Building Certification Institute (GBCI) and the United States Green Building Council (USGBC) carefully positioning their messages to honestly communicate the intent of their missions, processes and standards. Nevertheless, in the larger societal context, green design serves as a useful but imperfect set of rungs leading towards the broader, more complex and ultimately more impactful movement of sustainability.

Sustainability

On the other side of the Razor, sustainability exists as a shift towards a fundamentally new and powerful force that will reshape society at levels not seen since the beginning of the Renaissance. Now, society is beginning to develop a world view that drives integration at all levels of organizations, drives changes in manufacturing, in building design, in medicine, in food, in consumerism, in the very fabric of life. Such a paradigm jump will appear differently in different regions of the world. In theory, developing countries will see the benefits of higher standards of living through development that is balanced by environmental protection and increasing levels of social equity. Developed countries will see a migration from a "standard of living" to "quality of life" where happiness is not defined by material possession and maximized comfort but rather by the quality of experiences that shape empathic relationships and generate memories.

The Razor's Edge then defines a line between two different approaches to the expression of sustainability in the built environment. Green design expresses the societal goal of "wants" to "save the planet" and to "tread more lightly on the Earth" – while at the same time consuming vast amounts of resources, inflicting significant damage to the planet through deforestation, desertification, erosion, pollution and climate change. It is akin to taking vitamins with a Pepsi. The other side of the Razor's Edge is sustainable design. Over there one finds a profound movement towards a neutral, if not regenerative relationship to the Earth and its resources, as in the need to "do no harm," as the minimum condition. The concept of design based on "needs" offers a view of the role of the built environment professional who now responds to the planet's obvious need for healing itself through restorative design practices; through the need to conserve valuable resources via innovative design, construction, habitation and demolition strategies; and the need to continue to provide safe, secure, comfortable, buildable environments. Table 2.1 illustrates the expressions of green design versus sustainable design in the built environment.

Table 2.1 The Razor's Edge: *green versus sustainable*

Wants + (The Age of Information)		Needs (The Age of Integration)
Green design		Sustainable design
Relative improvements	+	Absolute performance
Mitigation of damage	+	Restoration of ecosystems
LEED® Silver ratings	+	Living Building Challenge
Energy Star homes	+	Passivhaus Standard
Environmental laws	+	Sustainable Sites Initiative
Green materials	+	Red list materials

The Living Building Challenge, which will be discussed later, offers a high bar of compliance that includes net zero energy and zero impact water goals (absolute performance). The Sustainable Sites Initiative goes far beyond LEED® and environmental laws to encourage the design and construction of zero impact landscapes. Notice the "plus" symbol between each column. This signifies the logical approach of "both and." For example, green design is still a desired result in comparison to a simple code compliant project. While the use of the plus symbol diminishes the metaphor of the Razor's Edge, the difference between greening and sustainability will become an important distinction later regarding the curriculum development process.

But to say that we can, as a society, or an individual, achieve sustainability is as naïve as it is dangerous. Currently there are only three Living Building Challenge Projects that are built and operating.[5] Like most paradigms, the promise of the proposition of sustainability exists as an ideal, a force that relentlessly demands both introspection (values) and physical actions (behaviors). The two are interrelated. In Figure 2.3 current design and construction practices fall somewhere between the lowest order of activity, conventional practice (one step ahead of jail), and the next step up, green high performance design. A movement higher on the scale indicates a sustainable or even regenerative level of impact. The reality is that a single building, no matter how well designed and how expensive, will struggle to achieve a net neutral relationship to nature, while larger approaches such as EcoDistricts offer a greater probability of success. Such realizations further call into question the notion that a single discipline contains enough knowledge and ability to tackle the complex task of designing a sustainable community.

The United Nations and sustainable development

In 1987, the Brundtland Commission of the United Nations published *Our Common Future*, which still stands today as the seminal document of sustainability. Unlike the Declaration of Independence or the Magna Carta or other documents that express a given philosophic change in direction for a specific country or region, *Our Common Future* is written from a global perspective that expresses the idea that issues of environment, economics and social equity, once relegated to specific borders, are now viewed from a bioregional and global perspective. Now, issues of pollution, climate change, deforestation and sea level rise have transcended political borders to become a more complex and demanding problem.

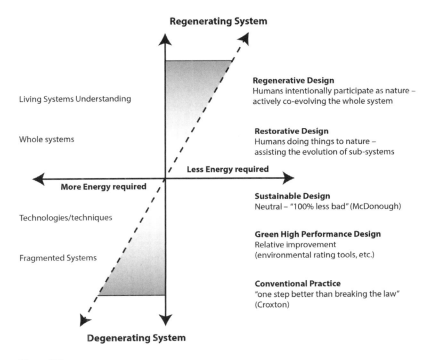

Figure 2.3
Trajectory of integrative thinking
Sources: *7group and Bill Reed (2009)*

The roots of the sustainability movement can be traced in part to a series of factors and events, including the publication of the alarmist *Population Bomb*, by Ann and Paul Ehrlich, which "warned of starvation of humans in the 1970s and 1980s due to overpopulation, as well as other major societal upheavals, and advocated immediate action to limit population growth."[6] In the same year the Club of Rome was founded, which describes itself as "a group of world citizens, sharing a common concern for the future of humanity."[7] In 1972, *The Limits to Growth* was published, offering a model to simulate the interactions between five variables – population, industrialization, pollution, food production and resource depletion – as a means to understand the dialectic between exponential human growth versus a linear growth of natural resources.[8] Lester Brown's 1984 publication, *State of the World*, began a series of yearly reports documenting the imbalance between the growing impacts of industrialism and a planet with declining resources.[9] For the purists, the roots of such views can be traced back as far as 1798 in *An Essay on the Principle of Population* by Thomas Malthus.[10]

Closer looks at some of the passages of the Brundtland Report, *Our Common Future*, reveal among other concepts a position that environmental protection and economic development are intrinsically connected. The passage below comes after the often quoted definition of sustainable development:

> Failures to manage the environment and to sustain development threaten to overwhelm all countries. **Environment and development are not separate challenges; they are inexorably linked.** Development cannot subsist upon a deteriorating environmental resource base; the environment cannot be protected when growth leaves out of account the costs of environmental destruction. These problems cannot be treated separately by fragmented institutions and policies. They are linked in a complex system of cause and effect.[11]

The clarity of this statement illustrates a powerful resolution of the competing doctrines of modern progress on the one hand, and environmental protection on the other. Such linkages transcend the typical level of awareness, but to link them "inextricably," as dependent upon each other, is a key theme of sustainable development.

> Environmental stresses and patterns of economic development are linked one to another. Thus agricultural policies may lie at the root of land, water, and forest degradation. Energy policies are associated with the global greenhouse effect, with acidification, and with deforestation for fuelwood in many developing nations. These stresses all threaten economic development. **Thus economics and ecology must be completely integrated in decision making and lawmaking processes.**[12]

The document goes on to link aspects of economic development with a more clear and specific set of environmental threats and drives home the call for integration. The underlying theme of integration as central to the framework of sustainability is profoundly impactful not just to the development of ethical frameworks but to the encouragement and adoption of higher levels of performance.

The power of this realization should not be underestimated and it has created strange bedfellows. The Blue Green Alliance between the Sierra Club and the Steelworkers Union is an unlikely but powerful alliance between labor and environmental groups and is a reflection of the shifting values and behaviors of organizations as they work to thrive within a new world view. The United Nations, in its adoption of *Our Common Future*, sends the message that economic development is not only tolerated but necessary to raise the quality of life for the many societies still struggling in poverty. It's an announcement that governments are limited in what they can achieve, and therefore the power of social and ecological entrepreneurship can deliver important services to otherwise struggling societies.

> It could be argued that the distribution of power and influence within society lies at the heart of most environment and development challenges. **Hence the new approach must involve programmes of social development, particularly to improve the position of women in society, to protect vulnerable groups, and to promote local participation in decision making.**[13]

This is probably the more controversial passage because sustainable development has now exceeded the obvious duality between environment and economics and calls for a further integration of equity as a fundamental component. On the surface, this passage could be interpreted as encouraging socialism and even communism. In the end, however, it is mostly viewed as a call for intergenerational equity.

However, the global nature of the term sustainability and the negative perception by many of the United Nations strikes fear into some. Libertarians and other conservatives in the U.S., for example, fear a "left wing plot" to form a world government built on social fairness and environmental protection that will include a plethora of rules and regulations that will threaten the foundations of free market economies.[14] However, the Brundtland Commission seems to address such criticism in advance:

> No single blueprint of sustainability will be found, as economic and social systems and ecological conditions differ widely among countries. Each nation will have to

63

> work out its own concrete policy implications. Yet
> irrespective of these differences, sustainable development
> should be seen as a global objective.[15]

Sustainability is positioned as an objective, rather than a mandate. The flexibility of each country to pursue the objective is clearly left open. The call for a world government simply does not exist. It is possible, however, that individual countries could enact severe environmental standards that could reduce profits and potentially hinder development in the short run, but such regulations will also pave the way for more balanced and less impactful development in the future. Some would argue that the Kyoto Protocol, a worldwide agreement on carbon reductions, is an example of such global collusion to control markets and impose constraints on free market economies. The opposition to carbon trading in the U.S. follows the same logic.

The second major counter argument against sustainability comes from the direction of evangelical religious institutions. Objections have been made that environmentalism is a *secular* religion, a force that will confuse young minds and cloud their vision of the gospel.

> Around the world, environmentalism has become an
> unbalanced, radical movement. Something we call "The
> Green Dragon." And it is deadly, deadly to human
> prosperity, deadly to human life, deadly to human freedom.[16]

Resisting the Green Dragon, while extreme in its proposition, expresses an underlying feeling among many in the religious sector who fear a diminished role of faith due to the political nature of sustainability and because of its association with ideas about ethics and moral behavior.[17]

Other detractors see sustainability as a Trojan horse, a set of hollow corporate promises that serve to obscure the continued practices of environmental destruction and exploitation of an increasingly powerless workforce. The seduction of naïve shoppers into buying "natural" products that are simply repackaged and rebranded without any environmental improvements is another example. It's unclear, for example whether Wal-Mart is an environmental hero through the greening of its value chains and products, or the Al Capone of social equity as scores of small businesses and small town main streets are wiped out by the presence of Wal-Mart's lower prices and high levels of convenience.[18] But to Wal-Mart's credit, sustainability has been viewed as an opportunity to rebuild its negative perception and build a new brand based on environmental responsibility.[19]

Lastly, many see sustainability as an unfulfilled promise, as something that has been relentlessly hyped, but rarely witnessed let alone participated in. The hype of the Green Jobs movement led by Van Jones never produced the millions of jobs promised nor an economic resurgence of the U.S. economy. However, conservative estimates place the amount of green jobs at 2.5 percent of the U.S population, a respectable if not impressive number.[20]

Triple Bottom Line sustainability

While *Our Common Future* provided a powerful vision for the future of humankind, it did leave plenty of room for interpretation and re-presentation. In 1998 John Elkington, in his ground breaking book *Cannibals with Forks*, laid out a rationale and organization of the now commonly recognized Triple Bottom Line. The importance of his work cannot be underestimated as he translated the lofty, lengthy and sometimes overly nuanced vision of sustainable development from *Our Common Future* and repositioned it as a simple triad of People, Planet and Profit. While this collection of words may seem simplistic and even embarrassingly trite, the power of the idea has gained traction in both the corporate and political sectors.[21] Many have moved towards the "Three Es": Equity, Economics and Ecology. The Triple Bottom Line reappears ad infinitum with slight variations in literally hundreds of publications. Ann Thorpe, author of the *Designer's Atlas of Sustainability* uses "Economy, Ecology and Culture."[22] The European Commission "offers a vision of progress that integrates immediate and longer-term objectives, local and global action, and regards social, economic and environmental issues as inseparable and interdependent components of human progress."[23] New Zealand's Ministry of Environment, a world leader in sustainable governance, defines sustainability "as a term that can be applied across a range of areas, such as the environment, society and the economy."[24] Society, culture, equity are all terms used to describe the human aspects of the sustainability equation.

While the three intersecting rings of people, profit and planet have been used repeatedly as a method to describe the Triple Bottom Line, the diagram on the right in Figure 2.4 offers a more authentic version of Elkington's original "tectonic sliding plates" of sustainable development.

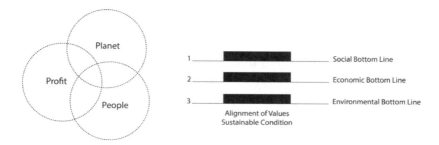

Figure 2.4
Triple Bottom Line diagrams

Source: *Image on the left: Re-drawn and adapted by author from a standard diagram that is frequently used*
Image on the right: Elkington, J. (1997)

Notice that the core social, economic and environmental values are vertically aligned, depicting an organization that has equally prioritized all the "bottom lines" in its decision making processes. Elkington writes, "Society depends on the economy – and the economy depends on the global ecosystem, whose health represents the ultimate bottom line."[25] Figure 2.5 below reflects a more likely scenario where the values of an organization do not align, creating an unsustainable condition. Elkington writes, "As the plates move over, or against each other, 'Shear Zones' emerge where the social, economic and environmental equivalents of tremors and earthquakes occur."[26]

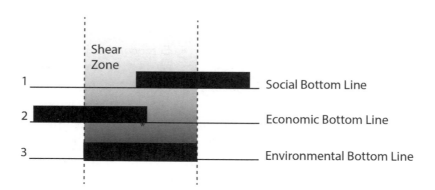

Figure 2.5
Triple Bottom Line diagram with shear zone
The Shear Zone is shown slightly differently than in Elkington's model for emphasis
Source: *Elkington, J. (1997)*

The BP oil spill in the Gulf of Mexico in 2010 was perhaps one of the most profound expressions of Elkington's Shear Zones. In the cataclysmic explosion and resulting spill, corporate demand for increased profits compromised normal environmental safeguards, leading to loss of life for 11 workers (social bottom line), the despoiling of the waters (environmental bottom line), and devastated tourist and fishing industries (economic bottom line). Corporate decisions made in the context of all three bottom lines would, in theory, have reduced the risk of the oil spill, prevented the disbursement of billions of dollars to victims by BP and in the bigger picture would have been considered more sustainable. The rapid response to the spill and to the making of reparations to the victims of the disaster suggest an evolution in U.S. culture in the form of increased transparency and accountability – key aspects of Elkington's sustainable future.[27] This is especially true given the pathetic response by Exxon after the Valdez Oil Spill in 1989.[28]

Impacts of the Triple Bottom Line on design and construction

In a world where executives from the corporate, governmental and nonprofit sectors (clients) are increasingly busy and spend less and less time pondering the sources of information they see and hear, the gestalt of the branded phrase Triple Bottom Line, offered originally as an accounting mechanism, resonates so clearly for so many as much more. Over time it has come to be a call to action, a mantra for organizations to reimagine themselves as twenty-first century evolving enterprises. Stuart Hart wrote in a 1996 article, "The more we learn about the challenges of sustainability, the clearer it is that we are at the threshold of a historic moment in which many of the world's industries will be transformed."[29] Indeed, William McDonough characterizes our time as the "next industrial revolution."[30] A 2012 *Sloan Business* report stated that over 75 percent of major corporations have a sustainability officer or plan to hire one.[31] While companies have increasingly invested in sustainability, government agencies have also assumed the mantle of leadership. The European Union has passed a requirement for all new homes to meet Passivhaus Standards by the year 2020.[32] The U.S. General Services Agency, the largest commissioner of design and construction in the world, has recently increased its minimum requirement for new construction and substantial renovation of Federally owned facilities to LEED® Gold Standards.[33] The passage of the International Green Construction Code reflects an important shift from green design as a voluntary act through the election to meet rating systems such as LEED® or Passivhaus to a new state of compliance through evolving building codes and zoning ordinances. The rise of large nonprofits such as USGBC to meet the demands for information and organization on green building, underscore the power of the emerging green economy and reflect the changes taking place in society.

Transcendent sustainability

The Triple Bottom Line may be a powerful shaping force for government and commerce, but it leaves some serious questions for those professionals that are responsible for the design of the built environment. While the argument can and will be made for the design professions to assume higher levels of economic responsibility, increasing levels of social responsibility and of course fundamentally new levels of environmental regeneration, the primary realm of the designer seems absent in the overall argument. Clearly aesthetics, place making, space making, proportion, scale, invention are all critical elements of design. And yet the invisibility of such issues as central to the sustainability debate in larger society is troubling. Elizabeth K. Meyer, landscape architecture professor at the University of Virginia, writes on the subject:

> Sustainable landscape design is generally understood in relation to three principles – ecological health, social justice and economic prosperity. Rarely do aesthetics factor into sustainability discourse, except in negative asides conflating the visible with the aesthetic and rendering both superfluous.[34]

The absence of beauty in the larger discussion on sustainable design can be explained in part by the still strong but waning existence of the more rational world view which has little space for the mystical, intangible qualitative aspects of existence and by default for design in the pure aesthetic sense. The emphasis on quantitative measurement and an objectified view of nature make it difficult if not impossible for designers to stake the kinds of leadership positions they once held in society. For example the continued obsession with cost and with financial measurement has pushed the design disciplines into an awkward position of having to defend the value of their work to clients who are less and less likely to either understand or care about the impact of smaller fees and tighter deadlines upon the aesthetic goals of a project. In fact, as will be discussed, the rise of the construction manager or owner's representative, in favor of the architect, as the "leader" of the construction and design processes is the most telling indication of a society that continues to hold onto a purely quantitatively understood universe. Strangely, those same clients are able to recognize the value of good design when they see it. The remarkable rise of Starbucks, for example, with its sophisticated color palettes, eclectic furniture and highly branded packaging, means it has been able to charge more for a cup of coffee than its competitors.

The fear then lies in the paradox of the sustainability argument made in this book. On the one hand it is argued that sustainability is the framework for an emerging, unified world view, a force that is driving a more integrated approach to a wide range of technologies, practices, processes and products. The scope of impact of sustainability is wide. From industrial designers who are conceiving of and making electric cars, to landscape architects making bio-regenerative site interventions, to food producers moving increasingly towards organics, to medical companies seeking to offer natural alternative healing techniques, the shift from environmentally destructive products and practices has not only begun but is in full force. But, surely the role of the designer in the twenty-first century must go beyond delivering the Triple Bottom Line? Aspects that designers hold dear – place making, space making, scale, texture and proportion – are all critical to design practice. Naïve logic holds that such elements must be on the table, if not central to the quickly coalescing definition of sustainability. The years spent in design studios during college followed by countless late hours in the office struggling for the perfect design resolution must hold some sense of "necessity" for society. Clearly the need to design satisfies our own internal yearnings to express our personal form of creativity to the broader community. However, the satisfaction of individual needs is not what is in question here. More to the point, the societal need for experiences that are intangible, immeasurable and evocative should go without question.

An interpretation of Abraham Maslow's Hierarchy of Needs would seem to support this assertion (Figure 2.6). Beyond the "deficiency needs" of breathing, food, water, Maslow begins to define a set of needs that are more psychological in nature and therefore more difficult to understand and measure. The needs of love and belonging link more directly to the small scale community of the family for example, and esteem links to the

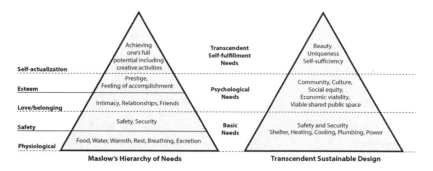

Figure 2.6
Maslow's Hierarchy of Needs repurposed for sustainable design

Source: *Image on the left: Maslow, A. (1964)*
Image on the right: Fleming, R. and Pastore, C. (2003)

scale of larger communities and networks. Lastly, and most importantly to this discussion, is the proposition that human beings possess fundamental needs that he categorizes as self-actualization. Maslow's description of such needs includes complex, metaphysical needs, such as *beauty, uniqueness, unity, aliveness, perfection and necessity, completion, justice and order, simplicity, richness, effortlessness, playfulness, self-sufficiency and meaningfulness.*[35] Repositioning these words as descriptors for design offers some intriguing insights and opportunities to expand sustainability into the realm of the poetic. The diagram on the right in Figure 2.6 expresses a reinterpretation of Maslow's Hierarchy of Needs from a sustainable design perspective. The lower level of physical needs is quite clear and reaffirms the critical role that designers play not only by providing basic shelter and security but also through the accommodation of plumbing, heating and cooling services. At the top of the pyramid one finds the nonquantifiable, irrational aspects of design: beauty and uniqueness. Interestingly, one of Maslow's descriptors of complex meta-needs includes the concept of self-sufficiency – a link directly to the ethos of sustainability.

Maslow's Hierarchy of Needs has received criticism because it is focused on the individual more than the collective, a manifestation of the American fixation on individualism. But if the Hierarchy is used in a more pure sense, as a framework to understand how organizational and personal values are placed into action through behaviors such as design, a deeper avenue for a more holistic, balanced conception of sustainability and sustainable design can emerge.

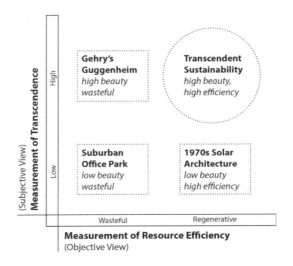

Figure 2.7
Transcendent sustainability

Source: *Fleming, R. and Pastore, C. (2003)*

In Figure 2.7, the objective of transcendent sustainability, developed in collaboration with Chris Pastore of Philadelphia University, is the result of an attempt to find a zone of design exploration that can work on multiple levels as promoted by the earlier discussions of Maslow's Hierarchy. The left side of the diagram is a measurement of the subjective aspects of design – aesthetics and sense of community. The bottom line of the chart reflects the objective aspects of design – environmental and energy efficiency. 1970s solar architecture, for example, was very efficient but left little for the soul, an expression of pure engineering. Frank Gehry's Guggenheim, while spectacular in its aesthetic form, is clad in the environmentally questionable material of Titanium. And yet the idea that such a building could ever be torn down is hard to imagine, reflecting a deep societal love for the project. In the lower left corner, the prototypical suburban office building is wasteful in its use of energy, destructive in its environmental practices, and offers very little aesthetic value and an even lower sense of community. As a result, such projects are an expression of unsustainability. In the upper right zone, transcendent sustainability begins to express a unification of the competing forces of efficiency (objective) and the forces of beauty, place making and cultural meaning (subjective).

Quadruple Bottom Line sustainability

Unlike transcendent sustainability which ignores financial considerations, the proposed Quadruple Bottom Line (QBL) of sustainability developed in collaboration with Philadelphia student Anne Sherman reflects a more integrated and a more balanced system. The addition of the fourth experiential bottom line catapults the soulless Triple Bottom Line into a full-fledged framework for the development of a more integrated approach. Anne writes in her 2012 thesis project entitled "Quadruple Bottom Line":

> The Quadruple Bottom Line uses experience as a means to address human behavior, and transform the human-biosphere relationship through physical, emotional, and spiritual consciousness development. At the highest level of this kind of relationship, sustainability is an authentic expression of the ways in which humans interact with the world.[36]

Anne's insights into the meanings of sustainability help to uncover the unseen driver of the QBL which can be found in the association of sustainability with quality of life, or with human well-being. This is an important distinction and expresses the statements in Chapter One that defined societal goals in developed countries as shifting from an obsession with increasingly higher *standards of living* to a set of goals focused on *quality of life*. The association of sustainability as defined by quality of life cements the fourth bottom line of *experience* into the mental model of Quadruple Bottom Line. Not surprisingly there is considerable push back to the idea of a qualitative and quantitative definition of sustainability. Authors Julian Marshall and Michael Toffell argue that "quality of life" should be removed from the equation, leaving sustainability to be solely about the relationship between ecosystem services and human consumption.[37] Such positions underscore the danger of purely objective logic and measuring systems. They deny a fundamental integral aspect to human functioning – subjective impulses. The QBL is not just for the designer, but for the owner's representative, the banker, the engineer and others who place contingency requests upon the designer. Armed with the QBL, designers can now interact with business leaders within economically dominated contexts and argue for the subjective aspects of a project such as beauty in a more legitimate way.

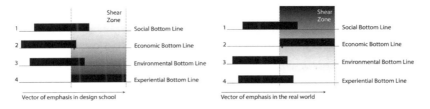

Figure 2.8
Quadruple Bottom Line Diagrams

Source: *Rob Fleming and Anne Sherman*

Figure 2.8 above illustrates how the QBL can become a useful framework in studying the effectiveness of prevailing pedagogic directions in design education. The vector of emphasis upon the "experience" of design far outweighs a focus on any of the other elements of the QBL and leads to a "shear zone" in the education process. Students gain very deep visual literacy skills, expertise in form making, and knowledge in the organization of spatial and functional relationships. However, they do so at the expense of knowledge and expertise in the the other three bottom lines – especially economics. Some would argue that a well crafted, well conceived, aesthetically sucessful building design will by default address the other bottom lines – that the sheer weight of a "masterpiece" provides a "get out of jail free card" for ethical transgressions. Jeremy Till, author of *Architecture Depends* writes, "In both the aesthetic and the tectonic of the ethical association is so far removed from the world of social dynamics, where ethics has to be situated, that it becomes phony ethics."[38] Indeed the proposition that a well-resolved design project that delights is somehow removed from the ethical oligation to address pressing economic, social and environmental issues cuts to the core of the disconnect between design studio professors who prefer to dwell in the poetic and tectonic versus the practitioners who are consistently beseiged by ethical dilemmas in the form of contingencies. At the same time, the argument here is not in any way to dismiss or ignore the tremendous need for society to be surounded by beautiful and evocative built and natural environments. Jeremy Till writes, "Arguing that aesthetics do not equate to ethics does not imply that one should throw away attention to the ways things look and are made."[39] In the end, the presence of an ethical shear zone between Till's "phony ethics" of experience versus social, economic and environmental bottom lines illustrates the challenge that lies ahead for design educators. The design studio may evolve from a place where issues of sustainability are "incorporated" into an otherwise aesthetically and spatially driven process to a location where well-designed experiences are "incorporated" into a much broader and by default ethically focused sustainability studio. This proposition then starts to attack the shear zone of the diagram on the left in Figure 2.8. In the "real world" the values shift from an emphasis on aesthetics to one of economics. The clear fact that most design students are financially illiterate upon graduation from design programs signifies a dramatic gulf between what the academies are offering as design education and what the real world is demanding. One could argue that such topics are better left to the professions, and even at that level many designers have found their leadership positions on projects eroded by the spreadsheet savvy owner's representative or construction manager. The shear zone in the real world also explains the continued presence of bad buildings or bad interiors or bad landscape projects. The severe imbalance between the economic demands of a project at the expense of the other three bottom lines creates a misalignment of values between the designer and owner, which leads to elimination of otherwise wonderfully poetic and aesthetically beguiling design moves through the value engineering process.

Sustainable design in the academies

It seems odd that 25 years after the Brundtland Commission's release of the definition of sustainable development, and 19 years after McDonough's powerful Centennial Sermon, and scores of subsequent publications on the topic, academics continue to lament the "confusing" directives of sustainability. The refrain, "how can we pursue sustainability if we don't know what it is or can't agree upon what it means?" continues to echo through the hallowed, if not procrastinating halls in the academies. But the confusion that grips the academics is so prevalent that it can, and often does lead to pedagogic paralysis, a freezing of the efforts of otherwise progressive design educators to pursue new methodologies. A few out there choose to learn how to teach sustainable design simply by jumping in the proverbial waters, without a life jacket, without the knowledge of how to swim and, worse yet, with no clear idea of where to find dry land. In that analogy, the emergence of sustainability has no real boundaries, no established educational methodologies and no clear end goal of the process: "How do I know when I've become sustainable?" Some would argue that those well intentioned, but confused early adopters may have done more harm than good to the overall sustainability movement because they put forth sometimes naïve and other times flat out incorrect information. Commonly uttered fallacies such as "Green buildings cost the same as regular buildings," promulgate two distressing responses. Firstly, young design students trust the rhetoric spouted by well meaning but misinformed green gurus and find their first green buildings are wildly over budget. On the other hand, skeptical designers cry "green washing" as they intuitively or realistically, through experience, know that such buildings in so many cases actually do cost more. Overall the definition of the terms green and sustainability are already clouded by mistrust by some and by flat out derision by others. The Quadruple Bottom Line is offered as a way to integrate the mandates of the Triple Bottom Line with the addition of aesthetics and experience as an integral component of design success. In this way the QBL can assist design professors by offering a clear framework that allows students to gain access to the big green tent of sustainability.

Notes

[1] http://www.ambasz.com/, Accessed: 8/1/2012 3:00PM

[2] http://www.merriam-webster.com/dictionary/environmentalism, Accessed: 8/2/2012 2:09PM

[3] O'Riordan, T. (1999) "From Environmentalism to Sustainability," *Scottish Geographical Magazine*, 115 (2): 151

[4] Ingram, A. (2012) "Toyota Prius vs 2012 Toyota Camry: Economy or Speed?," Green Car Report, http://www.greencarreports.com/news/1072442_2012-toyota-prius-vs-2012-toyota-camry-economy-or-speed, Accessed: 10/18/2012 11:50AM

[5] "Three Buildings Complete First Living Building Challenge Audits," *Ecostructure*, October, 2010 https://ilbi.org/about/About-Docs/news-documents/pdfs/three-buildings-complete-first-living-building-challenge-audits, Accessed: 7/3/2012 2:00PM

[6] Desrochers, P., Hoffbauer, C. (2009) "The Post War Intellectual Roots of the Population Bomb," *The Electronic Journal of Sustainable Development*, pp73–97, http://epsem.erin.utoronto.ca/desrochers/The_Population_Bomb.pdf, Accessed: 4/12/2012 1:09PM

[7] Club of Rome, http://www.clubofrome.org

[8] Meadows, D., Meadows, D. L., Randers, J. (1972) *The Limits to Growth*, Universe Books, New York

[9] Brown, Lester (1984) *State of the World*, Worldwatch Institute, New York

[10] Malthus, T. R. (1798) *An Essay on the Principle of Population as it Affects the Future Improvement of Society*, printed for J. Johnson in St. Paul's Church Yard, London

[11] *Our Common Future*, Chapter 1: Towards Sustainable Development: Report of the World Commission on Environment and Development (emphasis added), http://www.un-documents.net/ocf-01.htm, Accessed: 8/1/2012 4:28AM

[12] *Ibid*. (emphasis added)

[13] *Ibid*. (emphasis added)

[14] Chapman, R. (2010) *Culture Wars: An Encyclopaedia of Issues, Viewpoints, and Voices*, M.E. Sharpe, Armonk, NY, p265

[15] *Our Common Future* (11)

[16] Wanliss, J. (2011) *Resisting the Green Dragon; Dominion, Not Death*, The Cornwall Alliance, Burke, VA, p2

[17] Vucetich, J., Nelson, M. (2010) "Sustainability: Virtuous or Vulgar?," *BioScience*, July/August, 60 (7): 539

[18] Humes, E. (2011) "Wal-Mart's Green Hat: The company gets that a smaller carbon footprint is good for business," *Los Angeles Times*, May 31, p1, http://articles.latimes.com/2011/may/31/opinion/la-oe-humes-walmart-20110531, Accessed: 8/12/2012: 12:56PM

[19] *Ibid*.

[20] Muro, M., Rothwell, J., Saha, D. (2011) *Sizing The Clean Economy: A National And Regional Green Jobs Assessment*, The Brookings Institution, Metropolitan Policy Program, http://www.brookings.edu/~/media/Series/resources/0713_clean_economy.pdf, Accessed: 8/9/2012

[21] Kiron, D., Kruschwitz, N., Haanaes, K., Streng Velken, I. (2012) "Sustainability Nears a Tipping Point," *MIT Sloan Management Review*, Winter, 53 (2): 72, http://www.bcg.com/documents/file95002.pdf, Accessed: 8/9/2012 12:12PM

[22] Thorpe, Ann (2007) *The Designer's Atlas of Sustainability: Charting the Conceptual Landscape Through Economy, Ecology, and Culture*, Island Press, Washington, D.C.

[23] European Commission: Environment: Sustainable Development, http://ec.europa.eu/environment/eussd/ Accessed 8/12/2012 10:45AM

[24] Ministry for the Environment: Sustainability: A Definition, http://www.mfe.govt.nz/issues/sustainable-industry/tools-services/definition.php, Accessed: 8/9/2012 12:15AM

[25] Elkington, John (1997) *Cannibals with Forks: The Triple Bottom Line of 21st Century Business*, Capstone, Oxford, p73

[26] *Ibid*. p74

[27] Nostrand, J., Yahoo News, "BP vs. Exxon: The Oil Spill Cleanup: How BP's Reaction to Its Gulf Oil Spill Contrasts to Exxon's Efforts During Its Valdez Spill," http://voices.yahoo.com/bp-vs-exxon-oil-spill-cleanup-6137862.html, Accessed: 8/6/2012 3:05PM

[28] *Ibid.*

[29] Hart, S. (1996) "Beyond Greening: Strategies for a Sustainable World," *Harvard Business Review*, President and Fellows of Harvard College, p67

[30] McDonough, W., Braungart, M. (1998) "The NEXT Industrial revolution," *Atlantic Magazine*, October, http://www.theatlantic.com/magazine/archive/1998/10/the-next-industrial-revolution/304695/, Accessed: 11/4/2012 8:30AM

[31] Kiron et al. (21) p72

[32] "Steering Through the Maze #2, Nearly Zero Energy Buildings: Achieving the EU 2020 Target," European Council for an Energy Efficient Economy, November 2011, http://www.eceee.org/buildings/Steering-2-zerobldgs.pdf, Accessed: 11/04/2012 8:40AM

[33] U.S. General Services Administration: Sustainable Design, http://www.gsa.gov/portal/content/104462, Accessed: 8/8/2012 4:10PM

[34] Meyer, E. (2008) "Sustaining Beauty. The Performance of Appearance A Manifesto in Three Parts," *Journal of Landscape Architecture*, Spring: 6

[35] Maslow, A. (1964) *Toward a Psychology of Being*, John Wiley & Sons, New York, p94

[36] Sherman, A. (2013) "The Quadruple Bottom Line," A Thesis Presented to the Faculty of Philadelphia University, January, p70

[37] Marshal, J., Toffell, M. (2005) "Framing the Elusive Concept of Sustainability: A Sustainability Hierarchy," *Environmental Science & Technology*, 39 (3): 673

[38] Till, J. (2009) *Architecture Depends*, MIT Press, Cambridge, MA, p176

[39] *Ibid.* p177

3
DESIGN CONSCIOUSNESS

The notion of consciousness in design education is not new. In the 1960s and 1970s some designers worked hard to pursue educational strategies that prized social awareness and energy efficiency. So it would be inappropriate to argue that sustainability is a new consciousness for the design professions or for education. However, in the current pendulum swing towards ethical design there is a fundamental difference. Now, through Quadruple Bottom Line thinking, the once competing values of economic progress and social/environmental progress have been released from their dialectic relationship allowing academics in the built environment to teach a more unified conception of design – one that integrates the demands for ethics with the more typical aspects of form and function. The goal then is to develop an approach to tackle the challenge head on – not with hyperbole but with a raised consciousness, a set of evolving values and a tangible set of operational behaviors. M. W. Mehaffy writes:

> we argue that a much larger step-change looms ahead, one that must address much wider whole-systems phenomena.

New inter-disciplinary topics must include urban systems, evidence based design, qualitative and 'biophilic' factors. The role of existing and historic structures must also be recognised, and tools developed for their preservation and development. Students must learn 'meta skills' – collaboration, leadership, research – to overcome modern economic, technological and cultural limitations.[1]

Existing efforts to address sustainability vary greatly from institution to institution and from discipline to discipline. Designers are not the only ones trying to wrestle the elusive concept into submission. Almost all departments within colleges have appropriated sustainability and found ways to place their activities at the center of the equation. The emerging world view has caused a great restlessness among academics, causing elation for some and frustration for others. The need for a comprehensive model and methodology to pursue an integral approach to sustainability is needed to create a greater sense of philosophical alignment which will lead to more effective collaborations across disciplines and departments.

Ultimately, the goals of teaching design may lead to the discussion of *quality of life* and of the designer's role in the process. Design professionals have identified aesthetic quality as a major avenue towards raising the quality of life – instituting a more beautiful environment will make end users happier. All would be well if that simplistic view was enough, but given the changing world context of environmental degradation, depletion of energy supplies, dramatic imbalances in social equity and economic stability, the task before designers will be to widen their ethical frameworks to directly and consciously attack such important issues and opportunities. The emerging world context was hopefully established in the preceding chapters and now forms the basis of a more transparent, more equitable world – thus compelling the designer and the design educator to proactively enter the next age.

Early expressions of the new consciousness: the woven curriculum

On the surface, the efficacy of the *woven curriculum* seems logical and worthwhile. After all, the metaphor of weaving, or interlacing sustainability into an existing curriculum sounds hopeful. But such approaches demand deeper inspection. One of the weaknesses of the approach is that it relies on faculty who are committed enough to pursue the topic responsibly, and have the technical background to support such efforts. The relative freedom of the typical design studio creates an open door to a wide range of approaches and value systems that may be at odds with the stated sustainability goals of the program. The response among many faculty towards sustainability manifests in three ways.

The first response is reflected by the sentiment, "Sustainable design is *just* part of good design." This statement reveals that the professor clearly views sustainability as a set of practices to be integrated into an otherwise standard studio experience, a green approach. The message to the students is that green is a nice thing to do, but equal to other important aspects of design which also must be integrated. Students rationalize the inefficiency of their forms through the use of high performance glass or other technical solutions. Worse yet, the faculty member has failed to realize that his or her definition of "good design" is what has caused so much resource depletion and environmental damage in the first place. To argue then that sustainable design is akin to good design conveys a sad mixture of superficiality in terms of environmental awareness and a corresponding lack of urgency to look deeper into the opportunity.

The second response is typically expressed by the statement, "I am covering sustainability in my studio." If the understanding of sustainability is unclear because a set of common goals has not been established, the ability of students and professors to align their values towards some commonly agreed upon design approaches will be difficult. Furthermore, varying levels of technical proficiency and knowledge regarding sustainable design among the faculty may leave students with an inconsistent educational experience. Since the connection between building science courses and design studios remains tenuous at many institutions, the inconsistent tone of sustainable design education between support courses and studios remains an on-going problem. A 2008 study by R. M. J. Hillier revealed a disconnect between what the faculty believe they are teaching and what employers and students believe they are actual seeing.

> The survey queried faculty, students and sustainable design leaders to assess how well-prepared graduates entering the workforce are to practice sustainable design. Only 6 per

cent of design leaders believed recent graduates are very well-prepared as opposed to 23 per cent of students and 32 per cent of faculty. It is the students who give the highest ratings to their peers (17 per cent saying recent graduates are poorly prepared, versus 13 per cent for faculty for faculty and 6 per cent for design leaders). The higher percentage of students giving themselves lower scores on preparation suggest that they either have higher standards for sustainable design and/or that schools are not providing them with an adequate level of knowledge.[2]

The third response is the complete rejection, and in some cases, demonization of sustainability. Such studios serve to support a cynical view that is couched in terms of "healthy skepticism." Indignation towards the LEED® Rating System is the most common symptom of this condition. Lamentation about the point for bike racks in lieu of a larger discussion regarding ASHRAE 90.1, for example, does a disservice to young and impressionable students who deserve to have different aspects of green design, including the rating systems and other metrics, to be discussed in a minimum, at neutral tone.

In the woven curriculum, students receive a range of pedagogical responses, some of which serve to move students to higher levels of consciousness and to higher levels of integration, while others leave students in the lurch begging for more. Lastly, a danger lies in the use of words and their ability to brand perceptions internally and externally. Internally, faculty members may come to believe that they are in fact part of an interweaving of sustainability into the curriculum and will therefore remain content to perform at whatever level of sustainability they have established. Externally, the promotion of a program as being inherently green or sustainable suggests a benign level of green washing.

The dedicated sustainability studio

The dedicated studio is another avenue by which design programs pursue sustainability. This approach yields many benefits. It provides the typically lone green champion on the faculty with a place to dwell, thereby serving as a placating mechanism for slightly marginalized faculty members and a stalling tactic against larger adoptions of sustainability in the curriculum. After all, if the "green" faculty member is covering all the important aspects in his or her studio, then the other seven or nine studios are "free" to explore other topics and specialties. As a result, students may experience the attraction of sustainability in one studio, only to find it sadly missing or poorly represented in subsequent studios. In addition, the collecting of sustainability activities into a single course greatly assists the process of meeting accreditation requirements but once again allows other studios to ignore issues of environmental sustainability. And yet, despite all of the obvious shortcomings, I argue that the isolated, but dedicated sustainable studio may still be superior to the woven model discussed earlier. While the woven model is better reflective of the new integrated view in general, the lack of training, the ambivalence of some and the distrust of others can water down or even reverse the movement towards an integrated approach. The stand-alone studio, which pursues aspects of sustainability deeply and authentically, can serve as a proving ground for approaches that can be incorporated into the overall curriculum in the future. Such a statement underscores the earlier arguments, that lightweight greening will not be enough for the kinds of energy performance levels and environmental sensitivities demanded by well-established and widely accepted metrics such as carbon neutral EcoDistrict communities, a net zero energy house or a Living Building Challenge project. The Achilles' heel of the dedicated studio arises when multiple sections are taught. Now the "green champion" must oversee additional sections of the course, which may or may not be taught by faculty who share the same consciousness or values regarding sustainability and integration. Students in different sections are exposed to differing levels of commitment leading to a lack of internal cohesion.

Ultimately, both models serve the useful and important purpose of greening the curriculum – one side of the Razor's Edge. In order to reach the other side, the need to dig deeper, to look farther ahead and to discover and develop new approaches is incumbent upon us, if not for ourselves, then certainly for the next generation of design professionals who will be held to the task of dealing with the repercussions of centuries of environmental abuse as fostered by the benign neglect of the design community.

Integral Theory

As a beginning, it seems obvious to say that more integration is needed if we are to move to higher levels of greening and further towards sustainability. While integration is vaguely understood as an important, if not essential goal in design and design education, the specifics of what constitutes integration and the processes necessary to achieve such levels must be considered more systematically. The straightforward response would be to study systems thinking, an approach that on the surface would seem to provide all the answers. After all, some practitioners are able to boil down sustainability succinctly into the "proper and efficient use of resources in order to reduce impacts by humankind and to increase available eco-system services." But the addition of the social and especially the experiential bottom lines demands an approach that deals not just with measurable and definable systems, but also with the less predictable, less rational aspects of human psychology.

Transcendent sustainability, based on Maslow's Hierarchy of Needs began to crack open the complex and interdependent nature of sustainable design's quantitative and qualitative aspects, and the Quadruple Bottom Line serves as a culturally adoptable framework for sustainability. The emergence of Integral Theory, developed by Ken Wilber, holds the promise of an even tighter and perhaps better defined approach. As a start Wilber offers the following definition:

> *Integral*: the word means to integrate, to bring together, to join, to link, to embrace. Not in the sense of uniformity, and not in the sense of ironing out all of the wonderful differences, colours, zigs and zags of a rainbow-hues humanity, but in the sense of unity-in-diversity, shared commonalities along with our wonderful differences.[3]

Wilber's description contains a contradictory and complex view of the word and he is careful to avoid the impulse to clean up and streamline the definition. The approach is less rational and more complex than might be expected. Author Marilyn Hamilton in her book *Integral City: Evolutionary Intelligences for the Human Hive* explores another interpretation of the word: "*Integral* means whole, comprehensive, integrated, interconnected, inclusive, all encompassing, vibrant, responsive, adaptive."[4] She goes on to argue that integral is a word whose roots are related both to integrity and integration.[5] and finally, "In combining aspects of both integrity and integration, Integral subsumes the coherence of integrity and the blending of integration."[6] In short, Hamilton is arguing for a framework that acknowledges and unites the objective world view with the more subjective world view that emerged in the Information Age.

Ken Wilber's Integral Theory, as shown in Figure 3.1 below, offers such a framework. The right column focuses on the objective, measurable, quantifiable aspects of reality – the world and individuals as viewed from the exterior. The left column focuses on the subjective, the immeasurable and the undefinable aspects of reality as understood from an interior perspective. The difference between the two sides can be understood as the *map* (right side – objective view) and the *map maker* (left side – subjective view). The rows reflect either an "individual" point of view or a "collective" point of view.

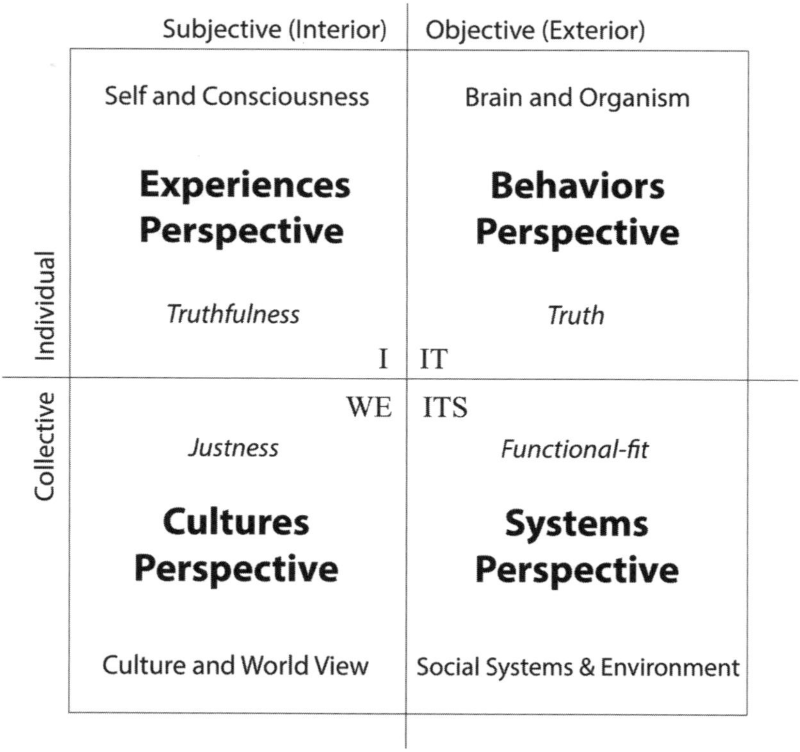

	Subjective (Interior)	Objective (Exterior)
Individual	Self and Consciousness **Experiences Perspective** *Truthfulness* I	Brain and Organism **Behaviors Perspective** *Truth* IT
Collective	WE *Justness* **Cultures Perspective** Culture and World View	ITS *Functional-fit* **Systems Perspective** Social Systems & Environment

Figure 3.1
Ken Wilber's Integral Theory
Source: *Wilber, K. (2000)*

As shown in Figure 3.1, the lower left quadrant in (the "WE" perspective) deals with the collective world views of a particular culture or organization. This is the zone that deals with the larger societal consciousness. In contrast the upper left quadrant (the "I"

84

perspective) deals with the personal consciousness, an interior experience in nonquantifiable terms. Beauty, which can never be universally agreed upon, is an example. Both of these zones address the subjective, nonmeasurable aspects of human existence. In the upper right quadrant (the "IT" perspective), the objective view of the individual is addressed as something tangible and measurable as in a set of observable behaviors (location and size). The lower right quadrant (the "ITS" perspective) reflects the measurable social and environmental systems.

The four quadrants of Integral Theory map well onto the four components of the previously discussed Quadruple Bottom Line (social, experiential, economic and environmental). For example, the environmental bottom line maps well to the lower right systems perspective. The social bottom line maps to the cultures perspective, especially when the word "ethical" is used as one of the defining attributes. The experiential bottom line directly matches the experiences perspective. And lastly, but a bit more awkwardly, the economic bottom line connects to the behaviors perspective. The quantitative, objective economic bottom line reflects this objective zone.

The Integral framework is different than the highly valuable and better understood *systems thinking* approach to sustainability which tends to focus on the set of relationships described in the lower right side of the framework shown in Figure 3.2 – an objective, measurable understanding of interrelationships and their impacts. Ecology, for example, is a classic approach to understanding very complex systems – an essential process necessary to pursue higher levels of overall environmental health. Integral Theory, perhaps, falls under the larger umbrella of "Soft Systems" as developed in part by Peter Checkland among many others and could have been influenced by the work of Enid Mumford (no relation to Lewis), who advocated for the participatory design process and the role of ethics in systems thinking.[7]

Furthermore, the use of Integral Theory is limited in this book to a focus on only the first two of the five elements of the AQAL approach – standing for all quadrants, all levels, all lines, all states and all types.[8] Lastly, Integral Theory is only beginning to be respected in wider academic circles and Ken Wilber himself has received his fair share of criticism from other integral thinkers,[9] especially in Jeff Meyerhoff's book, *Bald Ambition: A Critique of Ken Wilber's Theory of Everything*.

But if Wilber's frameworks are taken strictly at face value and stripped of their origins and influences, the potential for this holistic method for communicating sustainable design to students is one of the clearest and most compressive model developed to date. In Figure 3.2, the framework is used by Sean Esbjörn-Hargens to delve into an integral view of ecology.

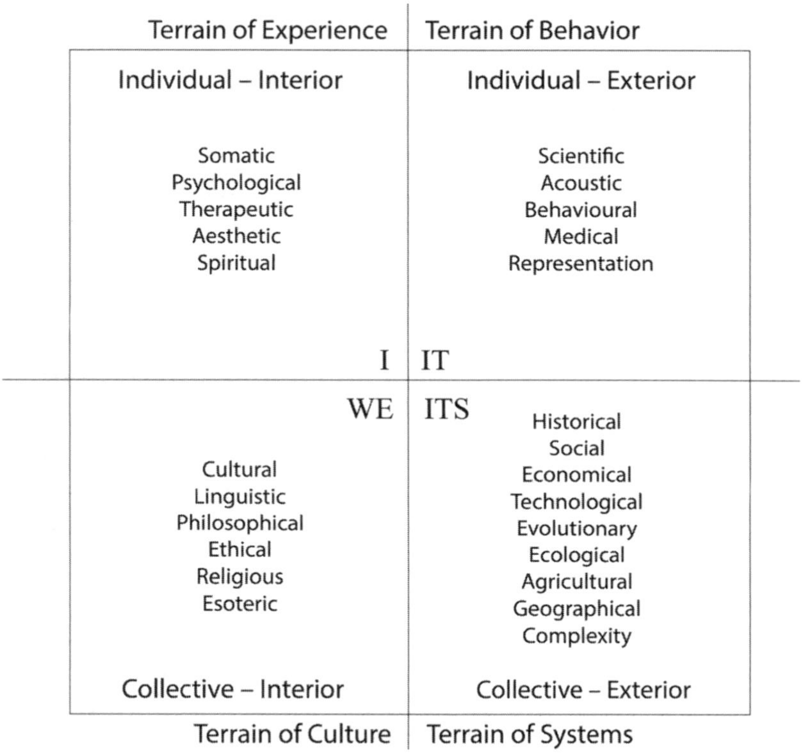

Terrain of Experience	Terrain of Behavior
Individual – Interior	Individual – Exterior
Somatic Psychological Therapeutic Aesthetic Spiritual	Scientific Acoustic Behavioural Medical Representation
I	IT
WE	ITS
Cultural Linguistic Philosophical Ethical Religious Esoteric	Historical Social Economical Technological Evolutionary Ecological Agricultural Geographical Complexity
Collective – Interior	Collective – Exterior
Terrain of Culture	Terrain of Systems

Figure 3.2
Integral Ecology

Source: *Esbjörn-Hargens, S. (2005)*

In Figure 3.2 above, the lower left quadrant contains the word *ethics* as one of its descriptors, a term used in the diagrams in Chapter One that described the different ages. Designers access this quadrant unconsciously all the time with a variety of overt and covert responses to ethical demands that vary from project to project. For professors, the four quadrant model allows students to access the opportunity of an ethically based design approach, not simply because it's the right thing to do, but more pointedly, because it is an *integral* part of an overall approach to design.

Integral Theory and the Quadruple Bottom Line begin to close in on a definitive framework for the pursuit of integration. Integral Sustainable Design, Figure 3.3, developed by Mark DeKay, adapts Wilbur's Integral Theory framework to convey a comprehensive approach for directly addressing the principles of sustainability in the design, engineering and construction of built environment projects.

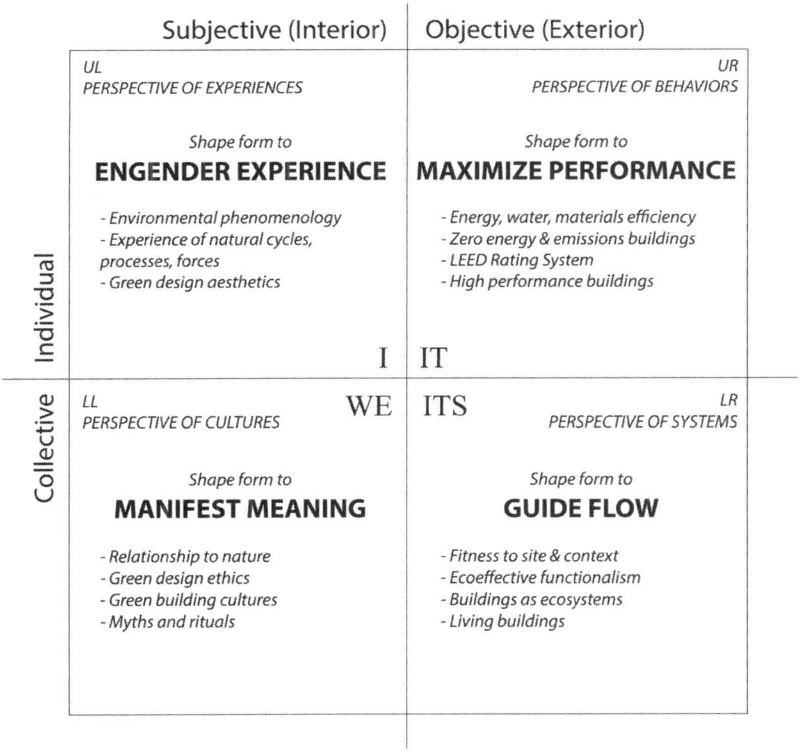

	Subjective (Interior)	Objective (Exterior)
Individual	UL *PERSPECTIVE OF EXPERIENCES* *Shape form to* **ENGENDER EXPERIENCE** - *Environmental phenomenology* - *Experience of natural cycles, processes, forces* - *Green design aesthetics* **I**	UR *PERSPECTIVE OF BEHAVIORS* *Shape form to* **MAXIMIZE PERFORMANCE** - *Energy, water, materials efficiency* - *Zero energy & emissions buildings* - *LEED Rating System* - *High performance buildings* **IT**
Collective	LL *PERSPECTIVE OF CULTURES* **WE** *Shape form to* **MANIFEST MEANING** - *Relationship to nature* - *Green design ethics* - *Green building cultures* - *Myths and rituals*	**ITS** *PERSPECTIVE OF SYSTEMS* LR *Shape form to* **GUIDE FLOW** - *Fitness to site & context* - *Ecoeffective functionalism* - *Buildings as ecosystems* - *Living buildings*

Figure 3.3
The Four Perspectives of Integral Sustainable Design

Source: *DeKay, Mark (2011)*

The framework of Integral Sustainable Design offers an opportunity to finally organize the typically disparate entry points to sustainability into an interdependent, cohesive and inclusive set of *principles* that can easily be translated into *strategies* which can all be fused together into one integrated system – a built project.[10] Mark DeKay writes, "My claim that each of these (four quadrants) is critical to the ultimate success of Sustainable Design and that leaving one out dampens the effectiveness and may lead to failure."[11] For example a LEED® Platinum building, which is high performing but possibly aesthetically displeasing, has a potentially diminished life span due to its lack of cultural appeal (LL) and thus a greater likelihood of demolition prior to the end of its useful life. DeKay further describes the different aspects of Integral Sustainable Design with parenthetical additions added for clarity, "Maybe you are technically oriented (UR) perhaps you see the world through the eyes of an artist (UL), or maybe you think in whole systems like an ecologist (LR), maybe you see buildings as full of narrative and symbolism (LL)."[12] Of course none of us can be completely relegated to one quadrant or another but our DNA drives us towards one of the four zones. DeKay argues that "You can expand to understand and take the viewpoint of the other major ways to see the world, and then you can look at sustainable design through all of these lenses."[13]

The **Upper Right Quadrant** (UR) of DeKay's model seeks to "Maximize Performance," the most recognized expression of sustainability, for architects and mechanical, electrical and plumbing (MEP) engineers at least. The LEED® Rating System is now properly placed in the larger context of sustainable design along with net zero projects, embodied energy, carbon neutral design and water efficiency. In short these are all measurable activities and therefore capable of objective description. Perhaps the over emphasis on this quadrant in the past is what frustrates designers who intuitively understand that sustainable design must be about more than just performance. Perhaps, now, with a clear framework, and correct positioning of systems like LEED®, designers can now more fully embrace third party metrics as nothing more than a well-defined tool to "maximize performance." Clearly this quadrant prizes knowledge-based design and empirical methods – a clear nod to building technology and building science courses as well as zero energy and carbon neutrality design studios as promoted by the Society of Buildings Science Educators.[14] The 2030 Challenge also serves as an excellent model to help students define performance goals.[15] For landscape architects, the amount of stormwater processed on a given site is directly measurable as a predictable phenomenon and therefore this aspect of design falls under this quadrant. For interior designers, the amount of daylight, in terms of percentages that reach each interior space would fall into this category.

The **Lower Right Quadrant** (LR), "Guide Flow," speaks to the domains of landscape architects and civil engineers as disciplines that must, on some level, guide the forces of a site for beneficial purposes, either to the local ecology, human activities or ideally both. The drive towards ecological design can be expanded into other scales of built environment projects – such as green infrastructure or landscape urbanism. The emergence of the Sustainable Sites Initiative which expands LEED's Sustainable Sites credits into a more robust and targeted approach helps to minimize impact on ecologies and environments. Taking the idea further, DeKay argues that "Design is an analogue or literal ecosystem participant."[16] The design of the route and treatment of stormwater (not the amount), falls into this quadrant, which is more concerned with the overall systems of the site and their interactions. An eco-architecture studio focusing on site response in terms of the manipulation of flows of water, wind patterns, sun angles and flora and fauna falls largely into this category.

The **Upper Left Quadrant** (UL), "Engender Experience," speaks to designers in a very direct way. The manipulation of space and form to create experiences for users that are understood on a phenomenological level is the cornerstone of this quadrant. The added aspect of connection to natural systems and biophilic design as part of this realm offers one path to *engendering experience*. In contrast the approach of bio-mimicry would appear in the lower right ecological quadrant as it is a more systematic approach to design: "What would nature do?"[17] It is behavior in its functionality as opposed to an emotional approach. DeKay's description is as follows, "Design's role is to reveal and express sustainable technology so people have a direct and indirect experience of the cycles of nature."[18] In that statement, the qualitative and quantitative aspects of reality are united. The cycles of nature are a measurable and observable phenomenon, but how those cycles are experienced from person to person and from culture to culture is also a critical aspect of the design process. Design as a connector between the subjective and objective realms, something that has always been present but not often verbalized, is now better understood and perhaps better explained using the framework, and thereby better taught in the classroom and studio.

Lastly, the **Lower Left Quadrant** (LR), "Manifest Meaning," speaks to the desire of designers to communicate a story or narrative through the design of a building, site or interior. The project can have a narrative that is expressed either covertly or overtly through the conceptual design of the project. DeKay's model clearly reflects a need to reconnect to nature as a central theme of the design process. Design, among many other activities, becomes one of the ways that humanity can begin to reconnect to the natural world on a very tangible and meaningful level.

It should be noted that Integral Sustainable Design requires the expression and or exploration of all quadrants at all times, at all scales in all phases of the design process. The flatness of the diagrams should not be misinterpreted as a sorting out and separating of the four areas of interest. Instead, they should be imagined in the same way that the Quadruple Bottom Line was presented – as tectonic plates that float on top of or below each other in a complex three-dimensional matrix. Lastly, the presentation of Integral Sustainable Design has been significantly abbreviated in order to save space for later discussions on design curriculum.

Examples

A green interior design studio may include the requirement for students to specify recycled content in materials using the LEED® system. Points for recycled content in the system are calculated by the amount of recycled content against a percentage of the overall materials budget for a project – a quantitatively driven process (UR). The subjective characteristics of a material such as color and texture, in terms of how an individual may react to them, will appear in the left column of the matrix "I like that material" (UL). Unfinished homosote is excellent acoustically (UR) and is made of recycled newspaper which is good for the environment (LR). The lack of paint helps to improve indoor air quality (LR). But exposed homosote may not be a culturally accepted material (LL) as it looks rough and uneven compared to drywall and the edges are difficult to finish, which may lead to the product being painted to better conform to cultural expectations for wall materials. This short example demonstrates that any design decision can be evaluated simultaneously by all four quadrants – leading to a more holistic design process. More importantly, it also leads towards a more understandable and teachable framework for students in design schools.

Understanding a given site for a studio design project offers an opportunity to use Integral Sustainable Design as a methodology to collect the traditional elements of analysis into a clear framework. A site can be understood as a dynamic ecology, as measured and communicated by a site inventory, which studies the contours, water flows, movement of flora and fauna, sun angles and so on (LR). The performance of a site is measured quantitatively, as in "amounts of stuff." How much rain hits the site? How many cars drive through the site? How many squirrels live on the site? What is the energy performance of the buildings on the site (UR)? In addition to the site inventory, there is also the process of *site interpretation*. How do I personally react to the site, how do I feel about it (UL)? A poem can be written, or a photo montage can be made to express a personal interpretation of a given site. Lastly, how does the community (We) feel about the site (LL)? Through interviews and collaborative design charrettes, the emotional responses to a given site can be studied. Integral Sustainable Design serves as a framework then to organize a "site analysis" of all the quadrants into a comprehensive and hopefully useful basis by which to make decisions.

The purpose of this example is to demonstrate that many of the activities that professors use in the design studio are already part of an overall sustainability approach – whether it is expressed overtly as Integral Theory or not. DeKay's model allows for a more prescribed and more importantly a *more communicable system* to students. This facet should not be underestimated in its power to elevate and organize a student's mental processes regarding sustainability, but it also offers a powerful framework for the development of course syllabi, learning objectives and design briefs – some of which will be shared later.

The definitions and understanding of the meanings of sustainability and sustainable design are coalescing into an increasingly clearer picture. The plethora of rating systems and accreditation requirements continue to express more focused and attainable definitions of sustainability. The lack of clarity up to now has been a significant force impeding progress. Integral Sustainable Design can be used as a framework or a methodology, or both, to pursue sustainability directly and with less confusion. If faculty members want to protect their "intellectual freedom" and not adopt the system proposed here, then the impetus to discover, select or derive their own comprehensive model is essential.

The key to sustainable design education: aligning behaviors with core values

This last section of the chapter looks at how we can move from the ideal of sustainability as a static framework to an active process of identifying the core values and behaviors necessary to achieve higher levels of integration and ecological performance. Stuart Walker, author of *Sustainable by Design* writes, "It [sustainability] represents much more than simply an analytical approach to environmental auditing or business accountability. It also represents a way of acknowledging our values and beliefs and ascribing meaning to our activities."[19] Integral Theory and Integral Sustainable Design offer a framework to organize those values and behaviors, but other frameworks and methodologies are needed to address the process of change itself. Simply stated, if the decision is made by an organization to leap over the Razor's Edge and enter the arena of authentic sustainable design, fundamental organizational change will be necessary. Imagine the typical design department at a large university. Senior and junior faculty each with different world views, different values and different teaching behaviors somehow all coming together regarding the movement towards sustainability. The roadmap would be confusing, with accident prone intersections, long dead ends and tempting shortcuts. In short, the ascendance of a single individual to a new level of consciousness is one thing, but an entire organization making the leap is quite another.

Richard Barrett's Seven Levels of Organizational Consciousness is a widely recognized framework and methodology for better understanding how groups can begin to change their values and behaviors towards higher levels of awareness. Barrett writes, "All human group structures grow and develop in consciousness in seven well-defined stages. Each stage focuses on a particular existential need that is common to the human condition. These seven existential needs are the principal motivating forces in all human affairs."[20]

In Figure 3.4 the lower tiers of the system are recognized as Maslow's Hierarchy of Needs and the top tiers are new, offering higher levels of functioning that begin to align and express the emerging Integral world view. The "Transformation Level" now serves as the platform for pursuing important goals for organizations such as *internal cohesion, making a difference* and *service*. These higher level values cannot be effectively pursued unless the lower level goals are satisfied. In other words, it is

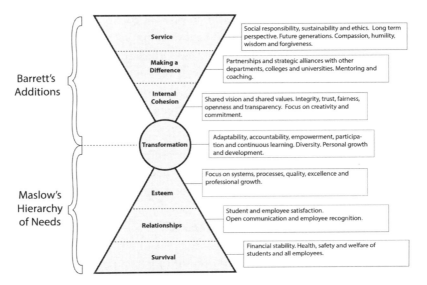

Figure 3.4
Barrett's Seven Levels of School Consciousness

Source: *Barrett, R. (accessed 2012)*

difficult to pursue "Service" when an organization is in financial difficulty or mired in bureaucratic log jams (ineffective relationships).

The tier of **Transformation** includes the attribute of diversity – a topic that is poorly understood and poorly addressed by design schools in general.[21] Moving towards higher levels of awareness and closer to integration is only effective if all stakeholders share the opportunity to move forward. Barrett writes, "The level of growth and development of consciousness in a school or educational establishment depends on the ability of the leaders to create a culture that enables the school to satisfy the needs of all stakeholders – students, faculty, and parents."[22] Therefore if some students have their needs met but others suffer due to the color of their skin, their gender or other differences, an inequitable condition exists making it impossible to effectively pursue higher level values. Chapter Four, "Inclusive Design Teams," will address the state of diversity in design education.

The fifth tier, **Internal Cohesion**, suggests an organization with aligned values – a shared vision of what is important and what matters. Design schools in general suffer in this area because of the collision of various world views, as held by different faculty members, and as expressed through design ideologies that are strongly defended. The misalignment of values can lead to a wide array of behaviors that serve to undermine larger attempts at addressing sustainability – comprehensively and authentically. In that sense, the earlier discussion regarding "woven curricula" and "dedicated sustainable studios" serve as early examples of a partial approach to a deeper and more impactful integral curriculum.

Making a Difference, the sixth tier, can be expressed by partnerships between departments, schools, colleges and universities across disciplines in pursuit of effective forms of collaboration. The benefits of collaboration are well known and understood, but the behaviors and values necessary for success are murky. For example, faculty members are happy to support group projects, especially those that cross disciplines, but such processes often occur without a clear plan for equitable power sharing, without any sensitivity training and without a design education process that is conducive to success. Faculty members in one discipline may perceive themselves as "superior" to colleagues in other departments based on long standing hierarchies in the professional world. Such misaligned values lead to dysfunctional control dramas that play out between faculty members and are transmitted to the students during competing desk crits or design reviews. Ultimately, more thought must be given to the interrelationships between disciplines in order to set the stage for effective and equitable power sharing in collaborative projects. Chapter Four will also tackle this opportunity head on.

Competition between faculty members, and between students, inhibits the pursuit of collaboration, a critical aspect to effectively pursuing integration. The traditional design studio is designed for the education of individual students who report to an individual studio critic. The emergence of collaborative teams that span departments in the physical sense and span ideologies in the psychological sense calls into question the efficacy of the standard approach to studio. A discovery process of new and innovative methods is in order. Chapter Five, "Cooperative Learning Environments," will examine the opportunities to move from a competitive, individualistic studio model to one that prizes cooperation as a means to reach internal cohesion.

At the top tier of Barrett's model is **Service**. Barrett lists a series of higher level processes including sustainability, social responsibility and ethics – the focus of this book and the end game of the transformational process towards higher levels of integration. In order to pursue sustainability effectively, the values as described in the lower levels of Maslow's Hierarchy must also be simultaneously pursued. Otherwise the efforts will be diminished. The success of the Rural Studio and the Solar Decathlon, for example, reflect, perhaps, the highest and best use of institutional efforts. The Decathlon's educational mission has served as a catalyzing force to engage students and faculty at all seven levels of Barrett's Organizational Consciousness in one grand project. The Landscape Architecture Program at Philadelphia University, which focuses almost exclusively on service learning and sustainability, is a reflection of Barrett's highest value set and a potential model for other programs seeking new educational formats.[23] The goal is to begin the process of defining values and shaping behaviors towards more authentic and effective levels of integration leading to higher levels of sustainability.

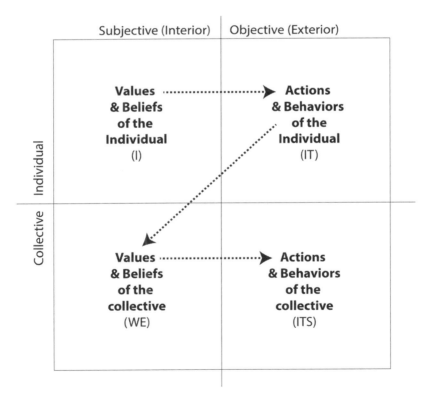

Figure 3.5
Barrett's Four Quadrants of Human Systems

Source: *Barrett, R. (accessed 2012)*

Wilber's four quadrants can also be used as a methodology to better understand how fundamental change can occur within individuals and organizations. Barrett links the four quadrants in the following way. He suggests through his diagram (Figure 3.5) that when individuals change their values and beliefs (UL), their behaviors change (UR). When sufficient numbers of people change their values and behaviors, a shift in the collective culture occurs (LL). This results in a change in the behaviors of the whole organization (LR).[24] From a sustainable design education perspective changes to design programs can occur through a variety of starting points. For example, Barrett's model plays out in the following sequence: a new Dean may be appointed to a college who comes to an existing academic culture with his or her own value sets or derives a new set of values as an effort to differentiate or elevate a program's position in the larger community. In turn, those value sets begin to drive the behavior of the Dean – which begins to impact the collective culture, which in turn drives the actions and behaviors of the organization through the development of curriculum, establishment of procedures and through a set of mission and vision statements. Another avenue of change can come from external sources such as accrediting bodies. A set of prescribed curriculum requirements (LR) which, temporarily at least, shift personal values and drive the behavior of the faculty to the creation of new learning outcomes for courses. Lastly, an effective behavior is the use of integrated design charrettes with all stakeholders – administration, faculty, students and staff – to conceive a set of shared or core values. Such processes, which will be studied in detail later, allow for the collision of personal values (world views) in pursuit of higher levels of consciousness for a given design program. This facilitated, organized and potentially equitable process is superior to a faculty meeting which is generally unstructured and allows for the domination of some faculty over others based on oral skills, loud voices, interrupting and other control mechanisms. The transparent and collaborative nature of a design charrette offers an excellent process for the development of new curriculum initiatives because it garners buy-in from the faculty and increases the likelihood of follow-through down the road.

Figure 3.6 offers an important framework for program administrators and faculty seeking to build a more cohesive and more consistent approach to sustainable design education that moves from the greening of the curriculum to the more aligned and integrated approach.

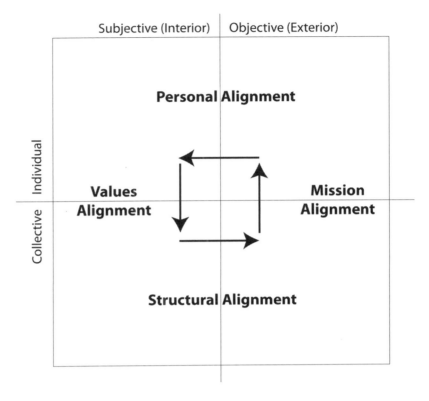

Figure 3.6
Barrett's Four Conditions for Whole System Change

Source: *Barrett, R. (accessed 2012)*

Assuming that an organization can move towards sustainability (and most have on some level), then the expectation among the stakeholders (those that are touched by the activities of the organization) will be to see alignment between the stated values of the organization and its actual behaviors. For example, if a university proclaims that sustainability is a core value or a top priority, then students and faculty would expect to see a variety of activities including, but not limited to: the construction of green buildings, the use of sustainable landscape practices, installation of energy management programs, and of course the evolution of the curriculum to more directly address sustainability. However, the alignment of personal values and collective values is very difficult for most design schools because of the wide range of consciousness levels: Rational, Postmodern and Integral. Departmental meetings often reflect a battle of ideologies as each world view fights for supremacy. But if the principle of transcend and include is valid, and all world views are both needed and valuable, the possibility exists for resolution. The matrix in Figure 3.7 was developed in part as a means to understand what an "aligned" department might look like as an aspiration.

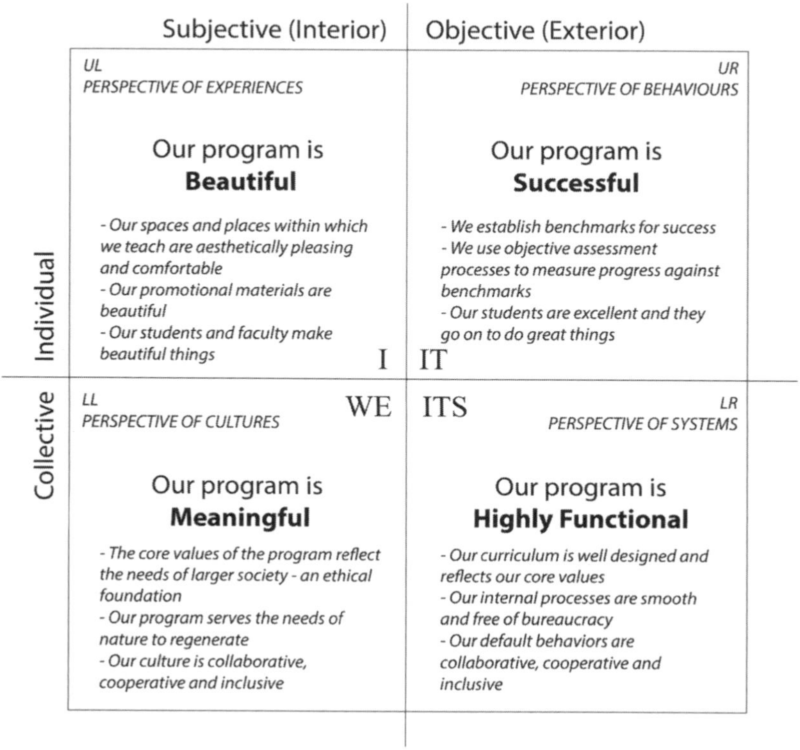

Figure 3.7
Philadelphia University's MS in Sustainable Design Program "aspirational": Barrett's Four Conditions for Whole System Change inscribed within Wilber's Integral Theory Framework
Source: *Created and drawn by author*

The program is understood from multiple perspectives which drive different outcomes. The right side looks at quantifiable and measurable aspects of the program and its functioning. The left side presents an interpretive aspect of the program. Ethics and beauty, for example, are difficult to measure but they serve well as ideals to be strived for. In Figure 3.8, the model for the Sustainable Design in the program is shown.

98

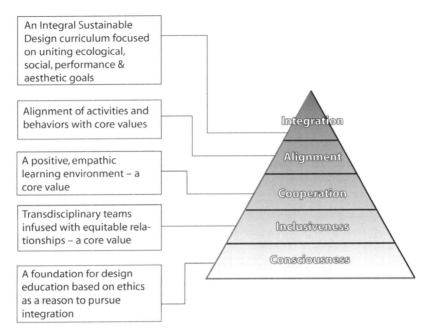

An Integral Sustainable Design curriculum focused on uniting ecological, social, performance & aesthetic goals

Alignment of activities and behaviors with core values

A positive, empathic learning environment – a core value

Transdisciplinary teams infused with equitable rela- tionships – a core value

A foundation for design education based on ethics as a reason to pursue integration

Integration

Alignment

Cooperation

Inclusiveness

Consciousness

Figure 3.8
Integral Sustainable Design Studio Curriculum Model at Philadelphia University

Source: *Created and drawn by author*

Figure 3.8 depicts a model for an individual design studio developed in Philadelphia University's MS in Sustainable Design Program. Consciousness, the focus of this chapter, forms a base for the expression of core values – such as inclusivity and cooperation (levels 2 and 3 above), which in turn help to change behaviors in the form of pedagogy and heuristics (levels 4 and 5 above). The behavior of alignment speaks in larger part to the previous discussion regarding the relationship between the stated values of the program or course and the actual practices or behaviors that follow. The collaborative development of the design brief, for example, is a behavior by which the ethical content of a project is aligned through the selection and scheduling of integrative activities in the design studio. Another example is the behavior of integrated design charrettes as a way to foster cooperation and inclusivity. The collection of consciousness, core values and integrative behaviors constitutes an attempt to form a more holistically connected and unified curricular model – one that demands significant evolution on the part of each faculty member's personal values (grassroots) and significant changes in mission, vision, policies and procedures that will serve to drive change (top down). The combination of both approaches can help to drive the development of new educational models that better reflect the emerging Age of Integration and by default begin to reverse the long course of environmental degradation caused by centuries of unsustainable design and construction practices.

Notes

[1] Mehaffy, M. W. (2008) "Architectural Education for an 'Age of Sustainability'," *The Oxford Conference: A Re-Evaluation of Education in Architecture*, WIT Press, Boston, MA, p59

[2] Dordai, P., Lander, J., Fleming, R. (2008) "Education Revolution: Empowering the Next Generation of Sustainable Designers," *Proceedings of 2008 GreenBuild Conference*, USGBC, p242

[3] Wilber, K. (2000) *A Theory of Everything: An Integral Vision for Business, Politics, Science and Spirituality*, Shambhala, Boston, MA, p2

[4] Hamilton, M. (2008) *Integral City: Evolutionary Intelligences for the Human Hive*, New Society Publishers, Gabriola Island, BC, p52

[5] *Ibid.*

[6] *Ibid.*

[7] Stahl, B. (2007) "Ethics, Morality and Critique: An Essay on Enid Mumford's Socio-Technical Approach," *Journal for the Association of Information Systems*, September, 8 (9) Article 3

[8] Esbjörn-Hargens, S. (2009) "An Overview of Integral Theory: An All-Inclusive Framework for the 21st Century," Integral Research Centre, http://www.integralresearchcenter.org/sites/default/files/integraltheory_3-2-2009.pdf, Accessed: 8/5/2012 9:27PM

[9] Visser, F. (2003) *Ken Wilber: Thought As Passion*, State University of New York Press, Albany

[10] DeKay, M. (2011) *Integral Sustainable Design: Transformative Perspectives*, Earthscan, London, p11

[11] *Ibid.*

[12] *Ibid.* pxxxvii

[13] *Ibid.* pxxxvi

[14] Boack Meyer, T., Guzowski, M., Wasley, J. (2008) "The Carbon Neutral Design Project," *The Oxford Conference: A Re-Evaluation of Education in Architecture*, WIT Press, Boston, MA, pp77–82

[15] The 2030 Challenge, http://architecture2030.org/2030_challenge/the_2030_challenge, Accessed: 7/5/2012 8:20PM

[16] DeKay (10) p13

[17] Benyus, J. (1997) *Biomimicry*, Harper Collins Publishers, New York, p237

[18] DeKay (10) p13

[19] Walker, S. (2006) *Sustainable by Design: Explorations in Theory and Practice*, Earthscan, London, p27

[20] Barrett, R. "The Seven Levels of School Consciousness," Barrett Values Centre, http://www.valuescentre.com/uploads/2010-07-06/The%207%20Levels%20 of%20Schools.pdf, Accessed: 6/3/2012 4:30PM

[21] Mitgang, Lee (1997) "Saving the Soul of Architectural Education: Four Critical Challenges Face Today's Architecture Schools," *Architectural Record*, May: 124–128; 125

[22] Barrett (20)

[23] According to Claudia Phillips, the Director of the program, over 70 percent of all design studios have an integrated service learning component and 100 percent of all courses in the program directly address sustainability as integral to the design process.

[24] Barrett, R. "Fundamentals of Cultural Transformation: Implementing whole system change," Barrett Values Centre, http://www.valuescentre.com/ uploads/2010-04-19/FCT.pdf, Accessed: 6/3/2012 4:35PM

4
INCLUSIVE DESIGN TEAMS

Everyone designs who devises courses of action aimed at
changing existing conditions into preferred ones.
(Herbert Simon, 1969)

The Age of Integration, as argued for earlier, suggests that a very
special phenomenon is taking place. The rise of an empathic civilization
reflects a shift from the individualistic and competitive world view that
fueled the industrial revolution to a new pluralistic world view that
continues the process of breaking down a wide array of gender, ethnic
and cultural barriers (women's liberation, gay rights, etc.). The current
drive towards a more multicultural world is underscored by observations
on the millennial generation from Jeremy Rifkin:

> Their nonhierarchical, networking way of relating to each
> other and the world, their collaborative nature, their
> interest in access and inclusion rather than autonomy and
> exclusion and their greater sensitivity to human diversity,
> predisposes the millennial generation to being the most
> empathic generation in history. A distributed,

collaborative, nonhierarchical society can't help but be a more empathic one.[1]

The connection between the value of inclusivity and the pursuit of higher levels of integration through the principle of sustainability is twofold. First, and foremost, the move forward must be a process by which all stakeholders have both the right and opportunity to participate in the process and to receive any benefits that may occur. If sustainability only exists under the purview of largely wealthy, Caucasian segments of society, the continued imbalance will prevent widespread change towards the attributes of Quadruple Bottom Line sustainability – a healthy environment, an equitable society, economic prosperity and a set of rich, healthy life experiences. The tackling of the ethnic, cultural, gender diversity question must begin, especially in the design academies, if overall progress is to occur. D. McClean writes in an article from the 2008 Oxford Conference: A Re-Evaluation of Education in Architecture, "The diversification of the UK Higher Education embodies a number of key strands; those of multiculturalism, socio-economic background, educational background, gender, motivation and aspiration, and learning style."[2] Theodore Landsmark, who chaired the AIA Diversity Committee, warns:

> The consequence of not [diversifying] is that the profession will occupy a diminished niche within the larger built environment and come to be seen to be providing services only to corporate and wealthy individuals, rather than the much wider range of people who are affected by good architecture.[3]

The second aspect of inclusivity, albeit subsidiary to the importance of diversity in education, is the role of interdisciplinary work as central to the success of integrated design. Without all the appropriate disciplines at the table, at the right time, each treated with respect and equality, the goal of higher integration leading to sustainability is placed in jeopardy. As will be discussed in more detail later, the linear processes by which the built environment has been conceived and realized is giving way to a new, more collaborative, more holistic process. Central to the success of the integrated project delivery model is the effective communication and cooperation between disciplines that traditionally have been separate and at times adversarial. It is incumbent upon the educational institutions that train the future designers, engineers and builders to not only learn to work together but to do so in a highly effective manner, setting the stage for a future in which disciplines will engage in deeply empathic relationships unified towards the common purpose of restoring the health of the planet through the design and construction of built projects.

A brief history of diversity in design education

Appropriately, the process begins near the start of the Age of Information, a time when many societies began to confront their own segregatory impulses. Alas, the design professions, and especially architects, remained out of touch, as evidenced by the now famous quote by Whitney M. Young, head of the Urban League to the AIA Convention in Portland Oregon in 1968: "You are not a profession that has distinguished itself by your social and civic contributions to the cause of civil rights … You are most distinguished by your thunderous silence and your complete irrelevance."[4] The statement, while painful for some to hear, reflected a sentiment that the cultural revolution of the 1960s in the U.S. had touched so many sectors of society and yet the design professions remained largely on the periphery. Perhaps the heredity of architecture as a rich white man's profession was still dominant. Perhaps the inevitable pull of the design studio, of creativity in its purest state, free of contigencies, beckoned so strongly, that the larger cultural revolution was unethically ignored.

John Saunders and a group of 12 black architects in 1971 formed the organization NOMA (National Organization of Minority Architects) at the AIA national convention in Detroit, to provide affinity for minority architects and designers and also to "champion diversity within the design professions."[5] The emergence of such organizations suggests a response to a vacuum in services from the long standing professional associations.

In 1990 the American Collegiate Schools of Architecture (ACSA) developed the "Code of Conduct for Diversity in Architecture" which offered the following reasons to diversify the students and faculty: promoting social justice, improving the climate of architectural education for all, recruiting the best talent from the widest possible pool, increasing sensitivity to the full range of clients, teaching students to work in a global marketplace and fostering diversity within the profession.[6] The list of goals is laudable, a set of intentions or values that clearly hit the mark when it comes to the important opportunity of diversification of the schools and professions. However, if a set of corresponding behavior changes does not take place, the words become hollow.

In 1991 Bradford Grant and Dennis Mann published the first edition of *The Directory of African American Architects*.[7] The *Directory*, now in the form of a web page, today is still active and chronicles the latest registered black architects and memorializes those that have died, a reflection of great compassion but also of the relatively small numbers of registered black architects in the U.S.

Also in 1991, the publication *Voices in Architectural Education* shed light on the on-going struggles for equality in design education and in 1992, Susan Maxman was elected as the first female president of the AIA. During the 128 years of the existence of the AIA, women had gained the right to vote, served in congress and the senate and led major corporations, and yet it wasn't until the 1990s, a time of continued rising cultural awareness, that a women was elected president of the organization. A 1993 landmark study by Mark Paul Frederickson, "Gender and Racial Bias in Design Juries" was published in the *Journal of Architectural Education*. The study followed three design programs over the course of a year and included the recording of numerous design juries. The results suggested two alarming patterns. The study found that minority students were more likely to be interrupted by their jurors and also received less overall time in the discussion of their projects.[8] Observations in the study prompted the following statement, "Remarks (towards minority students) appear to be couched in a diplomatic genre that renders them condenscending and insipid. Jurors tend to speak in simplified terms and interrupt the students with gentle prompting."[9] Part of the conclusion of the study underscored the problems and began to offer the call to begin the long process of improvement. In 1994, the AIA launched a series of conferences that would exist through the rest of the 1990s, moving diversity to a more prominent place in the mental map of the organization. The series marks the transition from hollow intentions to actual behaviors aimed at real change.[10] In 1996 Boyer and Mitgang championed the call for action in *Building Community: A New Future for Architectural Education* by first describing the ideal: "A just learning community is a place where the diversity of people's cultures and ideas is affirmed in the curriculum and the classroom, a place where differences in background and perspective among students are celebrated."[11] However, they were also quick to express the reality of the situation: "Thirty years after the dawn of the civil rights era, architecture remains among the less successful professions in diversifying its ranks."[12] In a follow-up piece in *Architectural Record*, Mitgang called for an end to "apartheid in architecture schools," and argued that the "race record of architecture education is a continuing disgrace, and if anything, things seem to be worsening."[13]

Kathryn Anthony, in one of the few publications on the topic, *Designing for Diversity*, writes, "For all tenured architecture faculty … only 14% are women and only 8% are persons of color."[14] Anthony goes on to express the distribution of African American students throughout the schools in the U.S.:

> recent figures show a disturbing pattern of racial segregation in architectural education. Of the 1,313 African American students enrolled in architecture schools in North America, 45% were students at the seven historically black schools with accredited programs – Florida A&M, Hampton, Howard, Morgan State, Prairie View A&M, Southern and Tuskegee.[15]

In a follow-up article in *JAE*, Anthony shares the following:

> My more recent research examines the turmoil and triumph that underrepresented architects – women, persons of color, lesbians and gays – experience in their profession from the past until the present. Many face special hardships: isolation, marginalization, stereotyping, discrimination, just to name a few. The same is true for underrepesented architectural educators.[16]

In her conclusion Anthony argues, "We architectural educators can remain passive, watching silently as underrepresented faculty and students struggle to succeed in an environment that is at best marginally supportive and at worst hostile and unfair," and that "A proactive stance towards diversity can help transform the profession in the 21st century."[17]

In 2004, Terrence O'Neal noted that, "In terms of diversity, the AIA is about 20 years behind the curve." He contributed to a resolution to help improve diversity figures in the "notoriously homogenous profession."[18]

In 2006, the AIA ran a series of articles by the late Stephen Kliment, FAIA, which looked at the progress of architecture programs in regards to diversity. The numbers are chilling. Kliment reported that:

> The number of black students at accredited schools declined between 1991 and 2003, and the number of graduates over that period actually dropped from 214 to 156, or 27 percent. The numbers for faculty aren't much better: between 1997 and 2003, full-time black faculty declined from 6.2 percent to 5.2 percent.[19]

Initial reactions by some argue that "qualified" blacks tend not to pursue architecture in favor of the more lucrative professions of law and medicine. Such arguments however continue a pattern of shifting responsibility from the individuals in power to other external factors. In the same series, Ted Landsmark opines on the subject:

> So until we adopt vastly more radical ways of addressing diversity by reaching outside of the traditionally defined architectural profession to include a wider range of people involved in the design and building professions, we will continue down a path that suggests that even if we triple the number of students of color who graduate from our programs over the next decade, we'll still only be at two percent of African-American architects in the profession.[20]

In the conclusions to the AIA series, Kliment writes:

> … educators such as Sharon Sutton, PhD, FAIA, and Ted Landsmark, PhD, Assoc. AIA, have carried the message to the profession, but much more needs to be done as this is one of the direst chapters in the diversity record. If blacks cannot dramatically raise the volume of black students and graduates, thereby boosting the pool of black graduates from which firms can recruit, white firms will continue to use this excuse for not hiring more black graduates.[21]

The last part of the quote suggests that a shift is needed in both attitudes towards diversity and the behaviors necessary to tackle the opportunity head on. In addition the quote reveals the need for white educators to join in the advocacy towards a more diverse and equitable learning environment — thereby diversifying the very movement itself and potentially increasing its probability of success.

Almost 40 years after Whitney's call for change, progress in the area of diversity and inclusivity remained limited at best. Hannah McCann, in a 2007 article in *Architecture Magazine*, writes:

> Kemba Mazloomian graduated from the University of Michigan in 1997 with a master's degree in architecture and now works as an editor in Chicago. "I worked in office after office where my white male co-workers, and even the clients we worked for, questioned my competence, rechecked my calculations, [and] dismissed my relevance on projects," she recalls in an e-mail. Her colleagues, Mazloomian says, "engaged in such a systemic campaign of emotional sabotage, that I invariably would seek work at another office – only to find that the office had changed but the dynamic remained the same."[22]

The temptation by the reader might be to dismiss her experiences as "her imagination" or that she was perhaps "oversensitive." Or, "It's hard to imagine that people would do that." Such rationalizations for abhorrent behavior on the part of majority groups serve to obfuscate the simple fact that discrimination, subtle oppression, stereotyping and a lack of inclusivity was present in 1997 and is still, by all accounts, present in today's design professions and schools.

Ted Landsmark suggests "we need to take a really hard look at what we've done in the past and how it has failed, and then adopt programs that are unified and focused on achieving real results. Indeed the benchmarking of the current and past levels of minorities in the professions is a beginning, a low water mark that can only go higher."[23]

Inclusivity

In 2012, The AIA defined inclusivity as, "The intentional act of being open, reaching out, removing barriers, and creating an environment so that all members of an organization can achieve their fullest potential."[24]

If design consciousness forms the ethical backbone of sustainable design education, then the principle of *inclusiveness* forms the functional backbone. The choice of the word inclusivity expresses the need to build a broader vision of interdisciplinary work that includes equitable learning environments that are welcoming to students and faculty of varying ethnic, gender and cultural backgrounds. This is critical as the quality of the collaborative experience must be useful and meaningful for each student. While all might agree that such empathic goals are both obvious and achievable, the process to get there is shrouded by a lack of awareness of the depth of the opportunity and by a dearth of identified strategies. Terminology is critical in the discussion of diversity and inclusion. For example, stating that diversity is an "issue" conveys the notion that it is a problem to be dealt with. It has negative connotations. The challenge then is to view such "issues" as "opportunities" to build a more equitable learning environment with the opportunity to develop higher functioning empathic relationships between students and faculty, between students and students and even between faculty and faculty.

While the perception of diversity as an issue is a default position of design programs in general, the lack of success of some student groups is symptomatic of a learning environment that is not inclusive – a learning environment replete with barriers – some more subtle than others. Inclusivity calls for the opposite – the conscious removal of barriers to allow greater chance of success for traditionally underperforming groups. For example, some design programs are extremely conscious of covering the accomplishments of minority designers in the history sequences. The inclusion of such expresses to students of similar backgrounds that the possibility exists for success. In sequences where predominately white male designers are featured, the message received by minority students is that the old boys club is not only alive and well but is perpetuated by the program and its faculty. Worse yet, if that perception is confirmed in the studio experience through marginalization or outright hostility, students will feel very strong barriers to their on-going success.

Inclusivity over diversity

The quest for higher levels of ethnic diversity, while important and useful, misses the fundamental goal of integration. It measures the level of diversity quantitatively, as in "we now have 17 percent minority students in our program." Such statements do not communicate the experiences of those students in the program nor does it communicate the graduation rates. A design school can increase its numbers of students of color through targeted recruiting strategies. However, if the social environment is not conducive to the success of those students the efforts are wasted. The fundamental challenge then is not to increase diversity, but to establish a culture of inclusivity. Such a culture not only will eventually have higher amounts of diversity but the educational experiences of everyone, including, the professors, students and administrators, will increase in quality – if quality is measured by a richer set of life experiences. Such experiences will become increasingly valuable as design programs continue to move from the isolation of the insulated design studio to the more contingent realm of community based design, service learning and design build. In other words, a more diverse set of students and faculty will have an increased likelihood of flourishing in a greater variety of learning environments – including those in the community.

Assimilation

Fundamental to this approach is the *rejection of assimilation* as the primary mode of diversification. Quite simply, asking students to adjust their values and expectations to accommodate existing social structures in schools that sometimes include subtle oppression and discrimination is difficult. The old model was one of adaptability, students either "fit in" or they don't. The new model advocates for change within the organization itself: the faculty and administrators begin to consciously engage in the formation of new *co-creative learning environments* that do not ask students to "fit in" but rather asks students to express their individuality and uniqueness comfortably and proudly. Such environments will challenge faculty to work *twice as hard* to understand each student and his or her unique attributes. Such a culture not only welcomes diverse students, but celebrates the uniqueness of each student. In this way, design schools begin to replicate the processes taking place in larger society. Multiculturalism and inclusivity became the expected norms of programs rather than the short lived special initiative spearheaded by a few "champions" on the faculty. This model shifts the responsibility from minority groups, who currently must advocate for equality (through groups such as NOMA Students), to the faculty and administrators who can begin to consciously develop an academic culture that is genuinely inclusive and equitable. Therefore it is incumbent upon those with privilege to initiate and sustain necessary changes. Female students, for example, should not need to advocate for inclusion of more female designers in the history sequences. Instead, such changes are meaningful if they come from above as part of an overall strategy to build an inclusive learning environment. In the 1993 study referenced earlier, Frederickson wrote, "Administrative leaders should learn to identify and empathize with those who have become alienated from the system and to envision and implement a mutually productive fit between them and the organization."[25]

An example of inclusivity (removing barriers) may be found at Woodbury's School of Architecture in Southern California, as described in an article in *Architect* magazine:

> Ramirez was also accepted at the more prestigious SCI-Arc but Woodbury's willingness to accept her work at Cerritos (local community college) was the difference. "Woodbury gave me credit for basically everything," she says, "I didn't start at the bottom like I would have at SCI-Arc."[26]

The mirror

As the call for diversity continues to drive faculty and administrators to grapple with the opportunity they are forced to confront their own deep seated feelings about class, race and gender. For example, most design faculty in the majority group (including myself) would like to perceive ourselves as socially aware and sympathetic to the challenges of underrepresented groups in school. While we carry an internal picture of ourselves as "socially progressive" and "current," the reality of our inaction regarding inclusivity as measured by the numbers (amount of diversity) and by the varying quality of shared experience of students of color suggests that the current practice of "benign neglect" is simply not working. Ted Landsmark, in an AIA series on diversity, has said:

> No architecture school that I've observed has developed that kind of systematic approach to recruiting and supporting more diverse student bodies. Only the University of Arkansas has put together a comprehensive diversity plan that begins to address those kinds of issues. By and large, design schools have addressed the issue with a kind of benign neglect.[27]

Benign neglect: a passive strategy

As the world becomes more desegregated and faculty members become more comfortable with those of differing ethnicities, sexual orientations or gender, design programs automatically benefit from these larger global trends. Therefore the temptation is to simply wait for the diversity problem to "solve itself," to just let the overall societal forces of "good" fix the exclusive nature of the design professions. Such an approach must be considered irresponsible at minimum and unethical at maximum. The scores of talented individuals that fail to see the light of day in the profession due to a lack of inclusiveness in educational programs is for them a disaster and for the design professions a missed opportunity.

While racism and other forms of bigotry appear to be on the decline, there is much work to be done, and the people that need to act are not the minority students, but the faculty and administrators in whom those students have placed their trust and with whom they have aligned their hopes and dreams. Intellectually it's an ethical proposition and emotionally it's a question of empathy. By increasing the ability to connect with students who may have a different set of life experiences we can begin to end the long cycle of exclusivity that is so prevalent in the design professions.

A diverse learning environment is good for everyone. The drive towards diversity and inclusivity is not solely pursued through the auspices of empathy, but also through the simple objective desire to improve design education in general. More diverse student sets and more diverse faculty can begin to broaden the learning experience of everyone involved and allow for deeper and more meaningful interactions. The end game of inclusivity offers the hope that design education and by default the design professions begin to reflect the larger changes in society. Rifkin argues that diversity is a critical aspect of successful organizations. He writes:

> It is expected that the extent to which these demographic workforce shifts are effectively and efficiently managed will have an important impact on the competitive and economic outcome of organizations. ... Only companies that have cultures that support diversity will be able to retain the talent necessary to remain competitive. [28]

The values and behaviors found in the corporate world support Rifkin's claims. He continues:

> While the motive might be expedient and instrumental to advancing corporate profits, the process itself does,

nonetheless, generally sensitize millions of workers to the unique realities of their co-workers, suppliers, clients, and customers and fosters a more cosmopolitan tolerance and empathic sensibility among diverse people. In a 2007 survey, nearly three out of every four U.S. employers said they planned on either increasing or maintaining spending on diversity-training programs.[29]

Moving forward

In Figure 4.1, Barrett's Organizational Change Methodology is inscribed within Wilber's Integral Theory Framework. Administrators can enact a set of organizational behaviors (LR) to "Foster an inclusive culture." While some schools administrators will argue that there is a dearth of qualified black architects, others take definitive action in

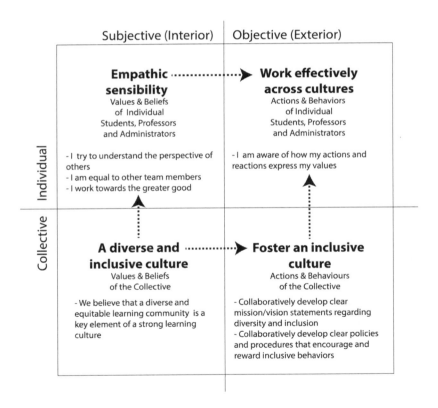

Figure 4.1
Approach to diversity and inclusivity

Source: *Created and drawn by author*

their hiring practices. Miami, Cincinatti and Auburn Universities advertise for faculty and campus positons on *The Directory of African American Architects* website.[30] Other schools demonstrate the beginnings of a commitment by spending time and money on specific events and their coverage in publications. Harvard's design school maintains an entire web page dedicated to stating the importance of diversity in education (values) and corresponding activities that support such statements (behaviors).[31] The presence of Harvard among other prestigious universities at student recruiting sessions at the 2011 NOMA conference sends the signal that diversity and inclusivity comprise the opportunity not just to do the right thing but also to gain a competitive advantage by recruiting talented students into their graduate programs. While institutional efforts can help, larger collective shifts among faculty and administrators towards inclusivity is critical because an inclusivity plan imposed from above without buy-in is doomed to failure. Therefore, the movement forward must also be as organic as possible and occur as an outgrowth of the adoption of an evolving set of values about the future of design education. Organizations in the corporate world hire facilitators to assist groups of employees in shifting individual values through sensitivity training and other initiatives. The same could be true in the academic setting within design departments, but only if an enlightened administrator or a dedicated group of faculty members actually takes the step forward to make it happen. The vision of the design profession free of disenfranchisement can start in the design schools, where lifelong values are identified and instilled. Faculty members and administrators possess both the intelligence and the opportunity to make a significant difference, but the will to change must be there. Dina Griffin, a 2011 NOMA attendee, expressed a vision for the future that is worth fighting for:

> When I first started attending the NOMA conferences, they were virtually all male. Incredible! Now, there are women's panels and the room is full. At present, there are only 276 black female architects in the U.S. And, oddly enough, I know my number – #6 in Illinois. But to walk into this room and see all these women who are smart, educated and driven – it was an amazing thing. And, each person spoke about having a mentor. I didn't have one, like many of my generation. But, I too see the future

> and I can't wait for the day when we start talking about
> 2000–3000 black women architects – so many that the
> number is meaningless because there are so many.[32]

Indeed, Dina's vision of the future will come true, and it will happen
much quicker and with less pain if the entire design community, faculty,
administrators, accreditors, practitioners and professional organizations
combine efforts to build truly inclusive learning communities.

Inclusivity in the collaborative teaching and learning process

While the call for increased diversity and inclusivity in design
education has on some level been made in the previous section, the
question of collaborative and interdisciplinary work requires deeper
introspection. As society moves further into the twenty-first century and
further towards an integral culture, the efficacy of a society built
around the primacy of the individual is now in question. While
individualism has provided numerous benefits to larger society, as in
the rise of democracy for example, the emergence of the "collective"
approach to design offers new possibilities for greater levels of
integration, and by default higher levels of sustainable performance.
With the advent of BIM software, collaborative design charrettes and
the integrated project delivery process, the design academies are just
now beginning to find their way into this new and exciting territory.
However, the dominant form of design education continues to be
delivered through individual professors who teach to a set of students
working as individuals. As a response, this section will focus on three
areas of interest: first, a brief discussion on the relative merits and
demerits of the solitary design educational processes will be provided.
Secondly, some proposals will be made to address the territorial
aspects of academic culture in general. And thirdly, an attempt will be
made to reconceptualize the design process to include a much wider
array of stakeholders. In fairness, an entire book is needed to delve
deeply into this topic, but time and space limits the conversation to the
passages below.

Values and behaviors of the individualistic design education process

The statement "My concept for my project is ..." is a commonly
uttered introduction by students at design juries. The student is
expressing his or her personal values and is informing the jury of the

fundamental approach that was used to generate the thrust of the project. While the utility of the design concept is not in question, the value of such an individualized and personal approach to a project reflects a number of concerns. Firstly, because the "collective voices" of the design studio are typically narrowly defined by both cultural and disciplinary diversity, the student has little to draw upon to sensitize and thereby improve his or her design. Secondly, the important aspects of systems functioning and high performance are subsumed under the larger dedication to the formalistic processes and products. Thirdly, and perhaps more disturbingly, is the characteristic of individualistic ownership of the project as if students are designing for themselves – "My concept for my project" – not for the client, or the larger community, or the larger environment within which the projects sits. The rising demand for ecological regeneration, energy efficiency, financial responsibility and social equity calls into question the continued effectiveness of this individualistic approach. Such limited approaches to design education are reinforced and perpetuated through larger cultural and institutional behaviors that include design awards for individuals (not groups), design awards for highly developed aesthetic responses to design problems (not environmental performance accomplishments), and through a grading process that places high value on aesthetic achievement. Figure 4.2 illustrates the cycle of design education that focuses primarily on the individual and his or her personal expression via the design project.

The conception that the design is in some way a personal search for the truth – the deepest and most cohesive formal resolution of the design project – creates a deeply satisfying and life affirming experience. In addition there is no doubt that high quality student work that is visually presented in evocative and seductive formats is a worthwhile outcome of design education. However, in the current swing towards a design pedagogy that emphasizes a wider range of deliverables, the emergence of collaborative teaching and learning is a prominent if not central behavior in the pursuit of a more integral design education. The principle of "transcend and include" helps us to understand that new models of collaborative work serve as overlays on top of the still relevant and still effective solitary design processes. The question might be asked, however, whether the current configuration of design education programs are structured to

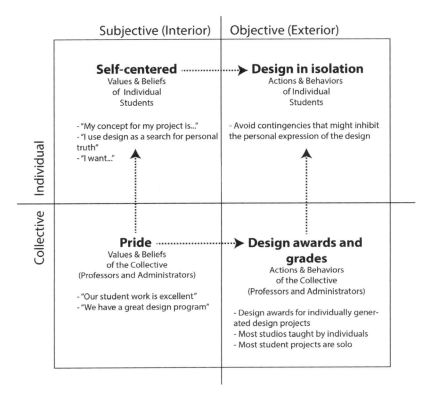

Figure 4.2
Approach to design education based on individual accomplishment

Source: *Created and drawn by author*

maximize the effectiveness of the approach. For example, it is problematic to force fit collaborative, multidisciplinary projects into the traditional design studio format which is optimized for individual student projects with individual faculty members who sit in individual desks and develop individually generated outcomes. The areas of concern regarding collaborative work fall into three distinct categories. Firstly, student to student relationships include the following elements that must be addressed, or at least acknowledged: differences of world view (consciousness); differences in values as expressed via power sharing arrangements; resolution of different learning styles; vocabulary; differing work efforts; and for multidisciplinary projects, differing perceptions of discipline hierarchies. Secondly, faculty to faculty relationships include the following aspects which must be addressed: world view alignment;

117

teaching style compatibility; digital methodology preferences; vocabulary; evaluation methods including grading; work pace agreements; power sharing agreements; and covert perceptions of discipline dominance or inferiority. Thirdly, the emergence of widespread collaboration has forced the attention to a number of institutional barriers including: schedule alignment; equitable credit loading for students and faculty; configuration of physical space that accommodates collaboration; agreed upon assessment standards; and lastly a reassessment of the criteria for tenure and promotion. Figure 4.3 reflects an attempt to sort out and connect the various aspects of collaborative work as a means of finding ways to move forward with thoughtful sets of values and behaviors geared towards effective collaborative teaching and learning.

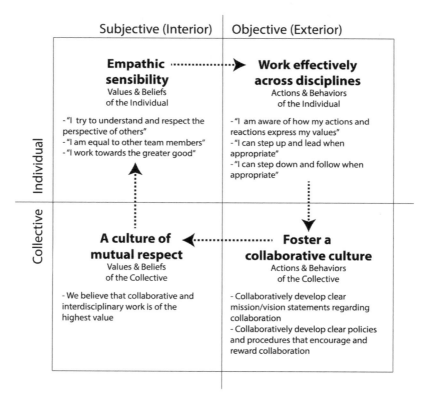

Figure 4.3
Approach to a collaborative educational culture

Source: *Created and drawn by author*

Figure 4.3 begins to unpack the complex factors that form the basis of effective collaborative work. As a starting point the process begins by understanding the all-important value of empathy (UL). Rifkin argues:

> Early evaluations of student performance in the few places where the new empathic approach to education has been implemented show a marked improvement in mindfulness, communication skills, and critical thinking as youngsters become more introspective, emotionally attuned, and cognitively adept at comprehending and responding intelligently and compassionately to others.[33]

Indeed, the need for empathic relationships as a prerequisite to successful collaborative work suggests that more focus and thought is necessary to uncover appropriate pedagogical approaches. Professors EunSook Kwon and Farrokh Attarzadeh provide a number of "steps" to successful collaborative work. They offer the following: "Step 1. Simple communication of ideas: The establishment of team communications usually generates frustrations when students detect others' deficiencies." It has been frequently described as "everyone on the other side is an idiot" or "the whole effort as a waste of time."[34] The professors rightly point out that communication is essential, which reinforces Rifkin's earlier statement. The question then arises as to whether we, as design educators, have the training and experience to facilitate the types of conversations that will yield the kind of results we would like to see (the next chapter will offer some processes to address this need directly).

Some of the behaviors associated with successful collaboration include the ability of the players to not interrupt while another team member is talking. Such a simple nonaction expresses a level of respect and tolerance for colleagues. Also, knowing when to step up or step down on a design team is a critical skill or behavior necessary for collaborative work. For example, if one student consistently tries to control all phases of the design project, important opportunities for others to learn how to lead and to share their core knowledge is diminished. Such processes demand a close look by professors at the personality types of each student, making sure to identify introverts and extraverts and prepare strategies to ensure equitable team participation. Furthermore, varying cultural expectations of design education from different cultures may mean that some students choose to defer in group settings for various reasons, causing again a loss of participation and by default lower learning outcomes for that student and for the group as a whole. It seems then that the beginning of semester for group projects is critical. As design projects become increasingly diverse in their deliverables (budget, schedule, energy performance) the need for different leaders at different times is critical. Lastly, faculty need to learn when to intercede in group conflicts and when to step back and allow the group space for resolution. Because training does not yet exist for faculty on this topic in general, direct experience and experimentation has been the primary vehicle for discovery.[35]

Collaborative behavior: vocabulary agreements

Kwon and Attarzadeh's second step of collaboration looks deeper into the understanding of the vocabulary of different groups. They suggest this is not just a way to improve communication but perhaps also to deepen the empathic connection between team members:

> Step 2. Piaget's reciprocal assimilation among the participating disciplines: Blurring of the boundaries between design and technology starts by asking each other to define technical terms and jargons. Reciprocal assimilation can be formed after asking endless questions about others' definitions and skills.[36]

Implicit in the statement is the need for time spent on the basics of team dynamics as a precursor to meaningful design collaboration. The professors continue:

> Step 3. Students' concentration on fruitful discussion areas: Team members realize how essential it would be to build good teamwork and construct fruitful discussions in every meeting. It takes time to form working relationships based on clarifying differences, defining sub-objectives, and creating a common language.[37]

This shows the importance of a deeper look at the behaviors necessary to achieve fruitful discussions. Group facilitation skills of the faculty and the students will become increasingly important as collaborative work becomes more common. The next chapter will look at some of the methodologies to structure interactions between disciplines.

The use of words in general connotes a sign of respect between team members. The "Political Correctness" phenomenon that took place in the 1990s suggested an approach to culture change not through an alteration of values but through changes in how words are used – a behavioral change.[38] For example, the way that men talk about women or how different ethnic groups describe each other was carefully considered during that time by some, regardless of actual feelings or thoughts. People became more aware of the use of the words and their impacts on the feelings of others, which, by default led to a more respectful environment, at least on the surface. The use of words symbolizes our feelings and values about different disciplines. Often heard derogatory terms such as "interior desecrators" or "landscrapers" serve to perpetuate the artificial rankings of disciplines – a significant barrier if not inhibitor to effective collaboration. Lack of discipline parity can be attacked via larger cultural and institutional behaviors, but also must occur at the level of each individual when a shift of values and behaviors is needed. Kwon and Attarzadeh offered the following observation at the completion of their study:

> Some students felt that his/her discipline was inferior to the other one when they encountered critical decision processes for the project. Based on the weekly progress report reviews, it was more than personal and team communication issues, but a disciplinary status conflict.[39]

Lastly, careless use of language and phrases by students in group discussions can be damaging. "That project is so gay," or "that project is so ghetto" are casually used as derogatory terms by students in group settings. It's up to the faculty to challenge such behaviors in order to create a more inclusive and equitable learning setting. Ultimately, the evolution of collaborative work compels faculty members to augment their facilitation skills.

Group project dynamics

The idea that a set of students joined into a team for the purposes of a design project will somehow "work out" any differences and share power equally is on one level naïve, and on a deeper level potentially damaging to the morale of the design studio and threatening to the acquisition of learning objectives. In design programs that feature a primarily competitive environment as fostered by the dialectic of the design review and by the artificial stimulation of effort via the threat of low grades or public embarrassment, the emergence of the collaborative, interdisciplinary model is highly problematic. It's one thing to manage such group projects within a single discipline, but when "others" are imported a clash of cultures and values is inevitable. For example, engineers and architects have very different processes. For designers the process is unfolding via multiple rounds of iteration – the design project is "never really complete." Conversely, engineers seek a more optimized efficient methodology and are content once the problem is "solved." Reaching net zero energy, for example, is a very clear goal, while maximizing the resolution of building design from an aesthetic sense through design development and detailing may seem foreign to some disciplines. The idea of "indoctrinating" disciplines from outside of design into the prevailing studio culture is problematic. "Others" who are not from the traditional design programs will struggle to understand the rigorous and strenuous design studio methodology, leaving nondesigners wondering why the designers are staying up late to continue work that on the surface, to them, seems complete. Worse yet, design decisions are made during those hours when all members are not present, causing rifts in team cohesion. The faculty members in charge must set the conditions for success by the way they set up the group projects and by the way they build bridges between disciplines.

A collaborative culture of mutual respect

Creating a departmental culture of mutual respect (LL in Figure 4.3) is a difficult process given the dramatic collision of consciousness (world views), values and behaviors of typical faculty and administrator groups. The idea that a set of collective values can be agreed upon regarding good design and good design education is hard to fathom. But if interdisciplinary and collaborative teaching and learning is to become a central feature of the twenty-first century design school, then the culture must shift in order to facilitate a smooth transition and an effective implementation of innovative curriculum. While an empathic connection between faculty members is a critical component of the process, the establishment of a nonjudgmental collective culture is also an important step. The same external elements that encourage us to elevate or lower ourselves in relation to others based on race, class or gender constitutes the same tendency to create artificial divisions based on disciplines. Architects, interior designers, landscape architects (LAs) and engineers, while all dedicated to achieving the highest quality built projects, operate out of different professional contexts and educational processes, and suffer or benefit from historical and artificial hierarchies in practice. Such hierarchies find themselves at play in the educational context pitting the disciplines against each other in a meaningless battle for supremacy.

In terms of discipline diversity, our tendency as humans operating under the industrial rational world view is to streamline, simplify and optimize our processes (behaviors). We do this on the pretence that time and money will be saved, convincing ourselves that a reductionist view via division of labor will lead to better projects or at least minimize the pain of the process. But design of the built environment is a messy process, fraught with stops and starts, entanglements between consultants, misunderstandings between clients and arguments with builders. The emergence of the integrated project delivery process will, in theory, begin to address the fragmentation of the process and reduce tension between disciplines. The professional environment is pre-disposed to pursue emerging delivery methods due to the need to constantly evolve practices to remain competitive. In the academies, however, the same kinds of pressures do not exist. Accreditation bodies ask for collaboration and interdisciplinary teaching and learning but not as a central theme to compliance. The accreditors understand very well the structural limitations placed upon programs that make it difficult to pursue wide scale collaborative multidisciplinary projects. Couple that with reticence among many faculty members to engage in such projects due to philosophic objections, or disinterest, the overall movement to widespread interdisciplinary collaboration is still a work in progress.

Crossing disciplines: architects versus interior designers and landscape architects

Architects have no hesitation to pursue interior design, product design or landscape architecture projects. The self-image of infallibility that architects possess stems from a particular educational approach that features a process stripped away from contingency and dependence to the point where total liberation is achieved. For the architect, the purity of design can be applied to any scale for any client, anywhere in the world. This is quite remarkable and there is much to be said for such an empowering educational model. However, when it comes to interdisciplinary work, the once powerful design hubris can become a significant liability. The natural desire and inclination to dominate or more politely lead a design process is simultaneously problematic and helpful. In certain groups of interdisciplinary students, a vacuum of

123

leadership and vision is quickly filled by the eager architect, who desires to see his/her visions come to fruition. If well coached and monitored, the entire team can rally around that student. On the other hand, strong interior designers, landscape architects or engineers who also are natural leaders can quickly come to loggerheads with the architect in a group project. For interior designers the contingency of the "given," in this case a pre-designed or existing shell of a building, serves as a consistent reminder, if not boundary to the limits of a project. Similarly, the landscape architect is so steeped in the "given" of the site, that their visionary moves are often tempered by the context. In any of the cases, whether it be architects freely taking a hand if not attempting to dominate the design discourse, or the interior designer's and landscape architect's self-imposition of boundaries, the resulting context for interdisciplinary work between the professions is challenging. As a response, the transdisciplinary environment is proposed, where students of varying disciplines can temporarily at least exist on design teams as equal members without regard to technical background or discipline specialty. Interior designers can and should participate on decisions regarding the site and landscape architects can and should involve themselves on decisions that shape interiors. The engineer can be free to discuss aesthetic options with the team — without concern of a deficiency in ability. In that sense the inclusion of nondesigners onto collaborative projects further levels the playing field in a transdisciplinary learning environment. The emergence of transdisciplinary design suggests a more equitable and less hierarchical model that increases opportunities for everyone to share ideas and promote specific solutions.

Policies and procedures in support of collaborative work

Professors who wish to collaborate within departments or across the larger institution require scheduling practices that make it easier to join groups of students at common times to share lectures or other educational activities. The university communicates its larger institutional values by accommodating schedule requests to foster collaboration. Administrators must understand that these are not trivial processes and that each step in the process towards higher levels of collaboration, if made easier, will stem faculty frustration and encourage more innovation. The issue also works in reverse. In some schools administrators seek collaboration, but faculty members may be unwilling or uninterested, thereby creating a misalignment between the mission/

vision of the program and the actual behaviors of the individuals – a tragic loss of opportunity. In addition, the process by which faculty can move proposals for cross listed and/or new courses through the approval process creates either barriers or gateways to increased collaboration. If the approval process is fraught with bureaucratic obstacles from either the faculty or the administration, the overall incentive to collaborate is diminished. Lastly, careful consideration of credit loading is an essential behavior to encourage collaborative work. If a six-credit team-taught studio is split in half, with each faculty receiving only three teaching load credits, that faculty will need to pick up an additional course to remain fully loaded, creating an overworked and frustrated faculty member. As a response, it's best to join two six-credit studios together, creating a 24 student course with two fully loaded faculty members. The increased numbers of students will increase the chances of more diverse learning groups and the faculty will be properly loaded. In many cases, different programs may feature the joining of courses with different credit assignments. For example a three-credit construction management course may be joined with a six-credit design studio. Such credit imbalances imply differing levels of commitment for different groups – leading to a misalignment of priorities among students.

The behaviors of grading and assessment become much more complex and require clear assessment outcomes for each student group and also clear grading rubrics. The intersection of accredited and nonaccredited programs further complicates the process. Kwon and Attarzadeh address this subject:

> Step 4. Complementing each other's skills. Students become aware of their own limitations and begin to complement each other's skills. Through great failures and frustrations the team members get to know each other, a meaningful collaboration is finally built which produces innovative problem solving.[40]

Indeed failure is to be expected and therefore the specter of lower grades must be removed to encourage risk taking by students and faculty.

The actual interior design of studio space in support of collaboration is critical. An institution expresses its values regarding how students work by the types of studio spaces provided, the types of furniture selected and the specific layout of that furniture. If, for example, a collaborative studio is asked to use space designed for the traditional model of individual students, working on individual projects and taught by individual professors, a disconnect occurs which inhibits the ability to successfully carry out a collaborative design studio. Rows of desks deny the ability to effectively meet as groups in an equitable power sharing arrangement. If a group must crowd around one student's desk, craning their necks to gaze at images on a computer, with students not facing each other, the dynamics are severely compromised. In fact, if a collaborative studio does have a shared conference table, the depth of the table itself is critical to foster the ability of all students to see and draw on the same base drawing – otherwise, certain students in certain physical positions will have the pencil and the power. While such discussions may seem trivial, the configuration of physical space is one of the many institutional behaviors that either supports collaboration or denies it. In a recent article in *Architect* magazine on the new spatial/ technical configurations that support design education, Brian Libby wrote, "Desks in straight rows and all eyes on teacher: These hallmarks of the traditional classroom are giving way to flexible seating, group work tables, and interactive technology." Indeed the same could be said for the design studio of the future, which will also require the same flexibility.[41] Charles Graham, Dean of the College of Architecture at the University of Oklahoma, presided over the installation and use of a prototype classroom – Steelcase's Learnlab Classroom. Dean Graham states, "It didn't take too long to realize we didn't want to go back to the 20th-century method of teaching."[42] He continues, "We just tried to acknowledge that kids are tech savvy and we don't want to discourage that."[43] The new studio spaces are used to increase digital integration and collaboration. Movable tables serve as independent desks or support group meetings and are interspersed with a wide range of digital technology including multiple projectors – a key to effective collaboration. The investment of time and effort on the part of institutions communicates a set of values that prize an emphasis on digital technology and collaboration – two fundamental components of the new horizons of design education.

While changes in physical space are one of the many indications of a changing set of values and behaviors in design education, the emergence of collaborative teaching and learning is placing considerable stress on the centuries old tenure and promotion process.

126

Originally conceived and carried out in an individualistic and competitive context, the new demands for cooperation and collaboration simply don't fit. Faculty to faculty competition continues to exist with lines drawn between territories of research and teaching. Such lines are drawn for reasons of promotion and tenure, where faculty are mentored into a clear focus and direction of research and teaching in order to increase chances of success. The drive towards specialization in research and teaching is antithetical to the widespread adoption of collaborative teaching where faculty must assume varying roles in team taught studios, share lead position on research projects and share authorship of publications. The strict allegiance to the measurement of individual accomplishment in the promotion process serves as a disincentive to such collaborative efforts and unfortunately pressures faculty into conformity with metrics in place literally for centuries. Furthermore, the groups that typically review for tenure and promotion fall within very narrow disciplinary realms and therefore can sometimes demand conformity towards established and predictable models of career development. Senior faculty now have the opportunity to change their values towards an appreciation of collaboration and change their mentorship and evaluation behaviors to reward junior faculty willing to take the risks of joint teaching, shared research and co-authorship.

The hiring behaviors of institutions also reflect their organizational values. Boston University hires "clusters" of faculty to attack sustainability. At Philadelphia University's MS in Sustainable Design Program the Fellows in Sustainable Design Initiative was incubated as a means to hire the greatest variety of disciplines from a single full time faculty line. Rather than hire an individual for a single full time position, two firms were engaged: In-Posse Engineers and Re:Vision Architecture. Each firm committed to a set amount of hours of participation and agreed to "send out" the appropriate staff member given the nature of the course and topics being covered. For example, one engineer taught the advanced energy modeling course, while another served as a co-teacher of the sustainable design studio and still another led the foundation course on sustainable systems. Staff from Re:Vision Architecture, a leading sustainable design firm in Philadelphia, co-taught studios and assisted with the Thesis Program. All in all, a total of seven individuals with different skill sets and interests were hired in the place of a single full time faculty member. The leaders from each firm attended faculty meetings and retreats.

127

While there are steps forward and changes are appearing on the horizon, the overall spirit of competition continues to exist in the academies. Studio professors vie for attention from their superiors, or argue passionately for their ideology in faculty meetings, or defend their particular territory of scholarship when such scholarship may be obsolete. Lastly, and perhaps more depressingly, the gulf between faculty members from different departments within a university runs even deeper. Lack of respect for disciplines or hostility between professionals is a recurring theme, where some are made to feel inferior or less important while others hold themselves up as the "superior discipline." Because the new emphasis on collaboration is forcing the connection between departments, schools colleges, universities, nonprofits and corporations, the negative aspects common in many institutions will begin to fade away. To end this section, the fifth and final step in Kwon and Attarzadeh's study on interdisciplinary teaching is reassuring and hopeful:

> Step 5. Integration of interdisciplinary study: Mutual integration of organizing concepts, methodologies, procedures, epistemology, and organization of research creates a new learning context for all of the engaged disciplines. The final learning outcome and document with collective inputs reinforce students' success in interdisciplinary studies.[44]

Everyone designs – the collective

The use of the word "collective" in the preceding quote is significant in that it expresses a new view of the design process – one that is not only transitioning from the individual to the group, but also from the group to the collective. Larger collectives of *designers*, as many as 60 or 70 at one time, can work on the conceptualization of a new building project through the integrated design process, which will be explored in the next chapter in more detail. The use of the word "designers" in the previous sentences suggests that the standard understanding of who designs and who should receive design education is now coming into question. Jeremy Rifkin writes on the subject:

> The shift into the distributed ICT revolution, however, and the proliferation of social networks and collaborative forms of engagement on the Internet are creating deep fissures in the orthodox approach to education. ... The result is that a

growing number of educators are beginning to revise curricula by introducing distributed and collaborative learning models into the classroom. Intelligence, in the new way of thinking, is not something that is divided up among people but, rather, the field of experience that is shared between people.[45]

The potential of the "collective mind" or of "collective wisdom" must be discussed if we are to move to a new model where stakeholders are not simply inheritors of design projects but actual co-creators. Sim Van der Ryn's Fourth Principle of Ecological Design supports this assertion: "Listen to every voice in the design process. No one is participant only or designer only: everyone is a participant-designer. Honor the special knowledge that each person brings, as people work together to heal their place, they also heal themselves."[46] Van der Ryn's principle is in line with other current thinkers on the nature of the design process, including Christopher Alexander and William McDonough who advocate for similar forms of participatory design. The collective is as good as the diversity of its participants. Research suggests that the greater the distance between the disciplines of the participants the greater the opportunity for innovation. This is borne out in a study by Lee Fleming (no relation), as reported in a *Harvard Business Review* article entitled, "Perfecting Cross-Pollination." In his study, Fleming analyzed over 17,000 patents for the correlation between financial value of the innovations that were patented and the level of disciplinary distance between the team members that worked on the patents. He concluded that if a team is made up of people that have very closely aligned specialties, the team is highly unlikely to achieve a patent that can be considered to be a highly innovative or breakthrough patent. If on the other hand a team is made up of highly diverse professions the team has a much higher probability of achieving a breakthrough patent.[47] Interestingly, the study went on to also document that teams that were closely aligned in terms of disciplines had fewer failures but also generated fewer ideas with high value (success).[48]

The same principle applies to the design of built environment projects. While the role and impact of stakeholders is well documented in the participatory design process, traditional design projects also feature a wide array of designers in the broader sense. The difference is simply nomenclature. For example, an engineer who "calculates" and

"specifies" a structural system is not considered a designer and yet his/
her decisions impact the aesthetic sensibility of a given project. An
engineer who develops a plan for the layout of ductwork, plumbing and
electrical systems will impact a design developed without consideration
of mechanical requirements at the beginning. The contractor who "value
engineers" a project is "designing" through the alteration of material
selection, the reduction of design complexity or the flat out removal of
formalistic elements. The client that decides the height of a building
based solely on financial return on investment is impacting its form,
massing and proportions. All of these participants and their wisdom can
be leveraged through a more consciously inclusive design collective.

If sustainable design by its very nature is best realized by a process based
on the harvesting of collective wisdom, then the traditional design studio
is limited in its ability to deliver what is needed. Academic organizations
are beginning to respond to the changing expectations of design
schools. Garth Rockville, former Dean of the University of Maryland's
School of Architecture, opined in a recent issue of the *IIDA Newsletter*:

> As with what we are discovering in cultural diversity and
> exchange, disciplinary diversity and exchange is often
> expansive and transformative and can enrich the work we
> do ... Universities can lead the way by opening
> classrooms and studios to more interdisciplinary
> experiences and experiments.[49]

By now all design programs have realized the needs and benefits to
pursue interdisciplinary teaching and learning. For many the process
occurs in an ad hoc manner, the collaboration of two friendly
colleagues who work in different departments. The ambitious
requirements of the Solar Decathlon drives collaboration by default. At
Philadelphia University's MS in Sustainable Design (MSSD) Program, the
design "collective" is brought in from the start through the admissions
process. There are no specific discipline requirements. Those who arrive
without design experience are asked to take some foundation courses,
not for the purposes of making them designers but in order to give them
enough skills to participate in the collective effectively. The pedagogic
strategy of "everyone designs" is a core value in the program and has
led to the use of the term transdisciplinary to descibe its culture. Such
horizontal organization allows, for example, the interior designer to
contribute to ideas regarding site planning decisions and the engineer

to participate in aesthetic as well as performance discussions. Central to the early success of the program was the decision to eliminate the boundaries that drive separation between disciplines and by default to reduce hierarchy. For that to occur the faculty had to model the types of nonterritorial behaviors that were expected of the students. The early results of the program are intriguing. One of the nondesigners who graduated from the program, Alex Dews, now works in the Mayor's Office of Sustainability in Philadelphia and one of his responsbilities, among many, is to write green building policy. Alex is clearly helping to shape the urban built environment and the processes by which those environments are created – design in the broadest sense.

At the core of the discussion for this chapter has been the underlying theme of empathy – an emotion that serves to change the way we view our colleagues, our competitors and our stakeholders. In turn, the core behaviors of the design and construction industry and the educational programs that serve them are changing, ushering in more equitable, more inclusive and ultimately more effective design teams. The potential for higher levels of integration and higher performing sustainable design projects rests squarely with the ability of design teams to not only learn to work together but to leverage each other's unique wisdom, differing world views and specialized training. The next chapter will focus on the types of cooperative learning environments and educational structures necessary to leverage the rise of the inclusive design team.

Notes

[1] Rifkin, J. (2009) *The Empathic Civilization: The Race to Global Consciousness in a World in Crisis*, Penguin, New York, p543

[2] McClean, D. (2008) "Architectural Education for an 'Age of Sustainability'," *The Oxford Conference: A Re-Evaluation of Education in Architecture*, WIT Press, Boston, p100

[3] McCann, H. (2007) "0.2%," *ARCHITECT*, March, http://www.architectmagazine.com/architecture/02.aspx, Accessed: 7/22/2012 8:5AM

[4] American Institute of Architects: AIA Diversity / Then+Now+NEXT, https://sites.google.com/site/aiadiversityhistory/, Accessed 8/6/2012 9:15AM

[5] National Organization of Minority Architects, http://www.noma.net/noma/history.aspx, Accessed 8/6/2012 9:20AM

[6] ACSA (1990) "Code of Conduct for Diversity in Architectural Education," Washington D.C., p2

[7] http://blackarch.uc.edu/

[8] Frederickson, M. P. (1993) "Gender and Racial Bias in Design Juries," *Journal of Architectural Education*, 47 (1): 38–43; 42

[9] *Ibid.* p42

[10] American Institute of Architects (4)

[11] Boyer, E. L., Mitgang L. D. (1996) *Building Community: A New Future for Architecture Education and Practice*, Carnegie Foundation for the Advancement of Teaching, Princeton, NJ, p96

[12] *Ibid.* p97

[13] Mitgang L. D. (1997) "Saving the Soul of Architectural Education: Four Critical Challenges Face Today's Architecture Schools," *Architectural Record*, May: 125.

[14] Anthony, K. (2001) *Designing for Diversity*, University of Illinois Press, Urbana, p15

[15] *Ibid.*

[16] Anthony, K. (2002) "Designing for Diversity: Implications for Architectural Education," *Journal of Architectural Education*, 55 (4): 257–267

[17] *Ibid.*

[18] Lubell, S. (2004) "AIA To Launch New Diversity Initiative," *Architectural Record*, September, Accessed: http://archrecord.construction.com/news/daily/archives/040901aia.asp, Accessed 10/22/2012 5:35PM

[19] Kliment, S. (2007) "Diversity: The Educators," *AIA Architect: The News of America's Community of Architects* (full text version), March

[20] *Ibid.*

[21] Kliment, S. (2007) "25 steps to Diversity," *AIA Architect: The News of America's Community of Architects* (full text version), December

[22] McCann (3)

[23] Kliment (19)

[24] American Institute of Architects (4)

[25] Frederickson (8) p43

[26] Lamster, M. (2011) "The Future Belongs to Woodbury," *Architect*, March, p88

[27] Kliment (19)

[28] Rifkin (1) p408

[29] *Ibid.*

[30] *The Directory of African American Architects* (7)

[31] Harvard Graduate School of Design, Dean's Diversity Initiative, http://www.gsd.harvard.edu/#/about/message-from-the-dean/diversity-at-gsd.html, Accessed: 8/7/2012 7:04PM

[32] Griffin, D. "IDEA at NOMA Part III," Idea Architects, http://idea8.com/site/blog/idea-at-noma/, Accessed: 7/5/2012 10:00PM

[33] Rifkin (1) p15

[34] Kwon, E., Attarzadeh, F. "Creating New Learning Contexts in Industrial Design Studio: Implementation of interdisciplinary learning tools and guidelines," *2011 IDA Congress Education Conference*, p46

[35] K. Dong and J. Doerfler from California Polytechnic State University San Luis Obispo, California have been working across disciplines and have conducted more than a few experiments, and there are many others, but where would you go for a workshop on how to develop, manage and assess an effective collaborative studio?

[36] Kwon and Attarzadeh (34) p46

[37] *Ibid.*

[38] Aufderheide, P. (1992) "A short history of the term 'politically correct'," in *Beyond PC: Toward a Politics of Understanding*, Graywolf Press, Minneapolis, MN

[39] Kwon and Attarzadeh (34) p46

[40] *Ibid.* p47

[41] Libby, B. (2011) "Studios on Steroids," *Architect Magazine*, March, p54

[42] *Ibid.*

[43] *Ibid.*

[44] Kwon and Attarzadeh (34) p47

[45] Rifkin (1) p605

[46] Van der Ryn, S., Cowan, S. (1996) *Ecological Design Tenth Anniversary Edition*, Island Press, Washington, D.C., p169

[47] Fleming, L. (2004) "Perfecting Cross-Pollination," *The Harvard Business Review*, September, http://hbr.org/2004/09/perfecting-cross-pollination/ar/1, Accessed 8/2/2012 10:00PM

[48] *Ibid.*

[49] http://www.iida.org/content.cfm/state-of-education

5
COOPERATIVE LEARNING ENVIRONMENTS

I remember one design review early in the first year of school. Our teacher was ripping us apart in his typical fashion, letting us know with no uncertain sarcasm that we were basically worthless and that we should redo the assignment. It hadn't occurred to him that perhaps the assignment was not very well defined nor were the deliverables clearly explained. As one of my colleagues finished a very shaky presentation, the faculty member reached into his pocket and handed the student a dime and said, "Go call your mother, you are changing majors."
(Anonymous design student)

Perhaps the student had been done a favor. After all, it was unlikely that he would make it through design school and even less likely that he would become a registered architect and even less likely that he would go on to start his own firm and make great architecture. The story, however, begs the questions: Why is design taught in this manner? Why is the studio experience in some moments so exhilarating and at other times so demoralizing?

The emergence of an integral design consciousness coupled with inclusive, empathically linked design teams is serving to reshape the playing field for the design and construction industry and for design education. Higher levels of collaboration and cooperation leading towards better integrated and more sustainable design projects is the critical feature of an evolving approach to design education. But what are the rules of engagement? How can such diverse groups be marshalled into a cohesive force that leads to the design of projects that generate more energy than needed, that clean the water and air, that restore the local habitat, that support culturally vibrant communities and provide much needed spiritual nourishment? While collecting a set of stakeholders, designers and domain experts in a room together is a requirement to attack such complex opportunities, the process by which collaboration occurs must also be considered just as carefully. Because the emergence of cross-disciplinary teams demands a flatter, more equitable learning environment, the fundamental tone of the studio must shed its dedication to competition in favor of new cooperative models that are based on deep empathic relationships. As a beginning, some of the cultural norms that have been held literally for centuries, such as the design jury, must be examined for their efficacy in new models of education. Later, emergent forms of co-creative processes will be explored as possible avenues towards more integrative results.

Studio Culture

Like most inherent problems, the process must begin by realizing that a problem exists at all. The refrain, "this is the way we've always done it," rains down upon those seeking internal change. The inertia for the current model of design education is very strong, as the classic formats for exchange of information, the desk crit, the design review and informal pin-ups have been handed down for centuries.[1] The proposal is not to abandon these methodologies, but to re-examine them. A recurring theme, this book is not a tabula rasa, but rather an ascension to new and higher forms of education that will ultimately better serve students and eventually the professions themselves. The emergence of new forms does not require the elimination of old forms. The mantra of transcend and include is in full force. While the traditional processes may remain, in one form or another, the larger question of the "tone" of the studio must be addressed. It should be mentioned that the following passages will not serve as an indictment of studio education in general.

Thomas Dutton and others write in *The Redesign of Studio Culture*, "Design studio teaches critical thinking and creates an environment where students are taught to question all things in order to create better design. Critical questioning is encouraged, visionary schemes are rewarded, and design-thinking serves as the base for exploration."[2] Indeed, design studio is not only a solid educational format but it continues to be more widely adopted, in general, across many disciplines and subjects.[3] Specialized MBA degrees are now offered which feature design thinking as the centerpiece of new approaches to business.[4] However, there is a difference between pedagogy in its pure form and the heuristics used by faculty to deliver educational content.

The competitive design studio

The hurdle of the competitive design studio as an inhibitor to cooperative learning environments must be jumped. Boyer and Mitgang offer the following: "in many design studios, competition is often regarded as the major motivating factor that pushes students to excel."[5] The authors go on to argue that, "Studio education should not be based on a concept of winning or losing, but instead on the process of learning."[6] Such statements serve to hint that the current studio teaching methodology is focused more upon product than process, leading students to compete for the best products at the end of the semester rather than focus on a series of enriching, life affirming experiences that are defined by the process of design. In a recent article, "Architecture School Confidential," author Tom Cardosa chronicles the experiences of first year architecture students at a Canadian School: "On the very first day, for the first assignment in September, I'd already pulled pretty much an all-nighter for the deadline," explains Rachel. "It's definitely hard on you. Sometimes you have two or three all-nighters in a row, and then coffee's your best friend."[7] Such statements are not only common among design students, but those kinds of "learning" experiences are expected. Professors take pride in the ability of their students to endure the punishing workload, all-nighters and caffeine induced states of reality. The author continues:

> Not everyone can keep up with the lifestyle. "[Last semester], one of the professors took pictures of every single one of his students, and then as they started dropping out, he would cross off their picture," says Rachel. "The pictures would be posted up in their section as well. So he started off with a group of 12 and ended up with a group of seven."[8]

The weeding out process, while necessary, perhaps, at some schools for space reasons, is taken much farther by some professors who seem to relish the competitive nature of the studio. Other faculty members, of course, take a more compassionate approach, easing students out of the studio and into a new major through advising. In either case, the weeding out process is a central part of the culture of design education. Faculty see themselves as "guardians of quality" as much as educators, meaning that great care is taken to make sure that only the best and most qualified students graduate from the program and go on to represent the school in firms and graduate schools. The importance of building a strong reputation for a given design program goes without saying, but do the ends justify the means? The weeding out process suggests a surreal play of social Darwinism, a struggle for the survival of the fittest, where the student experience is determined solely by an arbitrary or compassionate god – the design professor. Koch and colleagues write, "Architectural education based on the notion of survival and rite of passage should be an idea of the past."[9] Thomas Fisher argues that "There is the fraternity aspect of architecture, where the pressure on students and interns, in particular, becomes a rite of passage, or less generously, a weeding out of those unfit for membership in the club."[10] In short, the experience of design students, not just in architecture, is defined by cultural norms that are passed down from generation to generation. The continuation of that culture suggests a deep lack of awareness among design faculty and administrators, a tacit acceptance of the traditions of design education with little reflection and hence little action towards improvement.

The counter argument typically goes as follows, "After all, the design professions are demanding and competitive, and so the educational experience should prepare students for success in that kind of environment." Perhaps design educators have the opportunity to reshape the tenor and tone of design education to be more equitable, more inclusive and more empathic, which could over a long period of time begin to shift the actual culture of the professions themselves. Since changes in the professional world are already occurring as offices are moving to flatter less hierarchical structures in order to have the flexibility to attack projects more effectively, the efficacy of a corresponding change in the academic design studio is warranted.

Design juries

Design juries offer a venue for students to receive feedback on their design projects, but also to have the opportunity to practice presentation skills – a necessary and important skill for designers. In Ashraf M. Salama and M. Sherif T. El-Attar's most recent work, an exhaustive study of design juries and their relative effectiveness, they offer the following description of the purpose of the experience:

> Introduce constructive criticism of the students' designs, drawing the student's attention to the pros and cons of his/ her design. Provide general instruction on critical design issues that pertain to the student's projects under evaluation. Initiate scholarly dialogue, seminar-like exchange between faculty members, faculty members and students, and among the students themselves. Measuring the degree to which a student was able to acquire and apply knowledge in the form of a design solution in response to a hypothetical or real-life architectural or urban problem.[11]

The design jury stands as the culminating experience for students and faculty at the end of the year or as interim reviews during the span of a given semester. When the jury goes well, it is a sight to behold, as students and faculty dialogue about the relative merits and demerits of the projects. Jurors are typically happy to provide positive feedback, if warranted, and students are certainly happy to receive such feedback. In this way the design jury can be a reaffirming process – a process that students will continue to reflect upon for years. Negative comments can focus on a particular weakness of a presented project and students scribble down notes for their next steps – again, a life affirming process. As a culminating process, it's an opportunity for students to see the fruits of their labor pinned up on the wall, projected from a computer or displayed via beautiful models. However, not all juries are created equal, and the success of both students and faculty to produce great examples of work varies from year to year. Hence, there are many juries where things don't go as well as planned and can often become contentious, insulting and emotionally draining.[12] Koch and colleagues write:

> Unlike the studio, juries compress an enormous range of information and emotion into a twenty or thirty-minute ordeal, allowing little time to develop trusting relationships. In such critical moments, it is important that jurors and educators possess a repertoire of well-established communication, leadership, and idea-building skills, as well as knowledge of the effects of their personality and style on others.[13]

This begs a question regarding the amount of reflection and attention paid to the jury by design educators. While the design jury experience can be helpful to students to learn how to verbally present and to handle arbitrary criticism, it is limited in its ability to embody a sense of cooperation. In fact the jury model prizes a spirit of competition, a dialectic and in some harsher cases falls under the category of hazing.[14] The jury tells students that *product* trumps *process*, that seductive graphics and intriguing theoretical discourses that align with the professor's values and ideologies are more important than solving basic functional goals.[15] Such a route to success suggests a weakness on the student's part to find the easiest possible pathway to success, and a weakness in the faculty member who enjoys the reinforcement of his or her own design philosophy by the willing student. Salama and El-Attar identify the historical roots of the process:

> During the 1800s, the jury tradition was imported to North American Architectural Education since Europe was the model for the Americans ... Most schools of architecture in the US continued to have one or two "Paris-Trained Professors" to make sure that the system is in place ... It basically encouraged competition between students that was intense, and the end results were beautifully drawn projects in traditional and classical styles which were often defensible only on the grounds of "Good Taste and Intuition" ... Evaluation criteria were based on the quality of presentation and drawings, ignoring many of the variables that influence architectural design.[16]

The jury is much like a defense where the student must defend his/her project to a skeptical if not cynical audience comprised of designers who went through a very similar process in their education and so the heredity of design education continues to embody a largely competitive learning experience. The study by Salama and El-Attar found that:

> The majority of the students (75%) agreed that design and project priorities are changed during the jury process from what was intended and emphasized during studio instruction, commenting that this contributes to a continuous misunderstanding of what the project intentions were, and what aspects they should have placed emphasis upon, or whether there were true learning outcomes expected. Some

> students commented that this sometimes creates a lack of trust
> between them and the studio faculty who they expect to run
> the jury based on aspects kept emphasized throughout the
> project process. In essence, this result leads to the argument
> that the change of design priorities may lead to an anxious,
> defensive, and potentially hostile attitude toward the juror.[17]

In the first chapter a brief history was submitted as a means to place the current design education methodologies in better context. The jury process emerged from a rational world view, a world of competition, of individualistic expression and of little empathy for fellow human beings or the natural world. The design jury is a cultural behavior that expresses that world view very well. But the limitations of the design jury are well documented and reveal a lack of attention towards the educational value of the process. For example studies show that students' preparation for the verbal aspects of their projects is minimal at best.[18] In Salama and El-Attar's exhaustive study on juries, the authors found that when asked about the jury in general, "33% mentioned that there is always a contradiction among all members of the jury, while 55% mentioned that a competitive scene is what characterizes the discussion and intervention of jurors in the delivery of their criticism and viewpoints."[19] The contradiction among jurors is less worrisome and is to be expected. The "competitive scene" provokes concern. More worrisome is the following as excerpted from the study: "Only a few students (16%) stated that there is harmony and understanding among jurors."[20] While educators can and should come with their own value sets and world views – a critical aspect of diversity in viewpoints, the lack of harmony and competitiveness among jurors who promote their ideologies at the expense of student learning is troubling. Salama and El-Attar continue:

> This finding corresponds with the literature ... that jurors
> come to the juries with hidden agendas and that by some
> jurors, the jury is seen as a forum in which to set forth a
> certain ideological or philosophical approach to design or
> to respond to previous statements made by other fellow
> jurors at other juries.[21]

Perhaps the use of the term "hidden agenda" is problematic. More possibly, each juror comes to a jury with a set of personal values that have been shaped over decades, and they often come into conflict with the other jurors or the students or both. The behaviors used to express those differences in values come as a result of conditioning from decades of harsh design reviews which can include grandstanding – the promotion of one's personal philosophies or verbally abusive and dismissive language – a learned behavior which is used ritualistically by some. Not surprisingly, considering that the heredity model of studio pedagogy is still prevalent, the following quote from Koch and colleagues bears this out, "Faculty and visiting critics receive no formal training on how to conduct juries, and more often than not, they simply rely on the techniques their own professors used when they were in school, however good or bad they may have been."[22] The utter lack of reflection by design faculty upon the relative merits or demerits of the design review process serve to condemn the design academies as backwards and antiquated within the larger context of higher education, which has embraced and codified well defined and implemented assessment practices. Furthermore, the lack of structured facilitation by design professors of juries is cause for concern, as borne out by the AIAS Studio Culture Task Force:

> Because design can be a bewildering experience, the enigmatic quality of the process often provokes intense debate concerning what constitutes good design and good designing. The lack of accountability inherent in this dialogue allows many irresponsible comments to go unchecked or un-clarified and many design processes and products to go unexplained, thereby confusing students and making rational discussion difficult.[23]

Association of grades with design juries

The association of the design jury with the formulation of final grades is highly problematic. Grades themselves are a great concern in the search for more equitable and higher performing studio environments. Koch and colleagues state, "We fear that grades tend to heighten individualism and competition."[24] They go on to argue that, "grades are a form of control and shift responsibility for learning from the students to the professor."[25] The association of grading with the already highly charged design review adds fuel to the fire of the process. The risk for students is quite high as they seek to avoid embarrassment from being incomplete, avoid negative or harsh criticism from the jury, and also seek to obtain the highest grade possible for the entire 10 or 15 week semester. This is problematic on many levels. First, many design faculty do not provide much quantifiable feedback during the semester, leaving students to wonder how they are progressing (control mechanism).[26] Secondly, the jury becomes a make or break experience for the students. Those who are behind imagine the miracle of the positive final jury saving their semester. For the advancing student the jury could reveal chinks in the design armor leading to a lowering of their grade. The association of results of the design review along with the calculation of final grades undermines the potential of the review process to focus on aspects of students' projects that either need improvement or demand praise. Juries are teachable moments, not just for the students but for the faculty as well.

The schedule of the jury

The jury, which is the culminating experience in the entire educational process each semester, typically occurs at the end of the project when students have no opportunity to address criticism further. Furthermore, the timing and geometry of such experiences leaves much to be desired. The design jury typically features 20–30 minutes of discussion – 10 of which are typically taken for the presentation. An average of three outside jurors (typically also of the exact same discipline as the studio focus) spend a total of five to eight minutes each to reflect on the project. This is woefully inadequate considering that a project could last as long as 12–15 weeks. As a response to the limited time, juries can run six or seven hours, offering a great vehicle to test the endurance of the students, but the efficacy of such approaches from an educational standpoint must come into question.

The physical arrangement of juries as a reflection of power structure

Surprisingly, architects and designers, who are typically very specific in the layout of space and arrangement of furniture in professional practice, spend little if any time considering the impacts of the physical makeup of juries.

The typical geometry of the design jury limits the educational experience for students because the arrangement, acoustics and optics necessary for high class participation is inhibited. The "wall of jurors" blocks both view and sound from reaching the students in the audience and reflects a clear power hierarchy in the process.[27] This can hinder a sense of cooperation by all attendees of the review. It is often difficult to hear the discussion or see enough details in the drawings to understand the specific issue under discussion. In Figure 5.1 the classic formal review layout is shown. Students in the far reaches remain disengaged, or struggle to comprehend the conversation. Students in the middle background can be engaged, while student note takers and presenters are highly engaged. Reviewers will sometimes turn to the larger audience to share thoughts and comments but in most cases the conversations are muted and often uneventful, thereby gently caressing exhausted students into a deep slumber.

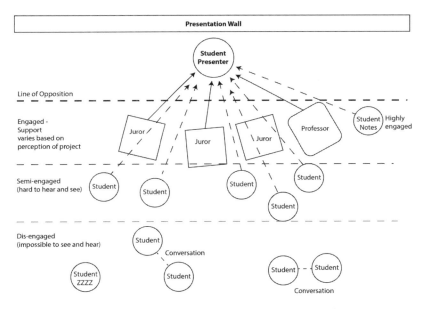

Figure 5.1
Typical spatial arrangement of design juries

Source: *Created and drawn by author*

Parnell and colleagues in their book, *The Crit: An Architecture Student's Handbook* explain the role that power plays in the physical arrangement of the jury:

> The relationship between presenter and listener is made more problematic by the unequal relations of power between the two. This is supported by the unequal spatial arrangements, the number of listeners in relation to presenters, the structure, which favors tutor voices, and

143

also, of course, the position of authority that tutors and visiting critics have in relation to the students (not least because they tend to hold the power of assessment).[28]

A more serious aspect of design jury geometry is the "trial like" atmosphere that standard arrangements connote. Salama and El-Attar state:

Anthony, Boyer and Mitgang among others all argue that the physical seating arrangements of the jury indicates that the students' work is on trial as they often present before rows of jurors. Such a setting as indicated by Boyer and Mitgang encourages the view of jurors as attackers and students as defenders, and this in itself can bring out the worst in both jurors and students where, as Sara states, a defensive attitude tends to lead to further attacks. These two aspects are coupled with the subjectivity inherited in any judgmental process and in the absence of clear measurements for evaluating students' performance. Therefore, it is not surprising that the current established jury practice is not as valuable as educators would like to think.[29]

In Figure 5.2, the design jury is presented as a collective behavior – a common methodology to review the quality of student work. The academic community's values are accepting of the process but without much reflection or observation. Individual students may fear the jury, which leads to unsustainable physical behaviors and draining emotional experiences. Part of the fear of the jury from the student's point of view is its unpredictability, its impact on grades, its potential for public humiliation and its impact on internal confidence. The associated behaviors expressed in juries fall very low on Barrett's model discussed earlier – Survival (physical and emotional health); Relationships (student satisfaction); while Esteem (professional growth and excellence) is met by the design jury. Barrett argues that lower level deficiency needs must be addressed in order to effectively pursue higher level values in education that include Transformation, Internal Cohesion, Making a Difference and Service (sustainability, ethics and social responsibility). The jury is an incomplete educational activity as it is not a structure by which higher level attributes of human development can be reached.

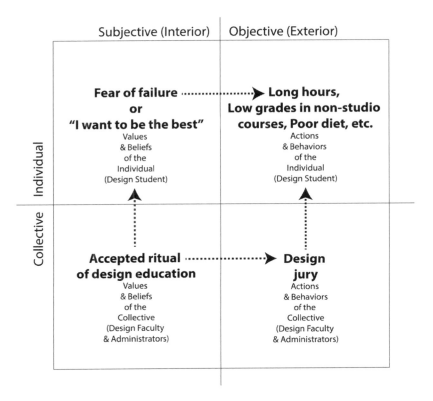

Subjective (Interior) | Objective (Exterior)

Individual

Fear of failure ······················▶ **Long hours,**
or   **Low grades in non-studio**
"I want to be the best"   **courses, Poor diet, etc.**
Values   Actions
& Beliefs   & Behaviors
of the   of the
Individual   Individual
(Design Student)   (Design Student)

Collective

Accepted ritual ·····················▶ **Design**
of design education   **jury**
Values   Actions
& Beliefs   & Behaviors
of the   of the
Collective   Collective
(Design Faculty   (Design Faculty
& Administrators)   & Administrators)

Figure 5.2
Design juries from an integral perspective
Source: *Created and drawn by author*

In wrapping up this visceral attack on design juries, some consistent strains of activity emerge: competition; lack of innovation in process; inconsistent grading and review procedures; lack of faculty role models; and hierarchical physical and social structures. All of these can serve to compromise the sense of cooperation in the design studio experience. A wide range of other aspects of design education that also serve to deny or inhibit cooperation include: the diminished role of support courses; the unhealthy exhausted student; and the imbalances brought on by lack of social equity. All these contribute to what has been identified as a necessary intention of moving design education to higher levels of performance. It should be noted that a core group of students will always be present who will stay up all night and starve themselves not for the reasons discussed above but for the simple love of the process. The opportunity to create beautiful works of art will always exist and continue to draw great amounts of effort.

The counter argument to the abandonment of the competitive atmosphere of design studio is that the profession is competitive, so "we need to prepare our students for such harsh environments." On some levels such comments make sense. Faculty have the responsibility to prepare students for success in the real world. However, those same professors also promote a litany of statements, strategies and techniques that are in complete denial of the real world. For example, design faculty do not pursue budgets for the studio projects. Design faculty ignore prevalent rating systems such as LEED®, a widely used tool in the professions. In that sense, to argue that the jury is a mechanism to prepare students for the real world is disingenuous since so many other aspects of design education do not align with the professional disciplines. Is it possible that the preparation for the harsh and competitive professional world is a self-fulfilling prophecy, that the design schools are partially responsible for the cut throat cultures found in some design firms?

The jury as an expression of values or beliefs

Parnell and colleagues state, "As a cornerstone of the design studio, the design review embodies and distils the values of architectural education."[30] Indeed with closer attention focused on the jury, the design education community can begin to consciously shape the experiences of the students, faculty and jurors, and thereby, the educational potential of the experience can become a more structured, more empathic experience. Frederickson concurs: "The jury is potentially a wonderful educational tool, and it could become a vehicle for realigning our professional attitudes and methods of communication."[31] The terms "attitudes" and "methods of communication" could be restated as "values" and "behaviors," which ties into earlier discussions of Integral Theory and Barrett's change matrices (see Chapter Three). Frederickson goes on to state that, "Instruction in these skills should be part of an educator's graduate education or professional up-dating."[32] The "skills" here refer to the "running of juries." This begs the question of where a faculty member might go to find strategies to improve the process. Kathryn Anthony's classic 1991 book *Design Juries on Trial*, is coming out in a new edition in 2012, suggesting that the book has staying power and also that little progress has been made in general on elevating the learning potential of design juries.

The integrative design processes

While the reformation of design juries is a critical part of building a more cooperative studio experience, new forms of studio experiences will emerge as a closer reflection of the rising tide of the integral consciousness. Koch and colleagues argue in reference to formal reviews that, "it may be that another kind of context needs constructing to facilitate criticism that is more reflective and more active or dialogical, etc."[33] Clues to the formation of new design educational processes come from Jeremy Rifkin, who argues in his book *The Empathic Civilization* that:

> Because empathic skills emphasize a non-judgmental orientation and tolerance of other perspectives, they accustom young people to think in terms of layers of complexity and force them to live within the context of ambiguous realities where there are no simple formulas or answers, but only a constant search for shared meanings and common understandings.[34]

In reflecting upon the classic studio experience, the constant questioning of assumptions is not far off from the process of discovering "shared meanings and common understandings," but the rise of a nonjudgmental tenor and tone in the studio has yet to appear. Because of the emergence of an increasing number of interdisciplinary group projects, such processes are more critical than ever. Koch and colleagues argue that:

> A challenging studio environment contains many aspects: relating knowledge to student experience and vision, a multiplicity of pedagogic and learning styles, a variety of student–faculty encounters and student–student encounters, the ability to take risks, and an opportunity to share power to construct new knowledge and transform thinking.[35]

Sharing of power is a recurring theme through the literature in terms of how the new landscape of design education will occur, while the ability to take risks is a key aspect of pursuing higher levels of sustainability. Disassociating design explorations from both the jury and grading can free the student from anxiety and open the door to a studio that is increasingly more cooperative, but also more grounded by the dynamics of a diverse group setting. Rifkin describes the emerging approach to problem solving:

> A "wiki workplace" refers to a collaborative venture involving scores, hundreds, and even thousands of people – some experts and others amateurs – usually across many different fields, which come together to share their ideas and problem solve. These new flat collaborative learning environments mobilize the collective wisdom of crowds, and their track record is impressive when compared to traditional hierarchically organized corporate learning environments.[36]

The advocacy for flatter and more equitable learning relationships is not surprising considering the drive towards a more multidisciplinary, more multicultural professional landscape. The rise of the integrated design process (the charrette) and the integrated project delivery process in the professional realm is a reflection of the changing world views in society and constitutes the emergence of new behaviors that engage stakeholders towards the goal of integration. As such, it is incumbent upon us, as ethically grounded educators, to seek and deliver the best possible educational programs for our students.

Origins of the integrated design charrette

Participatory design at the urban scale reflects the height of the Postmodernist plurality of the late twentieth century and constitutes a vast departure from the isolated design practices of urban renewal as supported by the industrial rational world view. The process is now evolving to serve not just urban design projects but also the creation of products, buildings, interiors and even organizational structures. One of the key characteristics of the process is the notion that there are no "wrong answers" or "bad ideas," and that the concept of authority, of who "knows better," is now downplayed in favor of the larger and more diverse voices of the community. Such processes prove unsettling for many designers who were educated through the mentor/apprentice process, where clear authority structures created mostly clear conceptions of what constitutes good and bad. The abdication of control and the sense of being the most knowledgeable person or the most creative person on the design team is difficult if not impossible to achieve for many designers, but if higher levels of consciousness and inclusive equitable design environments are necessary to reach higher levels of integration, then such psychological thresholds must be transcended.

148

Another term that can be used to describe the process is co-creation. Taken from the business world, the idea emerged as part of the realization that companies can offer products that customers buy, or companies can co-create value with customers that leads to greater alignment which in turn leads to higher customer loyalty and higher sales. In their seminal paper "Building the Co-Creative Enterprise" in the *Harvard Business Review*, Venkat Ramaswamy and Francis Gouillart describes the process as follows:

> Traditional process design strives to meet a defined set of customer requirements and focuses on streamlining existing processes. By eliminating steps and handoffs, it increases efficiency and saves time and money. It ignores the interests of all stakeholders but the firm and its customers. The co-creation approach, in contrast, aims to serve the interests of all stakeholders. It focuses on their experiences and how they interact with one another.[37]

In reinterpreting this as a critique of the linear design, documentation and construction process, the concept emerges of a more inclusive process where participants in the design of a new building such as the engineer, the builder, the maintenance staff have both a stronger *and* earlier voice in the process.

The authors go on to share the steps used in the co-creative process:

> 1. Identify all stakeholders touched by the process (employees, customers, suppliers, distributors, communities);
> 2. Understand and map out current interactions among stakeholders; 3. Organize workshops in which stakeholders share experiences and imagine ways to improve them;
> 4. Build platforms to implement ideas for new interactions and to continue the dialogue among stakeholders to generate further ideas.[38]

Before going further, a brief digression on the origins of the term design charrette is in order.

The charrette: a commonly repeated legend

During the days of the Écoles des Beaux-Arts, students would work in studio apartments near the school. When projects were due, carts would circulate around town to pick up student work. Students would place their work on the carts and grading would occur via juries, which were typically behind closed doors. As the legend goes, students were not always ready to turn their work in, and so as the cart moved past their "studio", they would jump on the cart and continue to work on their drawings. Students discovered that they worked very efficiently while on the cart, or "en charrette." The term "design charrette" typically came to mean working very hard for a short intense period, usually to meet a deadline – hence the verb "charretting". The realization that designers can produce and communicate ideas quickly is a cornerstone of the process as it is currently understood. In addition, the concept has been expanded to include the added requirement of multiple stakeholder input through a participatory design process. The speedy aspect of the charrette works well with such stakeholder driven processes because it is typically impossible to assemble the right mix of team members across a long spectrum of the design process. So, the shortness of the charrette is as much a reflection of thinking under pressure as it is a way to maximize the efficiency of stakeholders. At a deeper level, the design charrette allows for the temporary alignment of the values of the participants. For example, most sustainable design charrettes include the builder, who more often than not has a different set of values than the designer, who also has different values than the client and so on. The charrette is a collective behavior geared towards the alignment of values.

Better understanding the integrated design charrette

The efficacy of design charrettes is well established in the professional world. But, like sustainability, it is a word that is both poorly understood and often ill-defined. The design charrette presents many confusing and conflicting meanings. For clients and for design professionals there is a range of understandings that vary from "adding extra time to a kick-off meeting for more collaboration" to a week long intensive 20–60 person integrated design process.[39] For many designers, the term charrette is used either incompletely, as in using parts of the process, or incorrectly, as in using a charrette to get "feedback" on design ideas that were generated by the design team at an earlier date. Such mangling of both the terminology and functionality of design charrettes evoke a sense of "green washing" where clients and designers can claim that decisions were made as part of a collaborative transparent process when in actuality very little collaboration occurred and even less meaningful dialogue was experienced.

The charrette, when done properly, is the great equalizer of talent, maturity, discipline and skill. When done correctly it is a life affirming process that celebrates and activates the empathic impulses of the community, of the design team and of everyone involved. When done poorly or in an incomplete fashion the impacts can be extremely negative. The co-creative process is used by Re:Vision Architecture, a sustainable design and consulting firm in Philadelphia which has certified over 100 LEED® projects. They use the term "integrated design charrette" but the process and its goals are similar. For Re:Vision, the design charrette offers the possibility to engage all stakeholders (inclusivity) in a noncompetitive environment (cooperation) with the goal of raising the consciousness of the group to better pursue sustainability goals. Having completed over 25 major integrated design charrettes for a variety of clients ranging from corporations, to institutions, to private homes, the core processes have been perfected over those many projects. The passages below reflect the repurposing of the process to the academic environment. For the MS in Sustainable Design program at Philadelphia, the charrette is used as the pedagogic strategy for maximizing the potential of a diverse set of students and faculty. Figure 5.3 illustrates the approach. Because the MSSD program has instilled values of inclusivity and cooperation, the culture demands a methodology for bringing groups together – the co-creative process. In order for the process to reach its highest level of effectiveness, individuals will learn to "let go of control" and to form "supportive" relationships. Clearly this is a grand departure from the academic cultures described earlier in the chapter. Lance Hosey and Kira Gould argue that "Personal expression rules in education and practice both, and this makes it difficult to embrace sustainable design's emphasis on logical principles and communal values."[40]

Additionally, the lower left quadrant depicts the presence of a "culture of mutual respect and trust" within which the faculty, students and administrators work together with a minimum of hierarchy and a maximum of cooperation. The charrette switches the standard focus on the individual and moves towards a collective solution aimed at a given problem. In remembering Barrett's higher level needs for Internal Cohesion, Making a Difference and Service, the charrette begins to enter into those realms of cultural organization and as such serves as an effective methodology to attack sustainability. Of course, sustainability can be attacked effectively through the traditional design studio experience. The proposed charrette methodology is not posed as a replacement or revolution to the norm, but simply the next logical overlay of a new system.

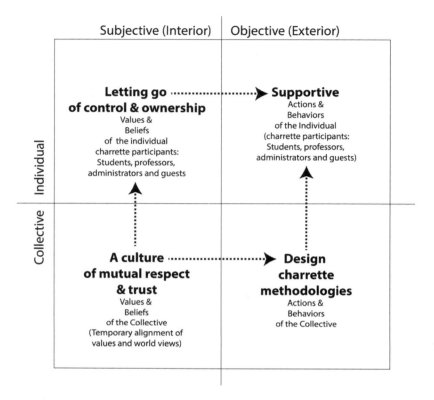

Figure 5.3
The co-creative or charrette process from an integral perspective
Source: *Created and drawn by author*

The professional design charrette translates well to the academic environment because it allows a space for different types of students, faculty, clients, experts and more to temporarily align values and to move collectively towards a defined problem. In Figure 5.4 an arrangement of charrettes to align with different aspects of a given design problem is illustrated. Charrette One starts appropriately in the lower left quadrant where the ethical and narrative aspects of a project are formed. The collaborative development of the "guiding principles" of the project explore the values of inclusivity and cooperation and communicate a "story" about the project that can be rallied around by the team. The second charrette finds its place in the lower right quadrant – the perspective of systems – and addresses the ecological aspects of the site in addition to the human social systems of circulation and other functional uses. The third charrette reflects an

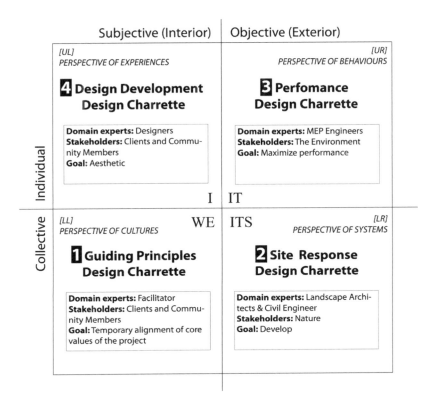

Subjective (Interior) | Objective (Exterior)

[UL]
PERSPECTIVE OF EXPERIENCES

**4 Design Development
Design Charrette**

Domain experts: Designers
Stakeholders: Clients and Community Members
Goal: Aesthetic

[UR]
PERSPECTIVE OF BEHAVIOURS

**3 Perfomance
Design Charrette**

Domain experts: MEP Engineers
Stakeholders: The Environment
Goal: Maximize performance

I | IT

WE | ITS

[LL]
PERSPECTIVE OF CULTURES

**1 Guiding Principles
Design Charrette**

Domain experts: Facilitator
Stakeholders: Clients and Community Members
Goal: Temporary alignment of core values of the project

[LR]
PERSPECTIVE OF SYSTEMS

**2 Site Response
Design Charrette**

Domain experts: Landscape Architects & Civil Engineer
Stakeholders: Nature
Goal: Develop

Individual / Collective

Figure 5.4
Integrated design charrette activities organized by the Integral Theory framework for an academic setting at Philadelphia University
Source: *Created and drawn by author*

expression of "pre-emptive" engineering, which will be covered in the next chapter in more detail. The goal of each charrette is to harvest the best and most creative ideas of the collective in order to "maximize performance." The engineer, for example, can lead an educational and collaborative process to explore various design approaches to yield the highest performance possible prior to the formal resolution of the design project. Lastly the fourth charrette seeks to more deeply explore the aesthetic potential of the project. It should be noted that each charrette has a pre-determined focus for the activities, but all quadrants are in play at all times. For students, the segmentation of focus for brief periods of time helps to organize their thoughts and sharpen their approach. The presence of end users and community members in all sessions helps to ground the activities in reality. For example, in the design of a school, student designers can query the end user (teacher) about a particular idea immediately, thus avoiding the highly problematic speculative nature of some design studio experiences.

Design charrettes, when done well, are comprised of inclusive and equitable team structures that feature the widest array of stakeholders possible for the project (stakeholders can and often do include multiple types of constituents). The concentric circles in Figure 5.5 reflect the scope of each charrette and its movement towards a final design solution. Notice the irregular aspect of each line heading towards the center. In theory the participants become more aligned and find more agreement as they move through each charrette. The alignment of values is useful in a charrette but the behaviors of each participant must follow a carefully developed set of ground rules that are enforced by the facilitator (students can be facilitators after some training). For example, interruptions, insults or other noncooperative behaviors must be addressed immediately.

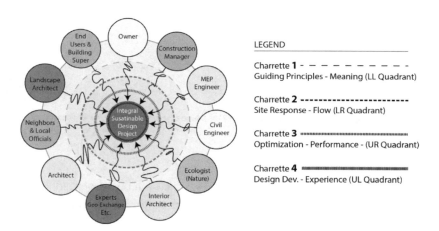

Figure 5.5
Interdisciplinary model of an integrated design charrette for an academic setting
Source: *Created and drawn by author*

Design charrettes are fast. Design teams develop ideas and concepts in minutes and hours versus days and months. It should be noted that the overall design process does not end at the charrette, but continues through several design development iterations. In an educational setting, charrettes are nonbinding. Student teams are not required to use the specific solutions from the charrette, but the alternatives generated by multiple design teams with multiple disciplines typically expand the opportunities for design teams to better pursue integrative ideas.

Design charrettes seek the widest array of design solutions rather than focusing towards a single one. No ideas are left on the table as not having been explored. The group never has to wonder whether a particular thought or idea could have been a better solution. And the speed minimizes the cost of the time committed by domain experts and the time volunteered by stakeholders (end users, community members, etc.)

Design charrettes are open source and transparent. Personal ownership of ideas is exchanged for achieving something much larger – an expression of a collective ideal. This allows for alignment between the client, designer, engineer and builder, a more streamlined process. Jeremy Rifkin writes:

> Similarly, the old adage Caveat emptor – "Let the buyer beware" – is replaced with the idea of transparency and openness. In a traditional business setting, one never divulges internal data that might compromise one's advantage over a supplier, competitor, client, or even a colleague. In a collaborative setting, by contrast, it is only by sharing data openly with one another that the players can optimize their collaboration together and create additional value for everyone in the network.[41]

Design charrettes are typically educational in tone, meaning that the end users learn from the professionals how such projects are approached and the design professionals learn from the end users about the functional requirements of the design. At the same time, the disciplines learn from each other as engineers, for example, explain how to optimize the energy efficiency of a building through orientation or through location of glazing. This aspect of professionally delivered charrettes makes the transition to academic use easier to accommodate.

The charrette is optimistic, uplifting and cooperative in spirit (when done well) which offers an avenue for educators to address the competitive nature of many design studios. It is common for design charrettes to feature multiple teams working in parallel in a friendly competition to develop the best scheme in response to a given challenge. In the educational environment, the presence of multiple disciplines and the inclusion of community members can temper the competitive yearnings of young design students.

The charrette builds a "transdisciplinary culture" where each discipline receives the respect it deserves through the establishment of domain expertise but also through the effective participation across scales in the design process. For example, landscape architects can begin to offer suggestions about the use of plants to purify indoor air quality or architects can make suggestions regarding a better layout of ductwork either for performance or aesthetic reasons.

Design charrettes are nonhierarchical in their spatial arrangements. This reinforces a sense of equity and encourages maximum participation. Figure 5.6 shows small groups who work closely with a faculty member, domain expert or other assigned facilitator during breakout work sessions. Over time students begin to lead the group as they gain comfort and skill in mediating group dynamics.

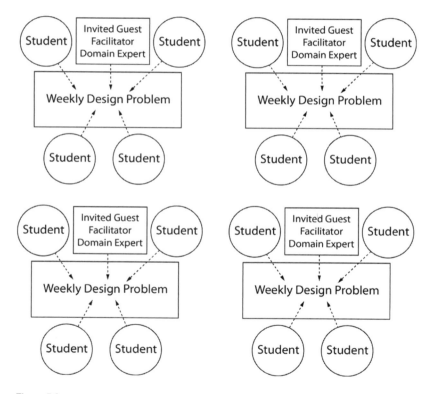

Figure 5.6
Typical arrangement of a breakout session in a design charrette
Source: *Created and drawn by author*

These breakout sessions encourage cooperation and collaborative problem solving. Notice the level of engagement between each student and with the expert participant or faculty member. Students are working together to solve problems through a facilitated process. The typical arrangement of an individually focused studio with 'L' shaped desks lined up is counterproductive to group work. Those program administrators seeking to promote group work should consider carefully the configuration of studio space.

Figure 5.7 illustrates the layout of a "vetting" session at the end of a design charrette. In this format ideas are presented and vetted to determine the "best" concept or approach to solve a pre-defined problem. The level of engagement is usually high. Notice the seating location of the participants and domain experts. They are part of the mix but not dominant in physical position. The vetting process, described in more detail below, emphasizes short comments to specific questions rather than a free form discussion. This allows educators to sharpen the conversation to the learning objectives at hand. Ideological rants have no place in a highly facilitated, pluralistic design charrette.

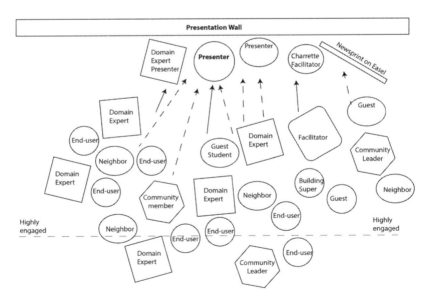

Figure 5.7
Typical seating arrangement for design charrette vetting session

Source: *Created and drawn by author*

157

Design charrettes are tools to reach higher levels of sustainability and integration for a given project because the collective intelligence or wisdom of the group will yield increased opportunities for the maximization of technologies, a more sophisticated response to a project's site and its ecology and a greater diversity of formalistic approaches. Most importantly it allows the differing approaches to design via engineers, experts, clients, neighbors and so on not only to co-exist but to thrive in a structure that is directional and yet still equitable. In other words, the process naturally eliminates ineffective ideas through the vetting process, which is described below.

The vetting process offers criticism in a spirit of cooperation within a set of shared values as developed in the guiding principles. In the vetting process, comments about a proposed design scheme occur within a defined framework that is collected via the following categories and in the following order. First, *Clarifying Questions* are asked by the participants. Facilitators are careful to make sure that no opinions about the project are offered in this part. Second, *Optimisms* are shared. Participants offer statements such as, "I am optimistic about the orientation of the building because it allows for maximum harvesting of the sun's energy." The facilitator is careful to maintain the discipline of the group to remain in the optimistic zone of discussion. Third, *Cautions* are shared. A comment from the same participant who was optimistic about orientation, may offer a comment here that is cautionary, "I am cautious about the amount of glass on the south side of the building because I don't see any shading devices in the section." Lastly, *Next Steps* are suggested. It is critical to note that the design team presenting does not reply to any of the comments except for clarifying questions. Instead, the comments from the participants are recorded on a computer projected onto a screen or on a note pad. This is a critical aspect of the process as the participants begin to feel that their ideas are heard – a critical element of generating an inclusive learning environment. The shortness of comments and lack of back and forth debate (a dialectic) greatly speeds the rate at which input is received and in turn the amount of feedback students receive on their projects. It should be noted that free form discussions like those that occur in jury formats can still occur at the end of the process when collaborative decisions are made.

Charrettes are carefully scheduled and orchestrated events. While they can break down, the attempts to adhere to the schedule help to reinforce a sense of structure for the participants, many of whom are unpaid. Figure 5.8 illustrates a typical schedule for a four hour charrette at Philadelphia University. Notice that each stage has clear directives. The efficacy of the schedule has been reaffirmed through five years of studio use in an academic setting and over 15 years of use in professional settings. Notice the clear steps in the process and time limits which must be adhered to if participants are to respect the process. The temptation to let the experience go longer than four hours should be resisted.

STEP **1** (30 Minutes) **Welcome & Information Download**	**Events** - Students present important information including site analysis results, project rationale, budget, guiding principles - Overview of the tasks to be accomplished for the day - Schedule for the day
STEP **2** (80 Minutes) **Break-Out Sessions** 3-6 teams of 4 people per team	**Events** - Facilitator led design sessions - Each team develops as many design options as possible in the time available - A task may be to develop different schemes for the organization of a project site, or develop 3 schemes for a building concept

STEP **3**
(80 Minutes)
**Vetting
Sessions**
	Events
	- Student or Facilitator led evaluation process
	- Each team presents quickly and receives:
	   - Clarifying questions
	   - Optimisms
	   - Cautions
	   - Next steps + discussion

STEP **4** (50 Minutes) **Collective Decision Making**	**Events** - Facilitator led discussion - Work together to make major design decisions - Use consensus process - Offer verbal proposal for final design direction - Seek any "paramount objections" - If resolution is impossible use voting process with three colored dots per participant - Closing comments

Figure 5.8
Typical schedule of a design charrette in an academic setting

Source: *Created and drawn by author*

In as many charrettes as possible, environmentalists or ecologists are asked to join the process to serve as advocates for natural systems to insure that the proposed design solutions will not be damaging to the local ecology, but also to uncover strategies to restore the local ecology to higher levels of functioning, such as stream bed restoration. The reality of consistently having such representation is unlikely, due to scheduling difficulties and financial constraints. For that reason, charrettes require well defined and ambitious environmental goals. In this way, society can benefit from enhanced ecosystem services on a pragmatic level and receive the biophilic benefits of a more beautiful natural environment. Furthermore, such approaches can move inside the building, bringing the same types of opportunities to indoor ecologies. The inside of the building now is seen as part of a larger ecological framework that is connected to the building, site and the region. The benefits of cleaner air with proper humidity levels and the absence of toxins will lead to greater levels of well-being for employees, which have well-established social and economic benefits.[42]

The guest facilitator plays a critical role in the charrette process. Typically, he or she will be seated with the following people: students from the sustainable design studio, guest students from other studios or courses, technical experts, end users of the project and faculty from the design studio. The facilitator must draw out participation from students who seem introverted or shy, and must curtail efforts by other students who tend to be vocal and dominant.

It is quite common for sustainable design studios using the integrated design process to invite students from other courses, especially those from disciplines that are underrepresented in the studio, to come and participate on design charrettes. For example, if a sustainable design studio is low in interior designers, it is likely that design students and their lead faculty will be invited to participate. Such "intersections" between courses can prove to be valuable for all parties. The visiting students receive a glimpse into the sustainable design process. The facilitator of the group will lead a discussion about the design problem at hand and may draw potential ideas while speaking. In many cases the facilitator will engage the visiting students and ask them for a proposal to solve the problem which can be articulated verbally or visually. Guest students should not be shy to participate given that the word "no" is forbidden in such processes. After each proposal is described a very quick collection of optimisms and concerns are developed. After that the team moves on to the next proposal. Another student may be asked to propose a solution. The students from the studio will either bring specific problems to be addressed or allow for a more wide open participation. Both have value for the overall development of the process.

The community members or end users are the most critical participants in the integrated design process in that they have first hand knowledge about how a particular organization or community actually functions. If accessed, they can remove the speculative nature of the design studio to one of direct service to the functional aspects of the project. However, end users or community members can also derail a charrette by stubbornly sticking to outdated ideas about how projects can function or overly conservative views of budget. The facilitators are the key players in managing the expectations of the community and are also responsible for making sure that charrette progress is maintained and that community members contribute to the dialogue in a useful way.

Domain experts play a key role on the charrette process as they provide a variety of services ranging from the roving expert who moves from table to table answering questions, to leading a sub-group of the charrette that is looking at a particular issue in the project, to participation in the vetting session at the end of the process. The experts return to the studio in subsequent weeks to reinforce the lesson learned during the charrette. Experts might assist with the following areas not normally represented in a typical studio: urban agriculture; geo-exchange systems; building envelope; green infrastructure; public art; value engineering; and acoustics.

Some of the benefits for students witnessed over the last five years of using this methodology include: students engage directly across disciplines and constituencies in a structured and equitable format; students learn to respond to various contingencies raised in the design process; they learn to place ego aside for the greater good; they learn to respect the views of other disciplines and stakeholders and some may learn how to structure and facilitate the integrated process. Faculty members learn how to facilitate complex and participatory design processes; learn how to step back and let the process drive the direction of design; learn to engage with the community and domain experts through scheduling and organization of charrettes and through the vetting process.

Some of the difficulties of the charrette process in academic settings include the relentless intersection with the contingencies of design in the real world. In a typical charrette, community members may advocate for higher levels of equity in design projects, developers may argue for more efficient building forms and less ambitious siting of buildings, or engineers serving as domain experts may call for reduced glazing on some walls and more on others. The pressures upon the student groups to synthesize and reflect a wide set of demands makes the process better suited to graduate and upper level students. For many graduate students who were trained as designers in the prevailing format, the co-creative process can be overwhelming. Students must synthesize or reject a multitude of contingencies in the design process. At risk is design paralysis – the inability to drive a project to higher levels of refinement due to a deafening roar of diverse forces. Bill Reed argues that too much diversity can also be a bad thing. The partners of 7group and Bill Reed argue in their book, *The Integrative Design Guide to Green Building* that "diversity can either be an asset or liability depending on how it is managed – depending on the process."[43]

A major criticism of the charrette is that it subjugates the genius of inspiration, that single brilliant idea which typically comes from the pain and suffering of a deep personal search for truth. Over the last five years of overseeing many versions of the charrette, I have seen that there is some truth in this critique. While the projects have reached remarkably high levels of community engagement, environmental performance and even economic feasibility, the level of pure aesthetic inspiration has varied. Over time, as more faculty members use this methodology, improvements may lead to better addressing this weakness.

As in the professional world where the front-loaded co-creative processes present significant financial challenges, the academic experience also begs many financial questions. The standard makeup of credit loads and staffing makes the accomplishment of a design charrette with high levels of diversity and expertise very difficult. One of the strategies used over the last five years at Philadelphia University was to take two 12-student studios and combine them. Then the professor for the second studio is sacrificed in favor of hiring a group of super adjuncts from a variety of disciplines who show up for charrettes and at other important times during the semester. This strategy has worked quite well because it aligned our staffing behaviors with our core values of inclusivity and as such generated confidence within the students that the expertise would always be available to support the completion of some demanding integrative activities.

Columbia's Building Intelligence Project (C-BIP) serves as another example of the kinds of studio approaches that will become increasingly common, as professors and administrators seek new methodologies to better address the complexity of Sustainable Design by engendering a sense of cooperation and exploring the potential of collaborative interdisciplinary design. The project, funded by a three year grant from Oldcastle, is described best by a quote from their website:

> The Columbia Building Intelligence Project (C-BIP) is a three-year pilot project designed to explore new forms of technology-enabled collaboration within and between the various sectors of the architecture, engineering, and construction industry. The project grows out of an interest in using emerging technologies and the increasing trends toward more integrated forms of practice to address the chronic adversarial atmosphere that has inhibited the progress of our industry for many years. In addition, C-BIP works with the premise that we cannot change the future of our industry without transforming the education of our future leaders, which begins with a renewed engagement between academia and industry.[44]

Of particular note is the desire of the creators of C-BIP to break down the "adversarial atmosphere" of industry in pursuit of a more collaborative model that can not only change the tone of education but perhaps begin to change industry as well. Emilie Hagen, a sustainable design consultant from Atelier Ten, who participated in C-BIP as an adjunct faculty (domain expert), saw the studio as "a model of collaboration and multidisciplinary work with diverse disciplines among the students and faculty including engineers, urban designers, real estate developers, artists and architects." Emilie finished her description, "C-BIP gave students the experience of working in a way that was as complex and nuanced as the professional work environment but still offered the freedom to create things that were not dictated by finance."[45]

Finally, more information from the C-BIP website parallels efforts at Philadelphia University as described earlier:

163

> The studio breaks the traditional model of architectural
> education in which 12 students are guided by a single
> studio teacher for a single semester ... three studios work
> together in a highly collaborative manner that encourages
> the sharing of information, the open exchange of ideas and
> a deep understanding of the need for collective teamwork.[46]

The use of the term "collective" is telling and serves as an apt descriptor
for the kinds of collaborations that occur in C-BIP. The evolution from
the standard studio model is an example of the kinds of risks that must
be taken to establish a new terrain of design in higher education, and
the founders of C-BIP clearly had that goal in mind as their program
description ends "with the goal of establishing a new studio model for
the future of architectural education."[47]

Conclusion

If the new context of design in the twenty-first century demands a more
balanced set of deliverables as defined by the Quadruple Bottom Line,
the expectation of what constitutes "inspiration" may be changing.
Furthermore, as other schools begin to share experiences and
techniques, the overall culture will begin to uncover the unrealized
potential of the co-creative process. Ultimately the movement towards a
more cooperative environment as supported by an inclusive culture and
integrative behaviors forms the nucleus of a design studio approach that
holds as much potential as it does uncertainty. Like most new
educational methodologies, time and experience will build the potential
of the process and help to increase levels of cooperation in design
studios. A quote from Boyer and Mitgang reminds us of the need to
move the evolution of the design studio further and quicker:

> To promote a caring climate for learning, schools of
> architecture must be places where students feel supported
> rather than hazed. An overly competitive, intimidating
> atmosphere takes away from this purpose. The point is that
> the education of architects must develop in students a
> sensitivity to the needs of and concerns of others from
> individual clients to whole communities.[48]

But in order for the co-creative process to be truly effective training is
needed. Frederickson wrote in the conclusion of his study on design
juries, "Group facilitation training should be part of the training of

design educators. Jury leaders would be expected to help set style, content, and purpose and to ensure more productive outcomes through the promotion of constructive juror and student behavior."[49] As a response, interested educators may seek training and certification at the National Charrette Institute. Also, most areas of the country contain design firms that use the co-creative process as a core part of their approach and could be hired as trainers for the process in the academies. Lastly, as will be discussed in the conclusion of the book, the professional organizations that support design educators could begin to respond to the changing face of design education by organizing their own set of trainings to be offered at yearly conferences. Finally, professors can begin to shift their values towards higher levels of collaborative interdisciplinary work and develop new educational behaviors as yet undiscovered.

Notes

[1] Salama, A., El-Attar, M. E. (2010) "Student Perceptions of The Architectural Design Jury," *Special Volume: Design Education: Explorations and Prospects for a Better Built Environment, Archnet-International Journal of Architecture Research*, July–November, 4 (2–3): 175

[2] Koch, A., Schwennsen, K., Dutton, T., Smith, D. (2002) *The Redesign of Studio Culture: A Report of the AIAS Studio Culture Task Force*, American Institute of Architects Students, Washington, D.C., p3

[3] Carroll, T. (July 2012) "STEM Learning Studios: Transform Schools from Teaching Organizations into Learning Organizations," *Ashoka Changemakers*, http://www.changemakers.com/stemeducation/entries/stem-learning-studios, Accessed: 8/8/2012 7:00PM

[4] Specialized MBA degrees are now offered which feature design thinking as the centerpiece of new approaches to business, for example, California College of Art's MBA in Design Strategy and Philadelphia University's Strategic Design MBA

[5] Boyer, E. L., Mitgang L. D. (1996) *Building Community: A New Future for Architecture Education and Practice*, Carnegie Foundation for the Advancement of Teaching, Princeton, p22

[6] *Ibid.*

[7] Cardosa, T. (February 2012) "Architecture School Confidential, A heartbreaking tale of sleepless nights, severed fingers, and a shitload of hard work," *The Varsity*, University of Toronto's Student Newspaper, 136 (23), http://thevarsity.ca/2012/02/06/architecture-school-confidential/, Accessed 8/8/2012 7:20AM

[8] *Ibid.*

[9] Koch et al. (2) p11

[10] Fisher, T. (1991) "Patterns of Exploitation," *Progressive Architecture*, May: 9

[11] Salama and El-Attar (1) p180

[12] I wrote this from my own perspective after 20 years of sitting on literally hundreds of design juries.

[13] Koch et al. (2) p20

[14] Anthony, K. (1991) *Design Juries on Trial: The Renaissance of the Design Studio,* Van Nostrand Reinhold, New York, p3

[15] Because the jury is so compressed, and because there are often very few metrics or indicators of what constitutes a successful project, jurors oftentimes latch on to the existing cultural norms for what constitutes good design – and in many cases fall on the qualitative aspects of a project.

[16] Salama and El-Attar (1) p175

[17] *Ibid.* p187

[18] Frederickson, M. P. (1993) "Gender and Racial Bias in Design Juries," *Journal of Architectural Education* 47 (1): 38–43; 44

[19] Salama and El-Attar (1) p188

[20] *Ibid.* p187

[21] *Ibid.*

[22] Koch et al. (2) p14

[23] Frederickson (18) p44

[24] Koch et al. (2) p29

[25] *Ibid.*

[26] I have been guilty of providing only a mid-term grade and a final grade to students during a semester. The students need to learn how to become independently satisfied with their work so that is not necessarily a bad thing. However, because they enter the jury unclear as to their position in the class, a great amount of stress is added to the process.

[27] Willenbrock, L. (1991) "An Undergraduate Voice in Architectural Education," *Voices in Architectural Education*, Bergin & Garvey, New York, p114

[28] Parnell, R., Sara, R., Diodge, C., Parson, M. (2007) *The Crit: An Architecture Student's Handbook*, Second Edition, Elsevier, Burlington, MA, p138

[29] Salama and El-Attar (1) p181

[30] Parnell et al. (28) p138

[31] Frederickson (18) p44

[32] *Ibid.* p42

[33] Koch et al. (2) p17

[34] Rifkin, J. (2009) *The Empathic Civilization: The Race to Global Consciousness in a World in Crisis*, Penguin, New York, p15

[35] Koch et al. (2) p16

[36] Rifkin (34) p529

[37] Ramaswamy, V., Gouillart, F. (2010) "Building the Co-Creative Enterprise," *Harvard Business Review*, October, 88 (10): 100–109

[38] *Ibid.*

[39] Re:Vision Architecture has conducted numerous week long design charrettes that include large evening meetings with the public and eight hour long work sessions.

[40] Hosey, L., Gould K., *Ecological Literacy in Architecture Education Report and Proposal*, American Institute of Architects and the Tides Foundation, 2006, p22

[41] Rifkin (34) p533

[42] Heschong Mahone Group, *Daylighting and Productivity,* http://www.h-m-g.com/projects/daylighting/projects-PIER.htm, Accessed: 8/8/2012 6:32PM

[43] 7group and Reed, B. (2009) *The Integrative Design Guide to Green Building: Redefining the Practice of Sustainability*, John Wiley & Sons, Hoboken, NJ, p64

[44] Hill, J. (2012) "Transforming the Architecture Studio with C-BIP", world-architects eMagazine, http://www.world-architects.com/en/pages/c-bip-studio, Accessed 1/20/2013 10:15PM

[45] Phone interview with Emilie Hagen, Architect at Atelier Ten and adjunct faculty/technical consultant C-BIP studio, 7/30/2012

[46] C-BIP website (44)

[47] *Ibid.*

[48] Boyer and Mitgang (5) p103

[49] Frederickson (18) p43

6
ALIGNMENT OF ACTIVITIES

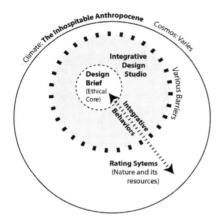

Integrative Design Studio Model
The Design Brief contains the ethical foundation of the project. Nature and its resources are the elements that need to be integrated into the design solution. The Integrative Design Studio is the place where this occurs through the Design Process (a sequence of integrative behaviors). Rating systems serve as useful collections of goals and serve as baselines to evaluate success of design proposals.

Figure 6.1
Integrative studio model: the design brief
Source: *Created and drawn by author*

The quality of life of humanity in the future will partially depend upon the next generation of designers to assume a leadership role in the creation of highly regenerative built environments. While the sentiment is overly dramatic, the concept that designers, like doctors possess a "dark knowledge" should not be controversial. After all, the ecological impacts of buildings, interiors and landscapes is now beginning to take shape in the form of climatic instability, resource depletion and environmental degradation. While the efficacy of a medical doctor's "dark knowledge" is witnessed in relatively short recovery periods, the design community's contribution regrettably must occur over the course of generations. Thomas Fisher writes about the call of our time:

> the period we are in holds some of the greatest
> opportunities for recent graduates willing to think broadly
> about themselves and their careers. We have several billion

people on the planet in desperate need of better shelter,
improved sanitation, and more secure communities. We
have half the species on the planet facing extinction
because of the thoughtless destruction of their habitat
through overdevelopment. And we have global climate
change that will remake where and how humans inhabit the
planet, requiring the redesign of almost every object and
environment based on how much water it uses, carbon it
emits, habitat it destroys, and waste it creates.[1]

And yet, despite the enormity of the task and the length of time
necessary to complete the process, many organizations and individuals
have heeded the call to action through a wide range of activities
including green living, volunteering to help a community, starting a local
sustainability committee, planting a vegetable garden and many other
tiny acts of faith. I offer that, for the design educator, the best and most
important place to begin is in the design studio. The alignment between
the core values of sustainability along with a set of integrative behaviors
will form a deep and lasting impression upon students thereby laying the
groundwork for the kind of mobilization necessary to "treat" an ailing
planet. The beginning lies partially in the most inauspicious of locations
– the design brief.

The expanded design brief

The collaborative development of the design brief requires the all-
important alignment of core values and integrative behaviors – a
precursor to an effective sustainable studio. The creation of the design
brief forms the guts of a project – the gravity that holds the otherwise
formalistic explorations close to the Earth and thereby serves as a
balancing or tempering force. Jeremy Till, author of *Architecture
Depends*, who will be quoted often in this segment goes further: "The
shift from the design of the object to the design of the brief ... inevitably
brings the social to the surface."[2] These words remind us of the relative
obscurity of the brief in its current role in design education. In fact, it's
common at many schools to reuse the same brief repeatedly for years
and even decades. Sadly, such unawareness of the power of the brief to
shape the ethical content of design projects has rendered it relatively
useless in the overall design education process. With the exception of
the occasional programming exercises as mandated by the accrediting
bodies, the program for the projects that students develop is almost

exclusively created by the faculty members or by the department – thereby exhibiting the hierarchical, inequitable learning environments that are so common. But what if the design brief emerged from its cocoon-like existence and began to flutter its new found wings as an integral aspect of design education? Till writes, "It is normally assumed that the most creative part of design is concerned with the building as object, hence the fixation with formal innovation, but it may be argued that the most important, and most creative, part of the process is the formulation of the brief."[3] Indeed the design brief offers an open avenue to address the new mandates of Integral Theory, a vehicle to begin to express the fullness and possibility of an integrated design process that addresses economic, social and environmental goals. Till continues:

> The creative brief is about negotiating a new set of social
> relations, it is about the juxtapositions of actions and
> activities, it is about the possibility to think outside the norm,
> in order to project new spatial, and hence social, conditions.[4]

Clearly, the development of the brief as a collaborative studio activity may on the surface seem uninspiring, especially to those faculty who dwell in provocation and the sensational, but the design brief offers an opportunity to engage a broader range of issues more directly and thereby create windows of opportunity for discussions that can involve race, class and gender. Till concurs:

> This process of evolving the brief may not provide the
> immediate rush of visual stimulation that is associated with
> creative design of an object – a rush which has proved
> addictive to architects over the ages – but it does have a
> much longer-term profound effect.[5]

The design brief is also where students and faculty can explore the emerging sense of empathy that underpins design activity. Issues of social equity can take strong form in the brief and serves to connect individual students to a deeper sense of purpose. Rifkin writes: "The new empathic teaching experience, though still nascent, is designed to prepare students to plumb the mysteries of an existential universe where the ultimate questions are not just 'how to' but also 'why'."[6]

The development of the design brief is the process by which the competing values of the Quadruple Bottom Line (QBL) – economics, equity, experience and ecology – are resolved through the act of critical thinking, writing and arithmetic – a boon to those faculty members and program directors looking for linkages to the liberal arts and to satisfy accreditation requirements. Figure 6.2 illustrates the power of the design brief to play a large role in the alignment of values as expressed by the QBL. Notice that the "shear zone" is relatively narrow in the diagram on the right compared to the diagram on the left, which is more reflective of the misalignment of values in the typical design studio. Notice also that the terms social, economic, environmental as bottom lines have been re-worded for the context of a design studio in the diagram on the right. This helps to place the nondesign values into a more tangible position for the students.

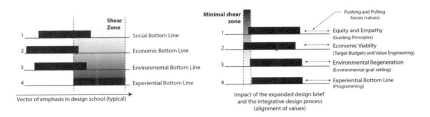

Figure 6.2
Comparison between typical design studio and proposed integrative model

Source: *Created and drawn by author*

Indeed, if the design project is to have an ethical foundation and if design is the process to better connect and integrate with the natural world, then the project brief can lay the groundwork for a deeply impactful educational process. The following passages will briefly explore each aspect of the brief to uncover opportunities for increased meaning in process and as a basis for higher levels of integration in the studio experience.

Guiding principles

Guiding principles, also known as Touchstones, are intended to create a unified vision among stakeholders, designers and other participants in the process. They represent the best intentions and the highest values for the project and are written in such a way as to encourage an optimistic frame of mind towards a unified goal. The Touchstones below were developed for a recent project by Re:Vision Architecture for the design of a new Living Building Challenge project building and the restoration of an 87 acre former waste dump in Lancaster County Pennsylvania.[7]

The Lancaster Urban Forest Center

- Create the healthiest environment imaginable at the urban forest center.
- Instil an environmental ethic through a safe and fun interactive experience with nature.
- Be the best example of integrated holistic sustainability through land conservation, restoration, preservation and green building.
- Educate and inspire about nature, stewardship, land protection and sustainable design through the building, site, program and process.
- Connect the community and the conservancy.

The Touchstones are relatively straightforward on the surface and reflect the approach of any designer who would take on such a project, but in this case they become an emblem for the entire team, a reminder of the core values that will drive the creation of the design. The trick, however, is to build a set of design based experiences (integrative behaviors) that lead to the attainment of the goals. In the case of the Lancaster County project, that meant a collaborative multidisciplinary design charrette of over 30 participants over the course of a single week. During the process, the Touchstones were used as an evaluation metric for different design proposals offered by each group in the charrette. This is a critical lesson for faculty seeking more definitive and by default more effective evaluation methodologies for the design studio. As Salama and El-Attar write, "[many scholars] agree with the view that faculty [typically] critique each project spontaneously without criteria made clear to the students who are asked to defend their work."[8] In the model under discussion, the guiding principles serve as the proverbial book ends of the project – setting the ethical tone in the beginning of the project that is also used at the end of the studio as an evaluation criteria during design juries or vetting sessions of charrettes.

In an academic setting, the collaborative development of the guiding principles for the studio project suggests that the students have some say in setting the goals for the project, but also allows opportunities for any community members, end users or domain experts involved in the project to include their voices in the processes. Kira Gould and Lance Hosey concur: "Students are becoming more involved in framing the questions, shaping courses, and interacting with practitioners and in the community."[9] Lastly, The guiding principles form the broad brush and aspirational goals for the project. The project brief is the vehicle to translate those principles into tangible goals, identified sustainable strategies, effective scheduling and appropriate team members – in short a set of integrative behaviors. The passages below will explore those behaviors in more detail.

Target budget

The development of a target budget for a studio based design project would, on the surface, seem to work against efforts to pursue the highest and best design expressions. Typically design studios are focused on a wide array of formalistic and functional concerns, but rarely, if ever, are project costs a significant consideration. The acknowledgment of cost and budget as a legitimate contingency to be integrated into the design process can be supported on several levels. Firstly, project budget is a direct and tangible reflection of the given project's ethical foundations. As an example, a guiding principle may drive the decision to pursue a LEED® Platinum rating which will on average cost more than a typical project. However, such distinctions in a typical design studio are meaningless because issues of cost are rarely, if ever, directly accounted for in the design process. As a response, students can research similar project types, scale and location and develop a target budget in dollars per square foot. That target budget can be lowered in the case of a publicly funded project or raised in the case of a privately funded project by a wealthy client. In any case the cost context of the project is set forth, allowing students to pursue design solutions within a very tight budget or a very lax budget. In either case a rationale is developed for the establishment of the target budget and later in the project early value engineering is used as a check. The domain expertise of the construction manager is critical in this phase. Although it is possible for design students to pursue the development of a target budget based on similar projects, the wisdom and experience of the construction manager offers a glimpse into a fundamentally different way in which built projects are conceived, and by default a window into the student's future career is opened. The efficacy of target budgets as developed in the design brief in relationship to the damage to the creative process caused by a perceived lack of design freedom is a price worth paying.

Environmental goals and identified strategies

The development of the design brief also includes the careful development of a set of environmental goals that support the ethical premise laid out in the guiding principles and reflect the target budget

173

also established in this phase. The decision to pursue a LEED® rating or to pursue the Living Building Challenge or to pursue a carbon neutral project as promoted by the 2030 challenge is a decision that should be made based on an analysis – a process of better understanding what each rating system requires. The goals must be in the form of quantifiable metrics so that students can later conduct building simulations and calculations to verify that their design approach achieved the desired results. Otherwise the goals are so nebulous that they will quickly lose weight in the mind of a student who is often seduced by the purity and imagery of aesthetically driven design decisions. Net zero energy is a clear energy performance goal. The goal of zero stormwater leaving the site is a very clear goal. Achieving a LEED® Platinum rating for a studio based design project will require the establishment of an ASHRAE 90.1 base building of the design to compare against the final design solution. Once a set of environmental goals is selected, a more detailed identification of proposed sustainable strategies for the project is pursued. In this way the identified strategies are tied directly to the larger environmental goals which are tied to the guiding principles of the project – a logic string formed through critical thinking. Students begin to avoid the arbitrary application of green technologies which occurs so typically in many standard design studios. Also, the set of strategies are clearly understood prior to the formal design process. This reduces the likelihood of the tacked on nature of sustainable technologies in many design projects. For example, a green roof does not always make sense in projects that are located in remote locations with plenty of site to work with. During this phase, the passive strategy of southern orientation with proper shading protection for fenestration is discussed up front prior to putting pen to paper. "Designing the design brief" allows for a reasonable process of decision making regarding sustainable strategies so that the probability of a tighter, more integrated approach to the final design will occur. At a deeper level, such processes speak to the *need* of design faculty to engage students in the kinds of rigorous and methodical processes they will encounter on the professional world. Lastly, a dialogue between the environmental demands of a given project and the desired target budget is both healthy and necessary to the optimization of each.

The roster

Students and faculty can work together during the creation of the brief to identify the appropriate players in the design process. The question may be asked by the professors, "who else should be involved in this process?" The students can then look at the environmental goals and the processes needed to achieve those goals and identify the types of disciplines that will be needed. For example, if "pre-emptive engineering" is used as a strategy, then certainly MEP engineers will be needed and more importantly needed at a specific point in the process. A landscape architecture studio may need an architect to join the team. An architecture studio may need an interior designer. All design studios could use the input of engineers, construction managers and artists. In the case of integrated charrettes, these professionals will bring their knowledge literally to the table over the course of structured interactive design charrettes. Through experience, early work by the design professor to line up some of the experts is an essential strategy to streamlining this process.

Site selection

The collaborative site selection process once again cedes some power to the students and helps to shift the responsibility for learning from the professor to the students. In essence the hidden agenda is for the students to take increasing responsibility for the project, and for the professor to play a more supportive role in the process. Of course in some studios specific sites must be pre-selected for accreditation or other programmatic objectives. But the lesson of site selection is important when considering for example optimum building shape for energy efficiency. Some sites are better than others.

Project program

The space programming task is not solely about describing a collection of rooms with square footage requirements and adjacencies. The ability to optimize human behaviors and the use of space with the need to reduce the amount of energy necessary to power a building, along with the reduction of corresponding embodied energy of materials construction, is a critical phase in the overall pursuit of a sustainable project. For example, a careful consideration of program in collaboration with a client or pseudo client in a design project could lead to a 20 percent reduction in built form as compared with the original square footage identified for a project. This also has significant budget implications. In addition, location of rooms relative to cardinal directions is key to optimizing the spaces that require the most amount of natural light in the best locations. While adjacencies are critical to human functioning, the location and disposition of the rooms also play a role in the overall project performance. As much as possible students should develop programming through direct interaction with clients, through research on comparable project types and through drawings and models if necessary. Janet Liao writes for the International Interior Design Association (IIDA) about the process that is used by the firm Little Diversified Architectural Consulting in Charlotte, North Carolina:

> The pre-design process entails interviewing stakeholders about strategic goals, as well as researching the makeup of the client's workforce to understand its culture. Taking time upfront to conduct interviews, site observations and focus groups may be tedious, but it pays off.[10]

The required drawing list

The list of required drawings contains the opportunity to reinforce the drive towards integration. The act of representation is well understood as both a process and a product. The process of constructing images reveals much about the desire to include or exclude contingencies that shape design decisions. Nicholas Pevzner and Stephanie Carlisle advocate for the "Deep Section" in a recent issue of *Landscape Urbanism*:

> The deep section designates a physical space in which a project's unknowns, goals and constraints can be drawn and tested. The "deep section" holds out promise as the graphic platform for convening the interdisciplinary conversation necessary to solve the complex and layered challenges of contemporary urban landscape projects within a medium that is native to landscape architecture.[11]

Like sections, which could reveal so much more of the complexity and interconnectedness of systems, plans offer the opportunity to present an existing site in varying levels of detail. The choice of what to add and what to extract is not simply a matter of graphic choice but is a reflection of a designer's approach to a problem. Pevsner and Carlisle argue that "contemporary landscape architects have re-embraced process and a hyper-connected view of nature through a re-engagement with the urban ground and its messy complexity."[12] The emerging interest in green infrastructure and EcoDistricts is a reflection of the idea that designers can attack a much greater level of complexity in studio projects – especially if the participants (students, faculty and guest experts) have a wide array of necessary skill sets. Furthermore, the types of drawings can help to support the collaborative design process. The authors continue:

> Developing a fluency with "deep sections," or sectional representation techniques that make visible the wide range of site complexity while providing a critical tool for interdisciplinary collaboration and design exploration, can be a start of a shift towards a deeper grounding in how landscapes perform.[13]

The schedule

Now that the set of key processes for a studio project have been identified, students and faculty can develop a more detailed schedule including the specific integrated design charrettes that will occur. The following question can be asked: if we know which contingencies to address in the project, when, in the overall schedule, is the best place to tackle those opportunities? For example, in an interior design studio, which includes the aspirational goal to reach a LEED® CI Platinum rating, the need for MEP engineers to enter the process early to conduct the formal environmental goal setting process is acknowledged and scheduled. Now, the LEED® Rating System becomes much more tangible and accessible to young design students who often see such rating systems as important but mysterious.

The design brief as a connector across the curriculum

Much space has been dedicated to the discussion of the design brief. In the end, the message is not to necessarily adopt the differing strategies presented above, but to begin a personal exploration into the potential power of the document that typically drives the studio project. The opportunities for engagement of professionals outside the design realm are very high – especially in the development of guiding principles (liberal arts), the development of a target budget (construction manager), the designation of environmental goals (engineer, environmental scientist) and the assignment of spatial size and adjacencies (client).

Designer as agent

At a deeper level, the involvement of students, faculty and participants builds a case for the project that is as much about the role of designers as agents for a wide range of causes including social equality, ecological health and economic viability. In that sense students can drive their design activities from a clearly defined ethical core and connect to a clearly defined set of environmental imperatives. Central to this accomplishment is the reorganization of the role of ego in the design process. While confidence is surely necessary to withstand the plethora of attacks that designers endure in their careers, the emergence of *agency* as an additional attribute can begin to reshape the mental model of who and what a designer is in the twenty-first century. Design processes that include nature as a stakeholder, if not a partner in the process, elevate the role of the designer to a potentially new found status in society. But as society moves further out of the comforts of the Holocene climatic period, and as the impacts of unsustainable industrial processes – including construction, habitation and demolition – continue to be placed into view, the efficacy of the designer as an "agent" and as the possessor of "dark knowledge" may serve to elevate the design professions as protectors of ecological health and as healers of damage inflicted by past generations. Figure 6.3 attempts to illustrate the design process as a search process with two answers: Goodness (ethical core) on one end and Truth (nature) on the other. Art becomes the vehicle by which the search is expressed by the designer/agent in three-dimensional built objects, spaces and places. Ultimately, the design brief serves as a powerful tool to focus the search by aligning the core values of the project (Goodness) with a useful set integrative behaviors (Art) and connected to the larger needs of nature (Truth). The end result is a design project unto itself, the formation of meaning in design through the collaborative creation of the design brief.

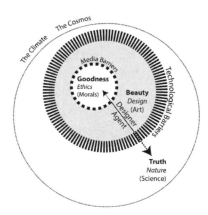

The Map
In this model the stereotypical ego driven designer in search of beauty also serves as the agent for the ethical core of the project (Goodness) and for the health of nature (Truth).
The collaboratively developed Design Brief is the location where the intentions and values for a project are defined and described. Actual integration occurs during the design process itself.

Figure 6.3
The designer as the agent
Source: *Created and drawn by author*

The involvement of students in the expanded development of the design brief shifts responsibility for learning from the faculty to the students and can set the stage for a more thoughtful, more grounded, more integrated subsequent design process. There are counter arguments to the expanded development of the design brief. Some professors will argue that valuable design time is lost and the student's projects will be less resolved at the end of the project. This is a valid claim and will require a shift in the expectations of design faculty, but if we are to become ethically grounded (sustainable) educators, the price may be worth it. In the next chapter some strategies are offered as a vehicle to create more time. Lamentations about loss of design freedom hearken back to a time when energy was cheap and plentiful, and to a time when formal manipulation of space and form along with the choreography of sophisticated exterior skins or interior design motifs was the primary focus of the design studio. In the emerging Age of Integration, the wider and more diverse set of principles (ethics), tangible goals and identified strategies must be encountered if projects are to reach the levels of regeneration necessary for a sustainable future.

Ultimately the expanded design brief offers the opportunity for students to delve deeply into the ethical foundations of the project (guiding principles and environmental goal setting, space programming, target budget), better understand the role of inclusive design teams (roster), organize the design process to meet the ethical goals of the project (schedule) and lastly, it offers an opportunity for students and faculty to express their personal values as part of a process to create a more unified set of collective values. In turn the design behaviors of individuals and the studio as whole will shift to higher levels of quality.

Notes

[1] Fisher, T., "Face of the AIA," *Practicing Architecture: Architect's Knowledge Resource*, American Institute of Architects, http://www.aia.org/practicing/akr/AIAB080529, Accessed: 8/7/2012 11:00PM

[2] Till, J. (2009) *Architecture Depends*, MIT Press, Cambridge, MA, p169

[3] *Ibid*. p168

[4] *Ibid*. p169

[5] *Ibid*.

[6] Rifkin, J. (2009) *The Empathic Civilization: The Race to Global Consciousness in a World in Crisis*, Penguin, New York, p15

[7] Touchstones developed by Re:Vision Architecture, 2012

[8] Salama, A., El-Attar, M. E. (2010) "Student Perceptions of the Architectural Design Jury," *Special Volume: Design Education: Explorations and Prospects for a Better Built Environment, Archnet-International Journal of Architecture Research*, July–November, 4 (2–3): 175

[9] Hosey, L., Gould K. (2006) *Ecological Literacy in Architecture Education Report and Proposal*, American Institute of Architects and the Tides Foundation, p76

[10] Liao, J. "Sense and Sensibility," International Interior Design Association, http://www.iida.org/content.cfm/sense-and-sensibility, Accessed: 8/1/2012 6:10PM

[11] Carlisle, S., Pevzner, N. (2011) "The Performative Ground: Rediscovering the Deep Section," *Landscape Urbanism*, Winter: 4

[12] *Ibid.* p3

[13] *Ibid.* p1

7

INTEGRATIVE BEHAVIORS

Integrative Design Studio Model
The line that links the Ethical Core (Design Brief) to the Natural World (Rating Systems) is populated by a series of Integrative Behaviors that demand new skillsets, new collaborators, new software, a new set of values and an evolving consciousness.

Figure 7.1
Integrative studio model: integrative behaviors
Source: *Created and drawn by author*

While the design brief serves as a powerful tool in the alignment of the ethical foundations for designers and helps to advocate for the needs of nature through the design process, other salient integrative behaviors are emerging and finding their niche within the larger design studio process. The behaviors are a manifestation of an integral consciousness and the adoption of values such as inclusivity and cooperation as cornerstones of the integrative design studio. One of the primary behaviors, the integrated design charrette has already been discussed in detail.

The technical aspects required to mitigate or reverse the impacts of the built environment upon the natural world must find their way into the otherwise normative, formalistically driven design studio. The studio is not only the place whether the various skill sets and techniques gained in support courses are synthesized and therefore mastered, it is also the genius loci of design programs – the heart and soul of the educational process. The faculty help to shape the values of the students and instil behaviors that will impact them for years to come. In this chapter, I leap over the "Razor's Edge" (from green to sustainable) to find the most effective and necessary activities possible to attack the ambitious goal of sustainability. Teaching sustainability in a coordinated and direct way in the studio communicates to the students that it is an important subject, and that requiring and supporting a series of integrative behaviors builds mastery of the subject within the students. This accomplishes the larger societal task of preparing "agents of change" but also serves to catalyze the integration between studio courses and all other support courses. The following passages seek to briefly touch upon the major integrative activities. The list is neither exclusive nor exhaustive.

Pre-emptive engineering

In the professional world, landscape architects, interior designers and architects are all directly impacted by the kinds of decisions that engineers make. Landscape architecture is tied deeply to civil engineering while architecture and interior design rely heavily upon structural, mechanical, electrical and plumbing engineers to make projects functional for human use. The current relationship between architects and interior designers and the engineers is sequential, meaning that form and layout are often determined prior to consideration of the spatial requirements and aesthetic impacts of necessary technologies for heating, cooling and so on, leaving the engineer to either stuff all equipment into shallow soffits, undersized closets and remote mechanical rooms or demand additional space from the designer to accommodate the technology. This approach, while typical, reflects a process that is free of contingencies for as long as possible for the designer, which serves to protect the purity of the design in its original conception. While many great buildings come to fruition through this approach, perhaps new models are needed to reach higher levels of performance and integration. The goal of higher performing projects as driven by an increased awareness of the impacts of energy use upon the atmosphere, for example, is causing a shift in emphasis in the design process towards the needs of the engineer to use short duct runs, straighter duct runs, larger ducts in order to increase energy efficiency and the special consideration of centralized mechanical rooms. All of those needs help to achieve maximum efficiency and are critical to reaching net zero. Such requirements will by default impact the design of the project. The consideration of duct runs and mechanical room location is just one example of the multitude of design opportunities that require consideration much earlier in the design process.

The proposal then is to "pre-engineer" a building design with the active mechanical and passive strategies as an early major design activity. In short the concept asks students to develop sites, locate buildings and scope out the major energy efficiency measure first, prior to giving shape and form to the project in the normative way. For example, an interior design student can optimize the location of the major spaces of the project for daylighting. This may mean the spatial sequences and room locations are different than is typically the case. The landscape architecture student can optimize the site for the most effective treatment and storage of stormwater and also consider the orientation and massing of a proposed building from a light and energy point of view. Architects can use orientation, shape and massing to optimize energy efficiency. All of these strategies communicate to the students that issues of energy and environment are not only important but central to the design process, a shift in values.

While such a proposal seems radical on the surface, the use of pre-emptive engineering does not automatically mean an aesthetically inferior product. It simply asks for the deeper aesthetic exploration of form, space and skin within a greater set of constraints and opportunities. Some design studios feature the inclusion of engineers in the design education process. However, in many cases they arrive after the majority of primary design moves have already been made: massing, orientation, disposition of rooms. Sadly, the engineer is left with "tweaks" of the form and shape of the building and perhaps the addition of shading elements to mitigate the wasteful use of energy that the typical project represents. Instead, the pre-emptive engineering approach asks design faculty, design students and the engineers to work together, typically through a design charrette to develop schemes that have the potential to reach high levels of energy performance.

183

Such a process reflects two different sides of the Razor's Edge as shown below:

Altering an aesthetically appealing design
to gain energy efficiency **(green)**

Versus

Altering an optimized energy efficient design
to gain higher levels of aesthetics **(sustainable)**

The fundamental premise of this flip is based on the simple fact that talented designers can create beauty, meaning, evocative forms and rich spatial sequences within a large set of constraints. For the educator, the "constraints and opportunities" of highly performative design are as much an expression of ethics as they are an added design challenge – a new area of exploration. Table 7.1 compares the typical design studio approach versus the proposed process as impacted by pre-emptive engineering.

Table 7.1 The impact of pre-emptive engineering

	Green Typical Design Studio (An object view)		Sustainable Studio with Pre-Emptive Engineering (A systems view)
1	Student pursues *highly resolved design* through the response to urban context, sight lines, proportions, massing, volume skin, spatial progression, etc.		Student pursues *highly performative design* through orientation, massing, volume, fenestration disposition, optimization of active mechanical components, shading, accommodation of solar in order to reach net zero energy
2	Engineer tweaks design to reduce heat gain, improve duct runs, relocate and treat fenestration, reorganize section to accommodate natural ventilation		Designer impacts the project to reflect urban context, sight lines, proportion and massing to generate a desired visual and experiential outcome
3	Resolution and development of the design continues		Resolution and development of the design continues – Calculation of energy performance – Designer determines amount of PV panels needed to reach net zero and compares to available roof area – Resolution and development of the design
4	Result: A beautiful project that is greener (less damaging)		Result: A net zero energy project that is beautiful (sustainable)

184

Neither column is an accurate representation of the real process as all designers are thinking about performance on some level. The overemphasis on engineering is used here as a metaphorical lever to shift the pendulum of design closer to a more balanced, more integrated approach where the aesthetic and performance requirements merge into a seamless design expression with each aspect reinforcing the other. For example, in a recent project designed by Andropogon Associates (with MGA Partners and Duffield Civil Engineers) for the design of a new community center for the Salvation Army in Philadelphia, rain gardens were used to manage stormwater from the roof but also used to frame the transition from one part of the site to another. Through the space between two rain gardens a level change was accommodated and a view towards a sculptural cross in the near distance was framed. Furthermore, the source of water for the rain gardens from the roofs of the buildings was celebrated via runnels that bisect the landscape every so often but terminate in the rain gardens. Such is the potential of a more integrated relationship between **performance** (zero rainwater leaving the site), **beauty** (spatial sequence), **ecology** (topography and natural systems) and **culture** (cross). In terms of interior design, the disposition of spaces based on the need for daylight can be a driver of the organization of a project, thereby eliminating the use of perimeter office walls, reducing the height of furniture partitions and the selection of reflective materials. A talented interior designer can work within that context to create a highly evocative and meaningful space, with the added benefit of using less energy to light the space. In this way the interior designer serves as an agent for the environment and participates in the co-creative design process.

Inherent in this discussion is a changing understanding of beauty by larger society. At one time rain gardens may have not been considered aesthetically acceptable but over time, as they appear more often, they become part of the "expected landscape" and will either disappear to the casual viewer or express beauty to the initiated. The same may be true of PV panels, someday. Right now they are considered a nuisance or visual noise, but like telephone poles, which eventually became culturally accepted, the PV panel, with its obvious societal benefits, may also be more accepted in the future.

Lastly, the additional tasks and technical skill sets reflected in the "pre-engineering" process suggest the use of integrated design charrettes as advocated for in the previous chapter, but also a renewed and targeted integration between design studio and technology courses. This union will be discussed later in the chapter.

On-going value engineering

The establishment of the target budget is a good first step to intersecting with the many contingencies that impact the design process. Adding a layer of value engineering early in the design process allows changes to be made by student design teams while the project is still in its early stages of development. This mimics the models being used in the sustainable design professions and as such will only help to prepare young minds for a critical aspect of their careers. Value engineering can be conducted by design students with minimal training and with the proper set of references. There are a number of publications that provide rough budget numbers for a variety of types of construction at a variety of levels.[1] Or, a group of construction management students can intersect with the design studio to assist in early budget estimates. The necessity to redesign in order to meet the target budget will be at the discretion of the students and faculty. The simple understanding that the design team has gone over budget is, in itself, a valuable event in the lives of young design students. Of course the emergence of building information modeling (BIM) software will begin to generate a digital process of early cost estimating, a boon to the student as long as he or she understands the inputs and outputs in a more direct way. BIM will be discussed later in this chapter.

Preliminary energy modeling

Directly associated with early value engineering is the process of early energy modeling of several schemes as proposed by the team. Whether a studio uses the charrette methodology or not student teams can generate multiple design schemes and then compare their efficiency. The use of simple energy modeling software packages such as Energy 10 or the Equest Schematic Modeler can generate a ball park estimate of energy performance for the purposes of comparison to other schemes. Of course only the relative relationship between the outputs really matters as it is widely understood that energy models are only as good as the inputs and even then their accuracy from an absolute energy use perspective is questionable. The use of BIM again comes into play as the digital model used for cost estimating, and understanding the three-dimensional aspects of a proposed project also can provide valuable information on energy performance and even carbon footprints via the use of Green Building Studio.

Wall section optimization

Interior designers have the ability to greatly improve the energy performance of their projects. The uncharted territory of the interior face of the exterior wall and the windows comprises an opportunity for designers to impact the overall energy performance of a project. In most projects new drywall or other finish materials are used to upgrade the interior space, offering an opportunity to explore the benefits of insulation, air sealing and the mitigation of thermal bridging. Simple software packages such as Energy 10 allow for the custom development and calculation of 'R' values of a given wall assembly. Design students can undertake the optimization process as a means to better meet environmental goals such as net zero energy, carbon neutrality or the energy reduction requirements of LEED® for Commercial Interiors.

Calculations and simulations

The validation phase is a critical element in the overall process towards legitimate design integration for sustainability. The process of closing the loop between the intentions to design for efficiency and the actual accomplishment of the task can be completed through calculations and simulations. The tables below illustrate some examples of the power of validation in the design process.

Table 7.2 The impact of calculations in an architectural design studio

	Typical Architecture Studio	Sustainable Architecture Studio
1	Student shows solar panels on roof in models and drawings (green)	Student shows solar panels on roof in models and drawings
2		Student calculates the total kWh generated by panels
3		Student compares the total kWh with the base electrical load necessary to run the building
4		Student calculates the gap between the two if any and recommends the amount of carbon offsets or purchase levels of renewable energy (sustainable)

Table 7.3 The impact of calculations in an interior design studio

	Typical Interior Design Studio		Sustainable Interior Design Studio
1	Student selects finishes with recycled content (green)		Student selects finishes with recycled content
2			Student calculates percentages of pre- and post-consumer recycled content and compares to 55% of the target construction budget. 10% = 1 LEED Point. This is one reason why a target budget needs to be set for the project at the beginning (greener)

Table 7.4 The impact of calculations in a landscape architecture studio

	Typical Landscape Architecture Studio		Sustainable Landscape Architecture Studio
1	Student shows rain gardens and green roofs as stormwater strategies (green)		Student shows rain gardens and green roofs as stormwater strategies
2			Student calculates the amount of rainfall that hits the site and then calculates the amount of stormwater treated by the rain gardens and green roofs (greener).
3			Additional strategies such as cisterns and under parking recharge beds to contain all run-off on site are added (sustainable)

These processes and behaviors could occur partially at least, through exercises and activities arranged through the technology sequences in design programs. The link between studio faculty and building technology faculty varies from school to school, but it is becoming increasingly clear that any separations between the two, whether they be logistical or psychological, must be dissolved in order for design students to receive the type of holistic and integrated design education that is necessary to pursue ethically driven projects. Before discussing the logistical aspects in detail, it is important to note that the values of the studio and technology faculty must be in alignment. If one half of the partnership is ambivalent about the need to connect, the partnership is doomed from the start. Aligning of values can occur through directives from above by Program Directors and Deans or it can be incentivized via seed funding, favorable course loading, favorable scheduling, and most importantly through changes in tenure and promotion procedures. All logistical incentives will automatically brush up against deeply ensconced patterns of institutional behavior which currently support the silo mentality towards the disciplines. However, small groups of individual faculty who have pre-aligned values can find ways to work through the maze of bureaucracy to form innovative partnerships despite the limitations posed by existing structures.

BIM as an integrative tool

The topic of building information modeling and its potentially transformative impact on the design and construction industry and by association design education is a subject for a book itself. The idea that a single three-dimensional model can generate a set of outputs ranging from perspective renderings, animations, daylight simulations, energy models, carbon calculations, structural analysis, cost estimates and construction scheduling suggests that the true digital revolution in the design of the built environment has begun in earnest. After all, standard computer aided design software served as a more powerful drafting board which increased the speed at which drawings were made but did not offer a fundamental revolution in the industry. The fact that BIM models are literally shared between the disciplines has partially led to the generation of new types of professional partnerships; new contract types; new mental models of how collaboration will occur in the future; and new relationships between the computer user and the software.

Cory Brugger, an architect at Morphosis and an adjunct faculty/technical advisor for Columbia's Building Intelligence Project design studio (discussed earlier) became quite animated in a recent interview for the book: "BIM is a complete reconfiguration of the way we work. It does not fit within an autocratic process, which inherently questions the practice of teaching architecture in the traditional sense." He went on to state that, "The new tools provide the opportunity for students to question the entire process of design, whether it be the application of algorithmic (scripted) processes or the exploration of federated architectural, structural and mechanical models; it requires a restructuring of our approach to the practice of architecture." Lastly, Cory saw reticence among some in the profession and academia: "change tends to inspire fear; people may not naturally drift towards BIM as it is true paradigm shift."

189

While the promise of BIM is high, many counter arguments and barriers remain before the technology can fully enter the educational arena. Complex BIM models require the purchase of superior hardware, a capital cost that only some institutions can bear. The training necessary to mine the depth of the potential of BIM is time consuming and also expensive. The total number of people who are deeply proficient in the software is low, leaving a huge gap between the potential of BIM as an integrator across disciplines and the actual reality of its use in the second decade of the twenty-first century. Added to that is the naïve perception that the standard BIM libraries will "entice lazy students to use standard doors and windows thereby short circuiting the creative process."

Design build as an integrator

Design build changes the hierarchical relationship between student and faculty and can begin to break down the separation between design students and students from other disciplines. It has the potential to build the empathic abilities of design students by giving them glimpses into the realms of the end user and into the territory of allied disciplines. Given that the values of inclusivity and cooperation are central to the success or failure of an integrative design course, design build offers a rich and rewarding avenue to the installation of values but also to the application of the integrative behaviors described earlier in this chapter. Clearly the small scale of the projects liberates students from requirements of a sophisticated parti development, programming, spatial organization, spatial sequencing at urban scale and more. While design build can exist as one form of operation, it cannot provide a complete educational experience for designers.

The other huge benefit of the design build curriculum is the opportunity to teach students the very real and practical concept of completion. In the nether world of the typical design studio, projects are never complete. They exist as a continual work in progress, and probably rightly so. Students continue to open up new doors of design opportunity through the description of construction details or through the integration of mechanical systems. But underneath the premise of the on-going, never ending design process is the powerful draw of the "perfect" as in the desire to reach a level of perfection in the process and product of design. Faculty instil the ethic of perfection into the minds of students right from the start, with juries, critiques and reviews that compel students to search deeper and work harder towards a "better" solution. On the surface there is nothing inherently wrong with this approach, but underneath lies the instillation of priorities within the design student that are unrealistic. Design build projects offer the premise that completion is not only desired but a requirement. The Solar Decathlon is famous for its sleek designs and well-resolved details. Such was not always the case. In the early years it had its share of structures that obviously needed more design time and better construction techniques. But if the goal of the Decathlon is as much or more about process and learning than it is about the "perfected" final product then such transgressions should be forgiven at every turn. Table 7.5 on p. 192 comprises a brief look at the integrative aspects of design build as viewed through the lens of the Solar Decathlon.

On-line education and the meta-studio

The preceding passages serve to both inspire and intimidate. After all, the depth and breadth of the behaviors necessary for a deeply integrative experience simply cannot be fulfilled by a single professor in a single studio course. The technical expertise necessary to support the effective use of energy modeling tools, the logical selection of environmental systems and so on, demand a collective of faculty with a variety of knowledge bases. Moreover, even if such a collective existed and could work together, the available time in a single studio simply is not enough to support such a wide range of activities. The standard response of expanding the studio into support courses such as building technology, visualization and structures has been blocked by the simple fact that the amount of information that must be conveyed via a live lecture is simply too time intensive to allow for meaningful linkages between studios and the aforementioned support courses. And yet, the call for more integration, for greater levels of sustainability and for higher levels of collaboration demands a dramatic solution.

The emergence of on-line teaching and learning may be the Holy Grail of said integration. The use of social networking and cloud based networks is revolutionizing the way we think about and the delivery of educational materials. Professors at MIT, Columbia and Harvard, for example, are delivering courses with literally thousands of students.[2] The Boston Architectural College is running a series of completely on-line degree programs including a Master of Architecture. All of my lecture courses are now taught live, broadcast live via the internet, and recorded for asynchronous on-line learning modules. Those examples

Table 7.5 Design build Solar Decathlon as an integrator

Design Build Solar Decathlon		Studio with Pre-Emptive Engineering (A systems view)
Consciousness		
	Biospheric and Integral	The Decathlon has a set of clear metrics for energy and environmental performance which connect directly to the larger issues of global warming, climate change and environmental degradation. The project serves as a connector between a student's ethical core and the larger biosphere via a set of values and behaviors as described below.
Core Values		
	Inclusivity	Students learn the value of inclusivity as they collaborate with students from different disciplines, different ages and different world views.
	Cooperation	Students learn the value of cooperation as they work through difficult technical and aesthetic issues to move towards final resolution.
Integrative Behaviors		
	Design Charrette	The design charrette enables engineers, architects, designers, landscape architects, and builders to work together early in the process to co-create design proposals that achieve high levels of energy performance, plausible construction systems and site systems, evocative forms and interiors and a broad narrative or concept that ties it all together.
	Pre-emptive Engineering	The inclusive design process suggests the addition of the engineer early in the design process.
	On-going Value Engineering	Cost estimating is a learning opportunity for students to understand that their decisions have real ramifications and that budgets are not something abstract but a link to an ethical foundation – assuming it's a low to moderate income project.
	Preliminary Energy Modeling	Software packages can assist in the visualization and early decision making – now that CFD is becoming more available via interfaces such as DesignBuilder or Vasari, the likelihood of early modeling is increasing.
	Wall Section Optimization	The design process includes a careful look at 'R' and 'U' values, thermal bridging, air sealing and hygrometric studies.
	Calculations and Simulations	Ultimately, final building simulations and calculations are necessary to ensure that the building design has met its performance goals.
	Construction	The process then moves into the next set of learning experiences – the actual construction of a built environment – which are not covered here.

are a small segment of the teeming masses of courses that are already on-line or in the planning stages. The writing on the wall (he wrote anachronistically) tells us that the rise of on-line teaching and learning is the biggest transformational force for higher education since the advent of the internet itself.

On the surface, the proposition of on-line teaching and learning seems antithetical to earlier arguments in this book that placed technology in the role of a villain, as the separator between humanity and nature and as a barrier between our ethical core and our technologically empowered ego selves. However, the principle of "transcend and include" reminds us that the addition of on-line teaching does not eliminate or preclude the traditional on-campus experience. Perhaps we can begin to view technology not as a barrier, but rather as a connector, as a series of hardware and software devices that actually allow for an overall enhanced and augmented set of educational experiences. There are two main tracks of on-line education that will be discussed in this section, each rousing the reader from the relative comfort of the present to the impending discomfort of the near future.

The first major thrust of on-line teaching comes in the form of the "flipped" or "blended classroom" experience. The basic premise according to Educause is that "The flipped classroom is a pedagogical model in which the typical lecture and homework elements of a course are reversed."[3]

The premise, while surprisingly simple, presents a profound shift in the way courses are conceived (see Figure 7.2). The typical three hour lecture, in a building technology course, for example, is delivered via a mixture of video recordings of previous lectures, podcasts, narrated PowerPoints, video recordings of specific technical tasks and readings. Students are required to watch the recordings prior to class and come prepared to engage in an integrative activity that links directly to, and reinforces the content of the pre-viewed lecture. In this way the professor is present and available to work with the students on the actual skill set in question. In short the homework is now completed during class time. As an example, the development of wall sections would be drawn in class, while the supporting lectures would be delivered prior to class electronically – including a recording of experts actually drawing and explaining the steps necessary to completing a drawing. For the student who is struggling to keep up with the live lectures, the on-line recording

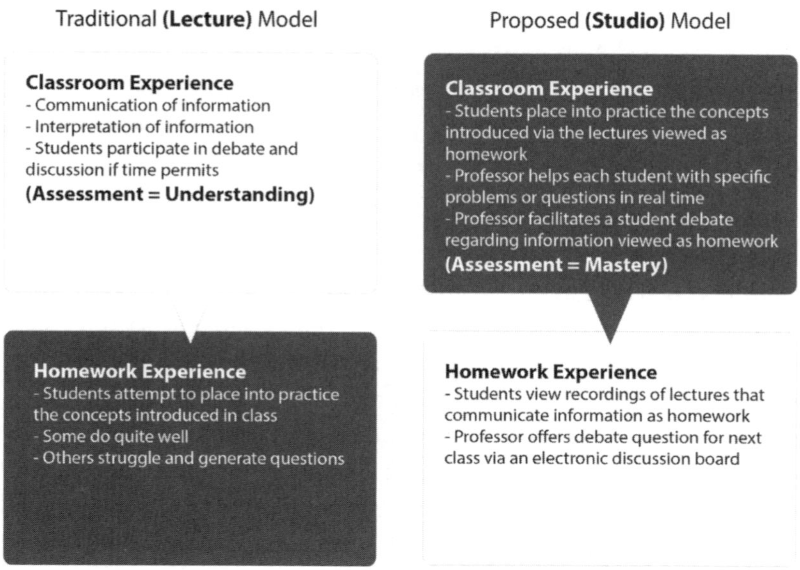

Traditional **(Lecture)** Model

Proposed **(Studio)** Model

Classroom Experience
- Communication of information
- Interpretation of information
- Students participate in debate and discussion if time permits
(Assessment = Understanding)

Classroom Experience
- Students place into practice the concepts introduced via the lectures viewed as homework
- Professor helps each student with specific problems or questions in real time
- Professor facilitates a student debate regarding information viewed as homework
(Assessment = Mastery)

Homework Experience
- Students attempt to place into practice the concepts introduced in class
- Some do quite well
- Others struggle and generate questions

Homework Experience
- Students view recordings of lectures that communicate information as homework
- Professor offers debate question for next class via an electronic discussion board

Figure 7.2
The blended or flipped classroom model for support courses
Source: *Created and drawn by author*

offers the ability to rewind, and repeat parts of the lecture that were difficult to comprehend. This can be quite an aid for students who are taking courses that are not delivered in their primary language, or for students who may need more time to digest and process the lectures, or for students who are typically slow processors. The recorded on-line lectures serve as an equalizer for large groups of students who may have typically struggled offering a potentially more equitable learning environment. Professors, now freed from the time constraints of verbally delivered lectures (which they probably enjoy) can move from the "understanding" level of learning that is typically associated with lectures, to the higher learning objectives of "comprehension, ability and mastery" via in-class exercises. The awkward first steps of developing a wall section now occur in a safe environment where the faculty helps to support student efforts on an as-needed basis – with the added potential of short impromptu lectures to address a commonly troubling aspect of the assignment – as supported by the Educause article below:

> The result is that faculty members can better detect the types of problems students are having, and the students begin to take on more responsibility for their learning. The

implications of this model to the average faculty member are deep and far reaching. The idea that includes a shift from the professor's focus on transmission of knowledge to the process of mastery through integrative learning offers new avenues to reconceive the way support courses are delivered in design programs.[4]

In the MS in Sustainable Design at Philadelphia University, Professor Chris Pastore, an engineer, teaches the principles and techniques of life cycle assessment via recorded lectures. He then uses class time to work with students in the development of complex spread sheets that are used to build an actual life cycle assessment. In addition, class time is used to shore up math skills for some of the students while the others move forward to more advanced concepts. The freedom from the lecture, while missed on nostalgic levels, allows Professor Pastore to attack a complex subject at a much deeper and more impactful level and also to deal directly with different learning styles and speeds.

The opportunities for curricular transformation leading to higher levels of integration are not limited to building technology or life cycle courses. The importance of eco-literacy calls for the immersion of students in the natural environment as often as possible. With lectures occurring electronically on a wide range of subjects, class time is liberated to experience the outdoors, learning to map watersheds, or better draw and understand contours. Repeated visits to a site over a semester create the possibility of higher levels of authenticity and connection to natural systems in support of integrated design projects. In other classes such as history of art and design, there is the potential for an increased number of field trips to local museums and to noteworthy design projects to achieve an augmented and, on the whole, an enlivened education experience.

Many mistakes must occur in order to tease out the primary digital processes and pedagogic strategies necessary for optimized student learning in a blended learning environment. The counter arguments to this approach are plentiful; some are well considered while others are impulsive. By shifting the lectures to homework, cloud based platforms such as Blackboard must be used to track whether the students have actually viewed the lectures. The typical amount of time spent on readings by students will by default need to be reduced as there is less overall time outside of class for homework which now occurs in class (at least partially). Already overburdened faculty must spend time learning new software packages in order to record, edit and process lectures. Tricks such as posting lectures in short 10–15 minute chunks with clear learning objectives allow the faculty to stay fresh during each recording; allow students to digest and process information; and place less burden on the internet connection. Other considerations include the need to align the way a particular program is marketed versus the actual experiences for students. Undergraduate campus based programs offer the traditional experience. Students may become frustrated and baulk at too much on-line interaction. In a pair of articles from *The Chronicle of Higher Education*, "Did Anyone Ask the Students?, Part 1 and Part 2," author Jeff Selingo writes that:

> Face-to-face education matters even more now. Because these students see the world through screens (mobile, tablet, and laptop), I expected them to embrace the idea of online education. Just the opposite. They want to engage with a professor and with their classmates, they crave the serendipity of classroom discussions, and they want the discipline of going to class. Even the adult students I met preferred a physical classroom. Online "you're pretty much paying to teach yourself," a Valencia student told me. "It's like text messages. There's no tone of voice."[5]

Such statements seem to indict on-line education. However, further reflections from students and the author reveal the following comments:

> That doesn't mean these students like everything about traditional higher-ed. They're over the lecture, they like the idea of "flipping the classroom," and they do seek out online resources to brush up on certain subjects. "A lot of professors are petrified by online classes," one Georgetown student said. "They really want to improve the classroom experience."[6]

In the end, formation of appropriate and effective uses of on-line education is still in development and requires both more thought and more experimentation. The typical response of design educators to "wait it out," can only lead to a yet another "lagging indicator" for our disciplines.

From my own experience over the last three years in delivering on-line courses, I ultimately enjoyed recording my classes live so that the recordings included student questions, laughter at jokes and the interpretation of information that is so important in these kinds of courses. Admittedly, it has placed limits in the amount I can move around the room and has forced me to be far more organized than I ever wanted to be. Frankly, though, now that I have embraced the new model, I will never go back. Last semester, thanks to a pair of recorded lectures, I was able to take my students, during class time, to two different LEED® Platinum buildings and receive a tour from the client and architect for each project – a priceless experience and far superior to any lecture I could deliver.

Lastly, the most concerning argument against this approach is the desire of universities to become more cost consciousness and thereby seize the on-line methodology as a means to reduce time in physical classrooms and studios. Because of this, it is incumbent upon the faculty, program administrators and Deans to remain ahead of the curve on this opportunity and become the "holders of knowledge" as a means to control the destiny of on-campus, live education. The flipped and blended classroom models still use class time and classroom spaces and also still require a living breathing professor for the total amount of class hours.

The dream of the meta-studio is dawning. The studio can now become the locus of integration: visual representation courses, building technology and construction courses, environmental systems courses, structural engineering courses, history/theory courses, lighting courses and even liberal arts courses can now converge with the studio via the emergence of comprehensive visualization tools such as BIM and through the use of on-line teaching and learning techniques. As stated earlier, with the time consuming live lectures now conveniently stored on a cloud server, the studio can, in essence move from a six credit experience to a 12 or even 15 credit "educational experience" of connected and integrative activities that are no longer confined to the studio.

The second approach to on-line education

The second and more controversial approach to on-line teaching and learning involves the creation and delivery of completely on-line programs – including design studios. Such programs already exist and have students enrolled. At the Academy of Design at RCC Institute of Technology, the Interior Design Program is accredited and is taught in a largely asynchronous manner, meaning that work is completed at a pace that is defined by the student. The website proclaims, "The online component is designed to allow students who, for reasons of geographic location or professional or family commitments, are unable to pursue in-class studies for some or all of their degree."[7] The benefits of the completely on-line program, according to their website include the "flexibility … of asynchronous learning" and "An online course may even involve more interaction between instructors and students, and between students themselves, than an in-class delivery method."[8] At Philadelphia University and the Boston Architectural College, the offering of completely on-line sustainable design degrees reflects a changing marketplace as students who are comfortable in the digital environment are increasingly expecting more avenues of study – including on-line. While the live interactions between student and teacher via eye contact offer one type of connection, the on-line environment offers the ability for teachers and students to connect in a different way, as many social norms that may inhibit participation in person simply don't exist in on-line communities. The use of on-line discussion boards, while awkward for uninitiated faculty, provide an intellectually free but also a relatively rigorous means of communication. For example teachers may require a series of responses to a posted question and in some case may ask for sources to authenticate and support the assertions. Such levels of rigor are not possible in a live, real time verbal discussion in a physical classroom. In my own experiences of teaching a sustainability seminar class on-line and on campus, the quality of the lecture experience was superior on campus, while the quality of the discussion in the on-line discussion boards was vastly more sophisticated.

The typical interactions of desk crits with faculty sketching on top of student's drawings, of mid reviews where students present their work and of final juries are all capable of either being recreated through the use of appropriate software and hardware or abandoned in favor of new methodologies not yet discovered. Scanners, for example, allow students to post freehand sketches to a website that allows multiple users to add comments or add drawings of their own through a cloud based program like Voice Stream. Participatory design charrettes are the next frontier for digitally enhanced education. Many software packages already offer "breakout rooms" for smaller groups of a class to work on specific problems or develop alternative design ideas.

Ironically, with the rise of digital work in general in the typical on-campus studio, many faculty find themselves sitting next to students looking at images on a screen without any paper at all.[9] Such interactions come closer to what would occur on-line than the traditional process of the faculty member sitting next to the student pouring over a set of printed drawings. Furthermore, as the world becomes more interconnected through digital networks, and as design practices use networks more and more, to complete projects around the world, it's only a matter of time before schools start to teach students to become highly functioning in such processes. In that sense, the seemingly negative aspects of on-line education switch to a positive as students become adept in the now common global and digital networked environments.

Moving forward

The promise of on-line teaching as a new delivery method may be disturbing to the uninitiated, but, as the rapid adoption of such methods are already underway, it's simply too late to casually opine on the topic from a safe distance. The speed at which technological diffusion occurs in society reminds us that sometimes it's better to jump into the proverbial waters quickly and accept the pain of the cold water rushing over our head and shoulders as a means to experience complete submersion in the new realm of on-line teaching and learning. Ultimately, the flattening of educational delivery shifts more responsibility to the students, who must watch the lectures or find themselves unprepared for integrative activities. At the same time the transition of support course faculty from *primary communicators of knowledge* via the lecture to the new found role as *studio professors, coaches and mentors* will be a difficult transition for some and a wonderfully liberating experience for others. The Educause report contains the following: "The flipped classroom constitutes a role change for instructors, who give up their front-of-the-class position in favor of a more collaborative and cooperative contribution to the teaching process."[10] P. Shah cautions in his essay for the Oxford Conference:

> The role of a teacher should be that of a facilitator. Imparting knowledge will no longer be considered important as electronic media and the Internet will shoulder that responsibility. But the real challenge will be how to bring out the student from the marshy land of over-choice and the ocean of information. The nuances of self-expression, psychological counselling and care taken by the teacher cannot be replaced by machines.[11]

Indeed, lamentations about the loss of the live lecture speaks as much to nostalgia as it does to fear of the unknown. The threshold on which the design education community now stands in regards to on-line teaching and learning is one that we can choose to jump through and embrace an uncertain and uncomfortable future, or, we can initiate the age old strategy of "benign neglect" and simply wait to be passed by.

The set of integrative behaviors which connects to the ethical core and reaches out into the natural world was offered as a partial list or as a set of examples to be used if desired. There are many others that are equally useful. The purpose of this chapter was not to instruct but rather to open a set of doors and windows just enough so that the reader might see something on the other side of the Razor's Edge. The building technology faculty are the "great unrealized bed of talent" waiting to be engaged for deeper performative design processes. A technically demanding studio curriculum along with increased time for collaboration via the flipped classroom, offers the promise of a *meta-studio*, a larger interconnected set of educational experiences that can engage the student's qualitative and quantitative mental map of design. The union of the two reflects a major theme that has run through this book and holds the promise of an educational model that is more reflective of the Age of Integration.

Notes

[1] *RSMeans Green Building Cost Data*, 2nd Annual Edition, 2012, RSMeans, A Division of Reed Construction Data Construction Publishers and Consultants, Norwell, MA

[2] Chea, T., "Elite Colleges Transform Online Higher Education ," *Huffington Post College*, August 9, 2012, http://bigstory.ap.org/article/elite-colleges-transform-online-higher-education, Accessed: 8/8/2012 4:12PM

[3] "7 Things You Should Know About Flipped Classrooms," *Educause Learning Initiative*, February 7, 2012, p13, http://www.educause.edu/library/resources/7-things-you-should-know-about-flipped-classrooms, Accessed: 8/9/2012 3:56PM

[4] *Ibid.*

[5] Selingo, J. (2012) "Did Anyone Ask the Students?, Part 1 and Part 2," *The Chronicle of Higher Education*, May 24, https://chronicle.com/blogs/next/2012/05/02/did-anyone-ask-the-students-part-ii/, Accessed: 11/04/2012 1:30PM

[6] *Ibid.*

[7] The Academy of Design at RCC Institute of Technology in Davisville Campus in Toronto Canada, http://www.aodt.ca/, Accessed: 8/8/2012, 4:15PM

[8] *Ibid.*

[9] It's common to see crits at a computer screen.

[10] Educause (3) p3

[11] Shah, P. (2008) "Toward Sustainability: Rethinking Architectural Education in India," *The Oxford Conference: A Re-Evaluation of Education in Architecture*, WIT Press, Boston, p92

8
NATURE'S ADVOCATE
metrics, standards and rating systems

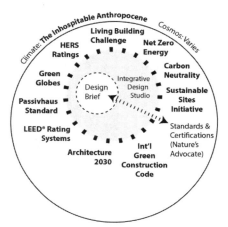

Integrative Design Studio Model
The collaborative selection of standards, rating systems and metrics in the design studio helps students to place their work in the larger environmental context and allows for the discussion of the role of the designer in larger society. Students learn that rating systems and metrics are tools for protecting the ecological health of the planet.

Figure 8.1
Integrative studio model: the collection of certifications, standards and metrics that serve to assist designers in understanding their impact on the natural world

Source: *Created and drawn by author*

The importance of design education to the professions and to the world at large is not discussed enough. The kinds of values and behaviors learned in design school set the stage for a lifetime of impact – both positive and negative. In that sense the four or five years of design education are critical not just for the student who is seeking employment and happiness, but for the larger world community that desperately needs a healthy environment and a deeper sense of social equity. The experiences in design school as provided by faculty, administrators and accrediting bodies holds the opportunity to develop talented designers *and* effective change agents.

While the collaborative development of the design brief and the pursuit of a comprehensive set of integrative behaviors form the nucleus of an integral studio experience, the representation of the voice of nature is a critical component. Individual faculty members, while dedicated and intelligent, typically will not possess the depth and breadth of ecological knowledge to serve as nature's advocate in the design education process. Furthermore, the optimum strategy of inclusion of ecologists, soil experts and biologists as a routine practice is excellent but difficult to maintain over multiple iterations of studio largely due to cost, scheduling, teaching loads and other logistical barriers. Rating systems such as LEED®, Living Building Challenge and the Sustainable Sites Initiative offer a pre-packaged set of values and behaviors that, in effect, serve the needs of nature to be protected, and regenerated. In return, a healthier natural world provides valuable ecosystems services to humans in the form of clean air, water and supplies of energy. The resistance on the part of some faculty to adopting outside standards is explained in part by Figure 8.2, which illustrates the curriculum development process as a collision of values – a clash between the wants of the faculty and the needs of society and nature.

Accreditations and rating systems deal very directly with *needs* while many design studios continue to focus on the *wants* of formalistic and tectonic expression. For those professors seeking to pursue sustainability more directly, they can either develop their own rubric that contains the wide array of "issues" to be integrated under the umbrella of sustainable design or they can adopt a pre-existing rubric that was developed and vetted by hundreds if not thousands of experts from diverse backgrounds – a rating system or standard. The rejection of LEED® and other metrics speaks to a deep and continuing sense of hubris among design faculty who view such ratings systems with a jaundiced eye. The frustrating bureaucratic nature of LEED® is more an expression of the inability of design professionals to police themselves than it is a need for control on the part of USGBC. Ultimately, LEED® and other rating systems continue to be adopted on a widespread basis. According to McGraw Hill, nearly 50 percent of all new commercial construction will be LEED® rated by the year 2015.[1] As discussed earlier, Harvard has completed its one hundred and fiftieth LEED® rated project. Lastly, the emergence of the International Green Construction Code reflects an increasing incorporation of LEED® credits directly into the code, with a special emphasis on ASHRAE 90.1, one of the most effective metrics in use today.

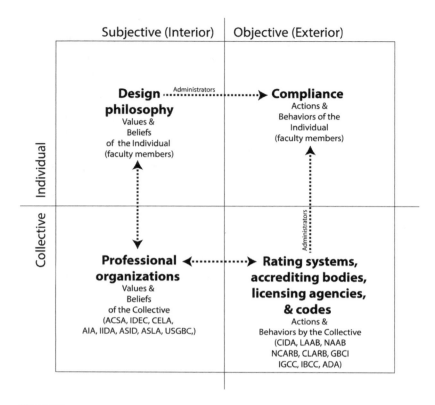

Figure 8.2
The forces that shape the development of design curricula
Source: *Created and drawn by author*

Just as the criteria for accreditation contain the seeds of an integrative comprehensive model of design education, the various ratings systems for green and sustainable design also offer a gateway for faculty to build more holistic and by default more effective models of design education. While the LEED® Rating System is a good start, it only offers half of the integral picture (the objective view) through the more quantifiable "right side" of the integral model (see Figure 8.3). In fact most of the LEED® credits fall squarely within the upper right quadrant "Maximize Performance" with Sustainable Site credits also occupying the lower right "Guide Flow" quadrant. The emptiness of credits on the left side of Figure 8.3 makes sense given that LEED® clearly deals with those aspects of design and construction that can be measured. The adoption of LEED® within the design studio can now be communicated to students quite clearly as a tool to objectively understand and communicate the performative aspects of a design project. It ties in well to the strategies explored in the previous chapter which focused on the establishment of baselines and the use of simulations and calculations to verify the levels of performance achieved in the design.

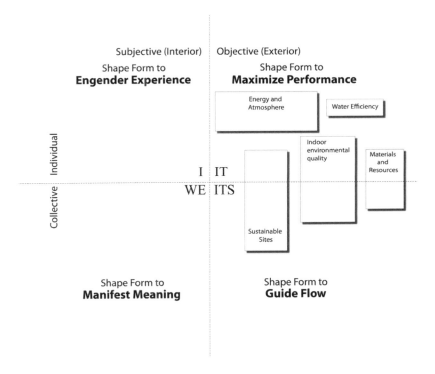

Figure 8.3
The LEED® Rating System categories organized within Mark DeKay's Integral Sustainable Design Framework
Source: *Created and drawn by author*

The Sustainable Sites Initiative (SSI) offers the opportunity to round out the LEED® system with a much more holistic and ecological focus. Criteria focus on "promoting equitable land use" (SSI 6.2), and "Protect and maintain unique cultural and historical places" (SSI 6.4). SSI is comprehensive and integrated in its approach and offers an excellent entry point for design studios to more deeply and authentically engage the natural world. Additionally, rating systems and third party metrics play an advocacy role in the design studio for the rights of nature. In Chapter Five, the inclusion of nature into the co-creative process was covered. As discussed in the section on design briefs, students can work with faculty to set environmental goals with the aid of existing rating systems. This common sense approach expresses the humility of relying on others with more experience and more effort to define sustainable design parameters as opposed to constantly recreating an approach to sustainability for each project or for each studio.

The Living Building Challenge (LBC) and Sustainable Sites Initiative (SSI) offer a more comprehensive and integrated model for design, with criteria intersecting all quadrants of the Integral Model. The LBC includes criteria that express a range of left side goals including *Civilized Environment, Biophilia, Democracy and Social Justice, Beauty and Spirit*, along with a set of right side goals: *Net Zero Energy* and *Net Zero Water* to name but two. Figure 8.4 illustrates the integral nature of the Living Building Challenge.

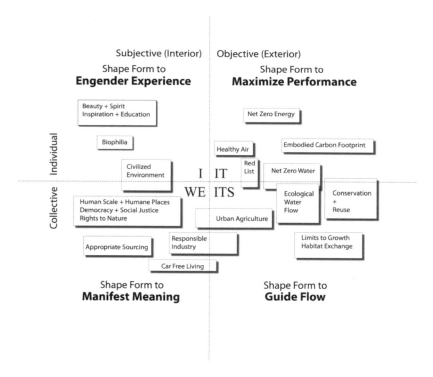

Figure 8.4
The Living Building Challenge's requirements organized within Mark DeKay's Integral Sustainable Design Framework
Source: *Created and drawn by author*

Accreditations

Design faculty members, in general, tend to look at accreditation as they would building code, a necessary evil and something to be avoided if possible. And yet the criteria themselves, if examined more closely, can become catalysts for deep levels of sustainable design and integration. the demands of the accreditors for "comprehensive design" is a powerful gateway to using each criterion as part of an integrative process aimed at creating projects that are more energy efficient, more environmentally sustainable and more socially equitable. A building with two means of egress, for example, is as much about meeting code as it is about teaching students how to take care of people in an emergency. A landscape plan with proper slopes allows people in wheel chairs to traverse outdoor spaces. There is a level of expression of empathy in the requirements for hand rails, accessible entries to buildings and even for functioning parking lots. Correspondingly the accrediting boards are stepping up their efforts to ensure that all students graduate with basic knowledge about how to make safe and accessible built environments, or how to design projects that use less energy, that pollute less, and that conserve valuable fossil fuels – an expression of intergenerational equity. The National Architectural Accrediting Board (NAAB) sets forth Comprehensive Design criteria for accreditation that group ten important points under one umbrella.[2] The result is an integrative model that maps well onto Wilber's Integral Theory as reinterpreted through the Quadruple Bottom Line. However, the absence of the lone Financial Criteria (B.7.) and the Professional Ethics Criteria (C.8.) reflects a still developing understanding of the complete picture of design in the twenty-first century.

In the Figure 8.5, the integrative components according to NAAB are evenly dispersed. The lower left quadrant contains the big picture views (Historical Traditions and Global Culture) along with criteria that deal directly with social equity (Accessibility and Life Safety). The lower right quadrant obviously includes Site Design and Sustainability, which is more akin to environmental sustainability in the NAAB description. The upper right deals with the measurable and technological aspects of the rigorous process of deriving and understanding a design (Documentation and Investigative Skills). Lastly the upper left deals with aesthetics through the use of Design Thinking and Ordering Systems. The use of a set of nested criteria within a single larger criterion reflects current thinking about organization behaviors as a set of nested experiences – a holarchy.

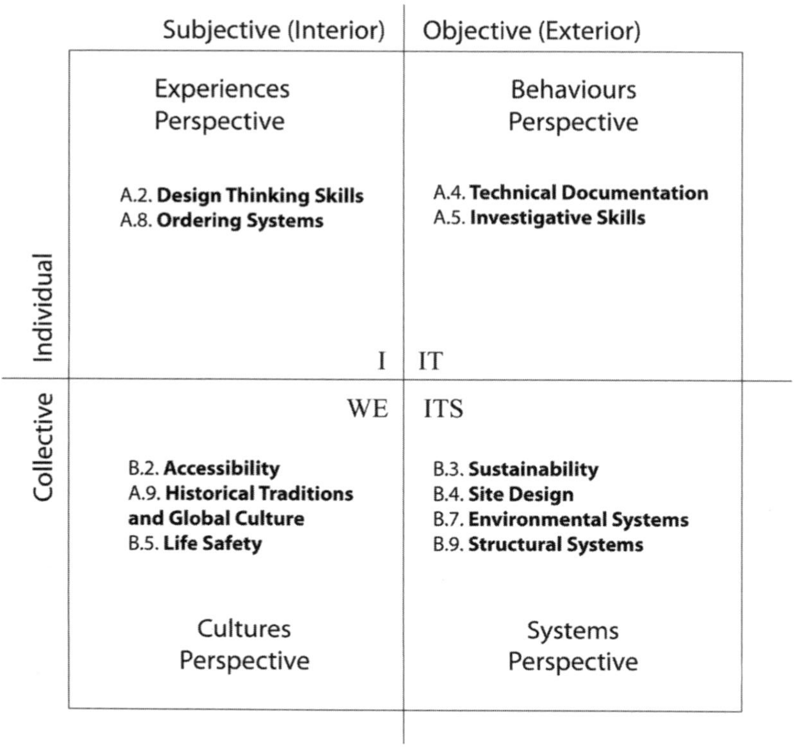

Subjective (Interior)	Objective (Exterior)
Experiences Perspective	Behaviours Perspective
A.2. **Design Thinking Skills** A.8. **Ordering Systems**	A.4. **Technical Documentation** A.5. **Investigative Skills**
I	IT
WE	ITS
B.2. **Accessibility** A.9. **Historical Traditions and Global Culture** B.5. **Life Safety**	B.3. **Sustainability** B.4. **Site Design** B.7. **Environmental Systems** B.9. **Structural Systems**
Cultures Perspective	Systems Perspective

Individual / *Collective*

Figure 8.5
Organization of NAAB criteria within the Integral Theory model
Source: *NAAB 2011 Criterion B.6. Comprehensive Design Ability (created and drawn by author)*

If the studio professor is uncomfortable accepting a system from a recognized authority, more straightforward options of net zero energy, carbon neutrality and ASHRAE 90.1 are available. As has been mentioned, setting clear environmental and energy goals with quantifiable baselines is critical. Otherwise students and faculty will struggle to comprehend the effectiveness of the selected sustainable strategies.

In conclusion, the use of rating systems and the acceptance of building code and accreditation requirements is a process by which design faculty members can inscribe their activities within a larger societal framework that is becoming increasingly more environmentally integrated and more ethically grounded. The fact that the development of rating systems, accreditation requirements and building codes are becoming increasingly transparent and more and more often developed as part of an inclusive process, means the opportunity for faculty members to join in the collaborative evolution of the systems is always present. Ultimately, the needs of nature must be reflected in the design process. Design faculty can express those needs abstractly and without detail in the studio or they can leverage years of work by thousands of experts and professionals through the adoption of standards and certifications that serve as frameworks and methodologies for the advocacy of the natural world. The choice, when understood in those terms should be obvious.

Notes

[1] "Construction Industry Workforce Shortages: Role Of Certification, Training and Jobs in Filling the Gaps," *SmartMarket Report,* McGraw Hill Construction, 2012, p5

[2] NAAB (2011) "Part Two (II): Section 1 – Student Performance – Educational Realms & Student Performance Criteria: Student Performance Criteria: B. 6. Comprehensive Design," *Procedures for Accreditation: For Professional Degree Programs in Architecture*, National Architectural Accrediting Board, p18.

9

TINY REVOLUTIONS

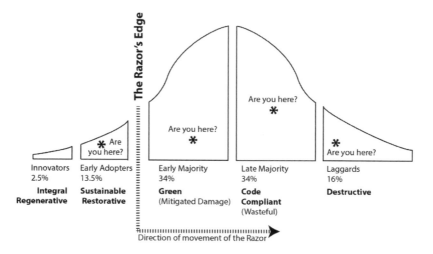

Figure 9.1
Rogers' adoption of innovation curve: adapted for Integral Sustainable Design

Source: *Re-drawn and adapted by author from Moore, G. (2002)*

Society stands at the precipice of the next great change – a change driven in part by new sources of energy, new forms of information delivery and dramatic climatic shifts. These forces are reshaping how we design and construct the built environment and in turn change how we develop and deliver design education. The negative environmental impacts of fossil fuel use and the threat of peak oil have partially led to the rapid rise of renewable energy systems. The combination of the two is changing the focus of design education, especially the studio, where the existing synthetic learning models now have the opportunity to more deeply integrate issues of economy, ecology and equity into an overall integral model. The rise of social media and cloud based networks is also driving the evolution of design education in two distinct directions. Firstly, social media among other forces has led to the emergence of an empathic civilization because the *amount* that we know about each other and the *way* that we know each other has led not only to a smaller world but a more connected world culture. Amazing acts of kindness in the form of service learning in local communities through design build (Rural Studio and Greensburg), and internationally (Haiti and Banda Aceh) serve as examples of how the values of inclusivity and cooperation play out among students, administrators and faculty. Secondly, the tremendous power of cloud based networks to store large quantities of information cheaply and efficiently allows faculty members to store vast amounts of data in the form of video recordings, readings, photos and other teaching materials. Interfaces such as Blackboard create frameworks to organize the materials, allowing students to gain efficient access. The rise of on-line teaching and learning stands ready to revolutionize the way that education is delivered, leading to the blended classroom, more opportunities for integrative activities and deeper learning. Completely on-line programs offer a huge benefit to students who could not normally take advantage of higher education. Lastly, and perhaps most importantly, the transition from the mild climatic conditions of the Holocene to the unpredictable and excessively hot climatic reality of the Anthropocene reminds that we are as much healers as we are creators – suggesting fundamental changes in our approach to design education. This profound shift in consciousness also opens the door to a deeper look at resilience as a design framework that shifts the focus from *reversal of damage* to the less inspiring but necessary process of *adaption*. Green infrastructure and EcoDistrics will become increasingly important as communities wrestle with the goals of zero energy neighborhoods and ambitious stormwater management strategies. In many countries the focus will shift from keeping people warm to keeping people cool and will drive an evolving set of passive and active strategies to provide basic comfort. At that point collaboration between disciplines will move from an interesting pedagogic innovation to a societal imperative. While sobering, the discussion regarding the impacts tells us that we are as much faculty who communicate information as we are shapers of values, and behavioral trainers. And as such we possess the unique opportunity to deliver enormously positive impacts to society, the natural world and to ourselves.

The evidence of change is all around us, if we choose to look. For some the Solar Decathlon is merely a seductive set of highly refined and remarkably sleek boxes lined up on the national mall. For others, it's the *form* that *follows world view*. Those tiny structures, each an amazing example of what can be accomplished by a university community, serves to remind us that moving from the green side of the "Razor's Edge" to the sustainable side is not only possible but probable (see Figure 9.1). The values of inclusivity and cooperation are so embedded in the collaborative development process of the Solar Decathlon projects that the magnitude of the cultural sea change is only now beginning to be fully understood. Those changes result in the wider adoption of new sets of behaviors that lead to integration. The design brief of the Decathlon was developed and vetted by literally hundreds if not thousands of individuals. The integrative activities ranging from energy modeling, to value engineering, to the resolution of beauty and performance provide a wealth of examples for faculty members seeking to develop their next studio course. Lastly, the pursuit of net zero energy, an *absolute* metric of success, reminds us that design now has a more complex, and more ethically grounded set of end goals – maximum beauty, *and* maximum power.

Despite the enthusiasm for the Solar Decathlon and for other ambitious sustainability projects, the harsh reality remains that many design studio professors have yet to cross the Razor's Edge, deciding instead to reside in the less ambitious but safer green space. The leap over the "Edge" begins first with the intention to jump and second with the acquisition of knowledge to make the leap. Herein lies the difficulty. While there is clearly a wealth of knowledge out there, and plenty of examples, the process by which one gains the knowledge is fraught with stops and starts with dead ends and wrong turns. Gaining LEED® accreditation will help but it is limited to the right side of the integral model. There are many books on the subject of sustainable design, but which ones to read first? Attacking a Living Building Challenge project in studio is great but also problematic if the expertise and knowledge is not present to support the endeavor. Going to a conference is helpful, but the sessions are "hit or miss" and not interconnected to present a cohesive vision of sustainable design education. As a response, Figure 9.2 is offered as a means to begin to frame the kinds of value shifts and behavior changes that will likely occur in the near future.

Transorganizational programs

While USGBC emerged as a new type of organization that reflected a biospheric consciousness, a corresponding leap has yet to be made in the design education arena. Of course the current professional associations such CELA, ASCA and IDEC continue to ramp up their offerings regarding sustainable design, but the great coalescence of the

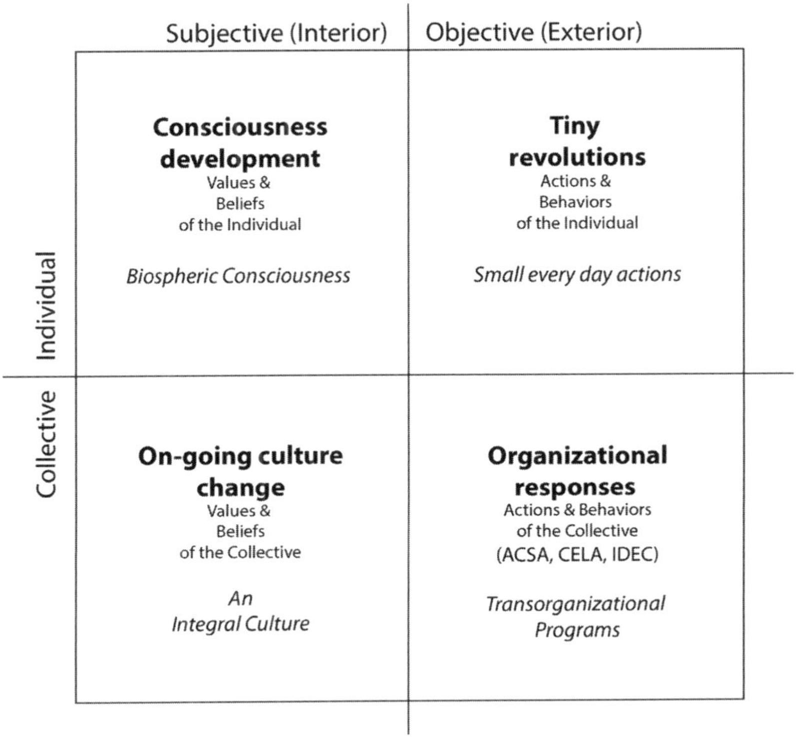

	Subjective (Interior)	Objective (Exterior)
Individual	**Consciousness development** Values & Beliefs of the Individual *Biospheric Consciousness*	**Tiny revolutions** Actions & Behaviors of the Individual *Small every day actions*
Collective	**On-going culture change** Values & Beliefs of the Collective *An* *Integral Culture*	**Organizational responses** Actions & Behaviors of the Collective (ACSA, CELA, IDEC) *Transorganizational* *Programs*

Figure 9.2
Culture change for design education: an integral perspective

Source: *Created and drawn by author*

organizations is still in dormancy waiting for enough individuals to gather the strength and energy to make it happen. By now the reader should understand the connection between the larger set of cultural values (world view) and the larger set of collective behaviors by institutions, accrediting bodies, professional and trade organizations, to name a few. The offering of a design competition with a focus on sustainability (collective behavior) reflects a larger adoption of sustainability as an important *value* in the organizational culture. The founders of the International Living Building Institute clearly possess a deep set of integral values which are expressed by the creation of the Living Building Challenge, a standard to help others align their values and behaviors. The Institute places the following statement on its website: "What if every single act of design and construction made the world a better place?" Ultimately, existing organizations could decide to join forces and start to offer joint programs in sustainable design education. This approach would express one of Barrett's core values of *Making a Difference* which advocates for building partnerships. Furthermore the opportunity to reach out to the organizations that govern the education processes of architectural engineers, civil engineers, builders and construction management will catalyze even more profound change. Transorganizational conferences offer the promise of deeper collaboration as paper sessions and panels are now much more diverse and also more interdisciplinary. The idea of a transorganizational conference sounds intriguing because of the need to find additional vehicles for the delivery of information to attendees. The "randomness" of content at conferences leaves the attendee longing for a more interconnected and focused set of experiences. Perhaps the time has come to pursue the offering of training programs and workshops that link directly to the needs that are emerging from the changing context of design education. Training programs can contain both content and activities, demanding more participation by listeners and by default more learning. Because the topics, as listed in Table 9.1, require very specific sets of strategies and detailed knowledge, the training format as opposed to the paper session or panel format is in order.

Table 9.1 Partial list of proposed sustainable design education trainings

Title of Proposed Training Session		Partial List of Training Deliverables
Effective design juries		– How to organize and facilitate effective design juries – How to use design juries as an effective assessment tool
Co-creative process facilitation strategies		– How to organize and develop the process – How to facilitate the process so that it is equitable – How to use the process as an effective educational tool
Community engagement practices		– How to initiate partnerships with local community groups – How to develop meaningful interactions between the institutions and community groups – How to ensure that students are having a quality experience and meeting learning objectives
Management of inter-disciplinary groups		– How to set appropriate learning objectives for collaborative interdisciplinary projects – How to manage student teams made up of different disciplines – How to build agreement between faculty members from different departments and disciplines – How to conduct assessment

Diversity awareness and initiative planning		– How to build awareness regarding diversity and inclusivity and why it is important – How to develop and carry out an effective diversity initiative – How to measure the success of the process
Sustainable curriculum and program development		– How to develop a set of shared values and integrative behaviors (processes and procedures) that drive the design and development of the curriculum – How to set benchmarks for success – How to measure success
Simulation and calculations		– How to understand the value of different types of simulations and calculations – How to perform them – How to integrate them into the studio or course curriculum
Cost estimating		– How to understand the value of cost estimating in design curriculum – How to perform simple cost estimates and integrate them into course work
The design brief		– How to manage and deliver the collaborative development of an integral design brief
Building information modeling as an environmental visualization tool		– How to understand the value of BIM as an environmental visualization tool – How to use BIM to perform simple simulations – How to integrate the practices into course work
Standards and rating systems		– How to understand the purpose and value of third party metrics such as LEED®, LBI, SSI, HERS, ASHRAE 90.1, Passivhaus, IGCC
On-line teaching and learning		– How to understand the purpose and value of on-line teaching – How to develop on-line curriculum – How to design and record on-line content

Departmental change

While larger professional organizations will continue to serve the needs and interests of their constituencies, and branch out to form collateral events, much work will also occur in the design departments, schools and colleges within the larger university. There are two major organizational behaviors that will be used to build the consciousness of the faculty. The first is the use of the co-creative methodology to develop mission and vision statements, core values and major curricular organizational structures. By using an inclusive and cooperative process

215

the extent to which individual stakeholders will align their values and beliefs will be determined in part by how involved they are in the process. For example, if a curriculum is mandated from above without early and meaningful input, the end result is a deep sense of disrespect and frustration that the collective wisdom of some or all of the faculty was not included in the process. The stakeholders for the process include administrators, faculty, students, employers, parents and others who may be touched by the results. The co-creative process, as discussed earlier needs an impartial facilitator, for obvious reasons, a tight schedule and clear objectives. Without a solid plan, the process can derail. As is usually the case, a set of "laggards" (see Figure 9.1) will be present during the process. Strangely the most knowledgeable faculty members are not always the ones most ready to embrace change (he said politely) suggesting that a high level of intellectual comfort has been achieved and that a specific world view is "locked in." Facilitated processes such as co-creativity are so valuable because they create a framework for interaction which allows the voice of the laggard, but is not derailed by it, mainly because other voices have equal representation and because the facilitator has the power to enforce an equitable process.

The second proposal is to occasionally replace faculty meetings, at regular intervals, with professionally developed and delivered training programs as described in Table 9.1. The topics of the trainings will relate to and support the mission and vision of the program. If, for example, the department has decided to pursue a more organized and targeted plan of increasing diversity and evolving the learning climate, a set of trainings is essential. When the mission of a program does not align with individual behaviors, the system becomes dysfunctional. As an example, a department decides to pursue collaborative studios that span disciplines. Without training on how to facilitate such educational models, the end result can be frustration. Trainings are only as useful as how well they fit into the system. If a department offers training on how to run a co-creative process but never provides the opportunity to use the knowledge gained, frustration ensues. Ultimately a wide array of training programs can be made available either on-site or at larger collateral conferences.

Transcend and include

It should be noted that in the spirit of "transcend and include" all previous organizational structures, if functional, remain intact. The addition of facilitated co-creative processes does not eliminate the need

216

for, or reduce the efficacy of faculty meetings. The development of a collateral conference on sustainable design education does not mean the existing professional organizations cease to exist. The use of on-line teaching does not mean that in-class experiences will disappear. There are no enemies, no evil doers, simply the constant and invisible push for progress, not in the industrial version that we typically think of, but rather through an emerging biospheric perspective and a reconnection to the very core of our ethical foundation.

Tiny revolutions

As the end approaches (the book, not the world), the big proclamations have been made. The advocacy for widespread and systemic change is complete. The relentless use of the words "values" and "behaviors" can now thankfully cease. The slate is clean and the subject has been laid bare. All that is left is the heart to heart, the direct line of communication, the appeal to the reader's ethical core.

Ultimately big changes are made by thousands, if not millions of small decisions, subtle shifts in attitude and seemingly small every day actions. They begin with a simple change of a word in the syllabus, the addition of a new concept here or there in the learning objectives, or the development of a new integrative exercise. They start with an empathetic wink towards a struggling student letting them know that you care, or an olive branch towards a long hated colleague in your department. They start by becoming aware of your own approach to design education, the jury, the design brief, the desk crit, the grading process and then beginning to imagine the next iteration, one that is shaped by the simple question, "why am I teaching?"

Sometimes the moves are bigger and more daring. A senior faculty member will breach the traditions of tenure and advocate for a new found emphasis on collaborative publications and cross disciplinary teaching. The registrar will find new ways to link support courses to studios. A junior faculty member will develop a new course on integration and share the results among colleagues. A Dean will reject "benign neglect" as a diversity strategy and lead the development of a targeted, well organized campaign for the establishment of inclusive learning environments. A faculty member will develop new cooperative models for interdisciplinary work and convince some like-minded colleagues in other departments to join in. Another will experiment with the co-creative process. Yet another will rearrange the furniture in her studio to accommodate team projects. A group of students will create a volunteer design build project to assist towns that have been decimated by devastating weather events. A faculty member will develop an on-line course and share it freely to assist those pursuing sustainability in faraway places. As the numbers and power of these and other tiny revolutions grow, the impact on our students will also grow, not because we taught them what we *wanted* them to learn, but because we taught them what they *needed* to know.

BIBLIOGRAPHY

7group and Reed, B. (2009) *The Integrative Design Guide to Green Building: Redefining the Practice of Sustainability*, John Wiley & Sons, Hoboken, NJ

Alexander, C., Ishikawa, S., Silverstein, M. (1977) *A Pattern Language: Towns, Buildings, Construction*, Oxford University Press, New York

Anthony, K. (1991) *Design Juries on Trial, The Renaissance of the Design Studio*, Van Nostrand Reinhold, New York

Anthony, K. (2001) *Designing for Diversity, Gender, Race, and Ethnicity in the Architectural Profession*, University of Illinois Press, Chicago, IL

Barnett, D., Browning, W. (1999) *A Primer on Sustainable Building*, Rocky Mountain Institute, CO

Benyus, J. (1997) *Biomimicry*, Harper Collins Publishers, New York

Birkeland, Janis (2002) *Design for Sustainability, A sourcebook of Integrated Eco-logical Solutions*, Earthscan, London

Boeker, J., Horst, S, Keiter, T., lau, A., Sheffer, M., Toevs, B. (2009) *The Integrative Design Guide to Green Building: redefining the Practice of Sustainability*, John Wiley & Sons Inc., Hoboken, NJ

Boyer, E. and Mitgang, L. (1996) *Building Community: A New Future for Architecture Education and Practice*, Carnegie Foundation for the Advancement of Teaching, Princeton, NJ

Brown, L. (1984) *State of the World*, Worldwatch Institute, New York

Brown, L. (2009) *Plan B 4.0, Mobilizing to Save Civilization* (1ˢᵗ edition) W.W. Norton, New York, NY

Brown, T. (2009) *Change by Design, How Design Thinking Transforms Organizations And Inspires Innovation*, HarperCollins, New York, NY

Burckhardt, J. (1985) *The Architecture of the Italian Renaissance*, University of Chicago Press, Chicago

Calthorpe, P. (2011) *Urbanism in the Age of Climate Change*, Island Press, Washington, D.C.

Chapman, J., Nick, G. (2007) *Designers, Visionaries & Other Stories, A Collection of Sustainable Design Essays,* Earthscan, London

Chapman, R., (2010) *Culture Wars: An Encyclopaedia of Issues, Viewpoints, and Voices*, M.E. Sharpe, Armonk, NY

Cziko, G. (2000) *The Things We Do: Using the Lessons of Bernard & Darwin to Understand What, How and Why of Our Behavior*, MIT Press, Cambridge, MA

DeKay, M. (2011) *Integral Sustainable Design, Transformative Perspectives*, Earthscan, London

Dutton, T. (ed.) (1991) *Voices in Architectural Education, Cultural Politics and Pedagogy*, Greenwood Press, New York

Edwards, J., McCommons, R., Eldridge, K. (1998) *Guide to Architecture Schools,* sixth edition, Association of Collegiate Schools of Architecture, ACSA Press, Washington, D.C.

Elkington, J. (1997) *Cannibals with Forks: The Triple Bottom Line of 21st Century Business,* Capstone, Oxford

Ellin, N. (2006) *Integral Urbanism*, Routledge, New York

Fisher, T. (2006) *In the Scheme of Things, Alternative Thinking on the Practice of Architecture*, University of Minnesota Press, Minneapolis

Fishman, R. & Fishman, B. (2006) *The Common Good Corporation, The Experiment Has Worked!*, The Journey to Oz Press, Philadelphia, PA

Fleming, J., Honour, H., Pevsner, N. (1999) *The Penguin Dictionary of Architecture and Landscape Architecture*, fifth edition, Penguin Books, London

Frampton, K. (1980) *Modern Architecture: A Critical History*, Oxford University Press, New York and Toronto

Friedenthal, R. (2010) *Goethe: His Life & Times*, Transaction Publishers, New Brunswick, NJ

Friedman, T. (2008) *Hot, Flat and Crowded, Why We Need a Green Revolution- and How It Can Renew America*, Farrar, Straus and Giroux, New York

Gebser, J. (1991) *The Ever-Present Origin*, Ohio University press, Athens

Goethe, J., Eastlake, C. (1840) *Goethe's Theory of Colours;* Translated from the German, John Murray, London

Gould, K., Hosey, L., (2007) *Women in Green: Voices of Sustainable Design*, Ecotone, Bainbridge Island, WA

Gropius, W. (1965) *The New Architecture and the Bauhaus*, MIT Press, Cambridge, MA

Hamilton, M. (2008) *Integral City: Evolutionary Intelligences in the Human Hive*, New Society Publishers, Gabriola Island, BC

Hosey, L. (2012) *The Shape of Green: Aesthetics, Ecology, and Design*, Island Press, Washington, D.C.

Hosey, L., Gould K. (2006) *Ecological Literacy in Architecture Education Report and Proposal*, American Institute of Architects and the Tides Foundation, Washington, D.C.

Johnson, B., Hill, K. (2002) *Ecology and Design, Frameworks for Learning*, Island Press, Washington, D.C.

Koch, A., Schwennsen, K., Dutton, T., Smith, D. (2002) *The Redesign of Studio Culture: A Report of the AIAS Studio Culture Task Force*, American Institute of Architects Students, Washington, D.C.

Kostov, S. (1985) *A History of Architecture: Settings and Rituals*, Oxford University Press, New York

Kruft, H. W. (1994) *Architectural Theory: From Vitruvius to the Present*, Princeton Architectural Press, New York

Leibowitz Earley, S. (2005) *Ecological Design and Building Schools: Green Guide to Educational Opportunities in the United States and Canada*, New Village Press, Oakland, CA

Lennertz, B., Lutzenhiser, A. (2006) *The Charrette Handbook, The Essential Guide for Accelerated, Collaborative Community Planning*, American Planning Association, Chicago, IL

Malthus, T. R. (1797) *An Essay on the Principle of Population as it Affects the Future Improvement of Society*, printed for J. Johnson in St. Paul's Church Yard, London

Maslow, A. (1964) *Toward a Psychology of Being*, John Wiley & Sons, New York

McHarg, I. (1992) *Design with Nature*, John Wiley & Sons, New York

McLennan, J. (2004) *The Philosophy of Sustainable Design*, Ecotone, Bainbridge Island, WA

Meadows, D., Meadows, D. L., Randers, J. (1972) *The Limits to Growth*, Universe Books, New York

Moore, G. (2002) *Crossing the Chasm: Marketing and Selling Disruptive Products to Mainstream Customers*, HarperBusiness, New York

Moos, D., Trechsel, G. (2003) *Samuel Mockbee and the Rural Studio: Community Architecture*, Birmingham Museum of Art, Birmingham, AL

Nabokov, P., Easton, R. (1989) *Native American Architecture*, Oxford University Press, New York

Papanek, V. (1995) *The Green Imperative, Natural Design for the Real World*, Thames and Hudson, Inc, New York

Parnell, R., Sara, R., Diodge, C., Parson, M. (2007) *The Crit: An Architecture Student's Handbook, second edition*, Elsevier, Burlington, MA

Rifkin, J. (2009) *The Empathic Civilization: The Race to Global Consciousness in a World in Crisis*, Penguin, New York

Roaff, S., Bairstow, A. (2008) *The Oxford Conference: A Re-evaluation of Education in Architecture*, WIT Press, Southampton and Boston, MA

Stevens, G. (1998) *The Favored Circle: The Social Foundations of Architectural Distinction*, MIT Press, Cambridge, MA

Thorpe, A. (2007) *The Designer's Atlas of Sustainability, Charting the Conceptual Landscape Through Economy, Ecology, and Culture*, Island Press, Washington, D.C.

Till, J. (2009) *Architecture Depends*, MIT Press, Cambridge, MA

Van der Ryn, S. (2005) *Design for Life: The Architecture of Sim Van Der Ryn*, Gibbs Smith, Layton, UT

Van der Ryn, S., Cowan, S. (1996) *Ecological Design Tenth Anniversary Edition*, Island Press, Washington, D.C.

Venhaus, H. (2012) *Designing the Sustainable Site, Integrated Design Strategies for Small-Scale Sites and Residential Landscapes*, Wiley, Hoboken, NJ

Visser, F. (2003) *Ken Wilber: Thought As Passion*, State University of New York, Albany

Walker, S. (2006) *Sustainable by Design, Explorations in Theory and Practice*, Earthscan, London

Wanliss, J. (2011) *Resisting the Green Dragon; Dominion, Not Death*, The Cornwall Alliance, Burke, VA

Wilber, K. (2000) *A Brief History of Everything*, Shambhala, Boston, MA and London

Wilson, D. (2007) *Evolution for Everyone, How Darwin's Theory Can Change the Way We Think about Our Lives*, Bantam Dell, New York

Yudelson, J. (2009) *Green Building Through Integrated Design*, McGraw Hill, CO

INDEX

Note: page numbers in *italic* type refer to Figures; those in **bold** refer to Tables.